M. 4. 72   With my p̶̶̶̶

THE SENATORIAL ARISTOCRACY
IN THE LATER ROMAN EMPIRE

THE
SENATORIAL
ARISTOCRACY
IN THE LATER
ROMAN EMPIRE

BY

M. T. W. ARNHEIM

FELLOW OF ST. JOHN'S COLLEGE, CAMBRIDGE

CLARENDON PRESS · OXFORD

1972

Oxford University Press, Ely House, London W.1

GLASGOW   NEW YORK   TORONTO   MELBOURNE   WELLINGTON
CAPE TOWN   IBADAN   NAIROBI   DAR ES SALAAM   LUSAKA   ADDIS ABABA
DELHI   BOMBAY   CALCUTTA   MADRAS   KARACHI   LAHORE   DACCA
KUALA LUMPUR   SINGAPORE   HONG KONG   TOKYO

PRINTED IN GREAT BRITAIN BY
WILLIAM CLOWES AND SONS LTD.
LONDON, COLCHESTER AND BECCLES

TO MY
MOTHER AND FATHER

PREFACE

THE aim of this study is to ascertain the political and social role played by the senatorial aristocracy in the period between Diocletian's accession in 284 and the death of Theodosius I in 395. Lecrivain's *Le sénat romain depuis Dioclétien à Rome et à Constantinople*, which appeared in 1888, is the only other full-scale published work on the subject. But it is a study of the Senate as an institution rather than of groups of senators. Lecrivain's view of the third century was obscured by his acceptance of the *Life* of Alexander Severus in the *Augustan History*, and his conclusion that there was 'une sorte de restauration sénatoriale qui a duré depuis le règne de Sévère Alexandre jusque vers la fin du troisième siècle' was later to be disproved.[1] As regards the fourth century Lecrivain distinguishes only between 'les sénateurs effectifs', who took part in public affairs in Rome, and those who preferred to remain on their estates in the provinces without bothering to undertake the burden of the republican magistracies.[2] In addition, however, as will be shown in the Introduction, it is essential to distinguish between those, whom I shall call the nobles or aristocracy, who were of senatorial birth and those who attained senatorial rank in the course of their careers. Since in the fourth century the holders of certain specified offices automatically received the clarissimate, the sign of senatorial rank, this title was as meaningless as an indication of social origin as a peerage is in present-day Britain. Yet no systematic distinction between noble and non-noble *clarissimi* has been offered by any writer on the period.

If I had referred in the notes as often as I might have to the following works, hardly a page would have lacked a reference to at least one of them: Groag and Stein's *Prosopographia Imperii*

---

[1] Lecrivain, *Le sénat romain depuis Dioclétien à Rome et à Constantinople*, 3. On the third century see pp. 32 ff., below. On the *Augustan History* see Sir R. Syme, *Ammianus and the Historia Augusta*, Oxford, 1968.

[2] On this see pp. 143 ff., below.

Romani, Pauly-Wissowa-Kroll's *Realenzyklopädie*, Barbieri's *Albo Senatorio da Settimio Severo a Carino*, André Chastagnol's *Fastes de la préfecture de Rome au Bas-Empire*, and A. H. M. Jones, J. R. Martindale and J. Morris's forthcoming *Prosopography of the Later Roman Empire*, a typescript copy of the first volume of which was kindly lent to me by the authors. References to secondary sources in the notes have on the whole been limited to points of disagreement.

When working on my Cambridge Ph.D. thesis, upon which this book is based, I was fortunate enough to have as my research supervisor the late Professor A. H. M. Jones, whose cool analytical intellect subjected every interpretation to the severest scrutiny. His knowledge of the period, born of an understanding as deep as it was wide, was coupled with the tolerance that is only to be found in a truly original scholar who has himself challenged accepted ideas. I have also benefited greatly from suggestions and advice given me by Mr. Peter Brown, Mr. John Crook, Professor W. H. C. Frend and Professor Sir Ronald Syme, all of whom have read the manuscript at one or other stage of composition. Not least, I owe a debt of gratitude to my parents, Dr. and Mrs. W. Arnheim, for their constant and unflagging encouragement, and it is therefore to them that I dedicate this book.

M.T.W.A.

April 1970

CONTENTS

APPENDIX: SELECTED PROSOPOGRAPHY

FASTI, TABLES, AND LISTS

ABBREVIATIONS

a.	ante (before)
AASS	Acta Sanctorum
AE	*L'Année Epigraphique*
a.v.p.p.	*agens vices praefectorum praetorio*
BC	Corpus Scriptorum Historiae Byzantinae, Bonn
BGU	*Aegyptische Urkunden aus den Staatlichen Museen zu Berlin, Griechische Urkunden*, I–IX, Berlin, 1895–1937
CIG	*Corpus Inscriptionum Graecarum*, ed. Boeckh, 4 vols. 1828–77
CJ	Codex Justinianus, ed. P. Krueger, Berlin, 1877
cons.	consularis
cos.	consul
CRP	comes rerum privatarum
CSL	comes sacrarum largitionum
CTh	*Codex Theodosianus*, ed. T. Mommsen, Berlin, 1905
Chron. 354	*Chronographus an. 354*, ed. T. Mommsen, MGH AA XI (*Chronica Minora*)
Cod. Veron.	*Laterculus Veronensis* (together with Not. Dig.)
Coll. Avell.	*Epistulae Imperatorum, pontificum, aliorum.* . . . Avellana quae dicitur collectio, CSEL XXXV
CSEL	Corpus Scriptorum Ecclesiasticorum Latinorum
D.	*Inscriptiones Latinae Selectae*, ed. H. Dessau, 3 vols., Berlin 1892–1916
Dig.	Justinianus, *Digesta seu Pandectae*, ed. Mommsen, Berlin, 1870
Eph. Ep.	*Ephemeris Epigraphica*, ed. Mommsen
Fasti	*I Fasti consolari dell'Impero Romano dal 30 av. Cristo al 613 dopo Cristo*, A. Degrassi, Roma, 1952
FHG	*Fragmenta Historicorum Graecorum*, ed. C. Mueller, Paris, 1874–85
Gr. Schr.	Die griechischen christlichen Schriftsteller der ersten drei Jahrhunderte
Hell.	Louis Robert, *Hellenica*
ICUR	*Inscriptiones Christianae Urbis Romae*, ed. G.-B. de Rossi, 2 vols., Roma, 1857–61; supplement ed. G. Gatti, 1915
IG	*Inscriptiones Graecae*, Berlin, 1872–

IGR	*Inscriptiones Graecae ad res Romanas pertinentes*, ed. R. Cagnat, Paris, 1901–27
ILAfr	*Inscriptions Latines d'Afrique*, ed. R. Cagnat and A. Merlin, Paris, 1923
ILAlg	*Les Inscriptions Latines de l'Algerie*, ed. S. Gsell, H. G. Pflaum, Paris, 1932–56
ILCV	*Inscriptiones Latinae Christianae Veteres*, ed. E. Diehl, Berlin, 1925
ILT	*Inscriptions Latines de la Tunisie*, ed. A. Merlin, Paris, 1944
Inscr. It.	*Inscriptiones Italiae*, ed. J. Mancini, Roma, 1952–
IRT	*The Inscriptions of Roman Tripolitania*, ed. J. M. Reynolds, J. B. Ward Perkins, Rome–London, 1952
Mag. Off.	magister officiorum
MAMA	*Monumenta Asiae Minoris Antiqua*, ed. W. M. Calder, Manchester, 1928–62
MGH AA	*Monumenta Germaniae Historica*, Auctores Antiquissimi
MGH Scr. Rer. Lang.	*Monumenta Germaniae Historica*, Scriptores Rerum Langobardicarum et Italicarum
NS	of certain or almost-certain non-senatorial origin
ns	of probable non-senatorial origin
Not. Dig.	*Notitia Dignitatum*, ed. O. Seeck, Berlin, 1876
Nov.	*Leges Novellae ad Theodosianum pertinentes*, ed. P. Meyer, Berlin, 1905
OU	origin unknown
p.	post (after)
PG	Patrologia Graeca, ed. J. P. Migne *et al.*
PIR[1]	*Prosopographia Imperii Romani saec. I, II, III*, ed. H. Dessau, E. Klebs and P. von Rohden, 3 vols., Berlin, 1897–8
PIR[2]	*Prosopographia Imperii Romani saec. I, II, III*, ed. E. Groag and A. Stein, Berlin, 1933–
PL	Patrologia Latina, ed. J. P. Migne *et al.*
PLRE	*Prosopography of the Later Roman Empire*, A. H. M. Jones, J. R. Martindale and J. Morris
P. Amh.	*The Amherst Papyri*, ed. Grenfell and Hunt, 2 vols., London, 1900–1
P. Cornell	*Greek Papyri in the Library of Cornell University*, ed. W. L. Westermann and C. J. Kraemer, New York, 1926
P. Fior.	*Papiri greco-egizii*, ed. G. Vitelli, 3 vols., Milano

P. Lond.	*Greek Papyri in the British Museum*, ed. Kenyon and Bell, London, 1893–1917
P. Oxy.	*The Oxyrhynchus Papyri*, ed. B. Grenfell *et al.*, Oxford, 1898–
P. Soc. It.	*Papiri greci e latini*, ed. Vitelli *et al.*, Firenze, 1912–
P. Thead.	*Papyrus de Theadelphie*, ed. P. Jouguet, Paris, 1911.
P-W	Pauly-Wissowa-Kroll, *Realenzyklopädie der klassischen Altertumswissenschaft*
PPO	praefectus praetorio
PUR	praefectus urbis Romae
QSP	quaestor sacri palatii
SB	of certain or almost-certain senatorial origin
sb	of probable senatorial origin
SEG	*Supplementum Epigraphicum Graecum*
Vic.	vicarius

NOTE: Plain Roman numerals followed by Arabic figures refer to inscriptions in the *Corpus Inscriptionum Latinarum*.

References to the ancient authors and to journal articles employ the abbreviations in common use. The works of modern authors are often referred to simply by the name of the author or by his name together with a brief title, thus: Chastagnol, *Fastes*. For full titles and details of publication the reader should consult the bibliography.

Where no reference is given for a consulate it must be taken as Degrassi's *Fasti*, and where this occurs in the case of urban prefectures, the reference is to *Chron. 354 (MGH* AA XI). The terms 'urban prefect' and 'prefect of the city' are always to be taken as referring to Rome unless Constantinople is specified.

INTRODUCTION

i. *The Problem*

'LA civilisation romaine n'est pas morte de sa belle mort. Elle a été assassinée'[1]. Such is the succinct conclusion of Piganiol, which is shared in essentials by both N. H. Baynes and A. H. M. Jones. A Byzantinist looking at the West, Baynes points out, is particularly concerned to discover 'the *differentia* which distinguishes the history of the Western provinces from that of the *partes orientales*'.

And so many of the modern explanations do not provide him with any such *differentia*. 'Die Ausrottung der Besten', civil wars, and imperial jealousy of outstanding merit did not affect the West alone: the whole Roman world suffered from these scourges: the brutality of an undisciplined soldiery was likewise an evil common to both halves of the Empire. Soil-exhaustion, climatic change, these must have affected the entire Mediterranean area. The oppression of civil servants, the decay of the municipal senates, the flight from the land—all these ills the Eastern provinces were not spared. Greeks and Orientals invaded the West and we are told caused the collapse of the Roman power there; but in the East these same Greeks and Orientals sustained the Empire against unceasing assaults for another millennium: it seems mysterious.[2]

Baynes's own explanation is one which, in his own words, 'is so humiliatingly simple that I am constrained to believe that it must be right'.[3] The *differentia* which Baynes sees between East and West is that, 'while the Danubian provinces were continuously ravaged, Asia Minor was for the most part untroubled by invasions: Asia Minor remained . . . a reservoir alike of men and money. It was this reservoir which the West lacked.'[4]

Far from settling the issue this explanation is only question-begging, forcing us back to those very factors which Baynes has dismissed out of hand. The lack of men and money in the West may well have been a factor in its fall, but on its own it is hardly a sufficient explanation. This poverty must itself be explained.

[1] A. Piganiol, *L'Empire Chrétien*, 422.
[2] N. H. Baynes, 'The decline of the Roman power in Western Europe. Some modern explanations', *JRS* 33 (1943) 34.
[3] Ibid.   [4] Ibid., 35.

Jones's explanation is at least logically consistent. The last sentence of text in his three-volume *Later Roman Empire* is a clear-voiced repudiation of internal causes: 'The internal weaknesses of the empire cannot have been a major factor in its decline.'[1] 'There is a very simple test', explains Jones in an earlier article, 'which Western scholars are prone to forget. It was only in the West that the imperial government broke down in the fifth century. Yet in the East Christianity was deeper rooted and more widespread, and monasticism was both more extensive and carried to greater extremes. The army in the East was fully as large and as expensive and the bureaucracy was swollen and corrupt. Yet at the very time when the Western Empire was staggering to its fall, the Eastern was making a recovery.'[2] 'These facts', Jones continues, 'indicate that the empire did not, as some modern historians almost assume, collapse from internal causes. It succumbed to persistent attacks by invading barbarians.'[3] Jones then goes on to describe the strategic advantages that the East had over the West: 'The greater part of the Eastern Empire—Asia Minor, Syria, and Egypt—was more or less immune from invasion, and provided the resources to maintain the imperial armies in the Balkans, which, though frequently invaded, were regularly recovered from the impregnable bridgehead of Constantinople.'[4] In the West the border between the Empire and the barbarians was both much longer and more vulnerable.[5]

The logic of this argument would seem compelling. How indeed can one attribute the collapse of the Western Empire to factors even more present in the East and yet causing no collapse there? Strategic vulnerability is one important respect in which the East and West differed. But is it the only one?

The answer given in the present study is 'No'. In the view of the present author there is a much more important difference between the two halves of the Empire, a difference which has not been noticed by previous historians. It is a difference in the power-structure of the two areas.

[1] A. H. M. Jones, *The Later Roman Empire*, ii. 1068.
[2] A. H. M. Jones, 'The decline and fall of the Roman Empire', *History* 40 (1955) 220.
[3] Ibid., 221.   [4] Ibid.   [5] Ibid., 221–2.

Both East and West are normally seen as ruled by an autocratic emperor, but this study will show that 'dominate', 'autocracy', 'absolute monarchy', 'oriental despotism', 'military tyranny' and the like are terms much less applicable to the West in the fourth century than to the East, though they tend to be used to refer to both halves as if there was no difference between the power-structures of East and West.

The 'Dominate' is seen in two main ways by historians. Some, following Gibbon, see no change in the real power of the emperor in the transition from Principate to Dominate; just a change in style. Others see imperial power gradually growing from the beginning of the Principate onwards, with a sudden culminating spurt in our period.

> Like the modesty of Augustus, [writes Gibbon] the state maintained by Diocletian was a theatrical representation; but it must be confessed that, of the two comedies, the former was of a much more liberal and manly character than the latter. It was the aim of the one to disguise, and the object of the other to display, the unbounded power which the emperors possessed over the Roman world.[1]

The other view is well put by J. B. Bury:

> From the very beginning the Princeps was the predominant partner [i.e. as against the senate], and the constitutional history of the Principate turns on his gradual and steady usurpation of nearly all the functions of government which Augustus had attributed to the Senate. The republican disguise fell away completely before the end of the third century. Aurelian adopted external fashions which marked a king, not a citizen; and Diocletian and Constantine definitely transformed the state from a republic to an autocracy.[2]

Diehl places the responsibility for the change directly on Constantine's shoulders:

> ... Long before this [viz. the founding of Constantinople], a new conception of the monarchy had been astir in the Roman Empire. The transformation came about at the beginning of the fourth century through contact with the Near East. Constantine strove to make of the imperial power an absolute domination by divine right. He surrounded

---

[1] E. Gibbon, *The Decline and Fall of the Roman Empire*, i. 373. Cf. H. St. L. B. Moss, *The Birth of the Middle Ages*, 21–3; E. Stein, *Geschichte des spätrömischen Reiches*, 2.   [2] J. B. Bury, *The Later Roman Empire*, i, 5.

it with all the splendour of costume, of the crown, and the royal purple; with all the pompous ceremonial of etiquette, with all the magnificence of court and palace. Deeming himself the representative of God on earth, believing that in his intellect he was a reflection of the supreme intellect, he endeavoured in all things to emphasize the sacred character of the sovereign, to separate him from the rest of mankind by the solemn forms with which he surrounded him; in a word, to make earthly royalty as it were an image of the divine royalty.[1]

Ensslin, writing in the *Cambridge Ancient History*, also discerns a 'transformation of the first citizen into an autocratic monarch,'[2] and Rostovtzeff goes so far as to attribute the Dominate to Constantine's pro-Christian religious policy:

[Constantine] offered peace to the Church, provided that she would recognise the state and support the imperial power. The Church—to her detriment, as many scholars believe—accepted the offer. For the first time the imperial power became firmly established on a solid basis, but it lost almost completely, save for some irrelevant formulae, the last remnants of its constitutional character as the supreme magistrature of the people of the Empire. It now resembled the Persian monarchy of the Sassanidae and its predecessors in the East, the monarchies of Babylonia, Assyria, Egypt and the rest.[3]

To round off our anthology on the Dominate here is A. H. M. Jones's succinct summary of imperial power in the later Roman Empire: 'Both in the theory and in the practice of the constitution the emperor's powers were absolute.'[4]

It will be noticed that none of the historians quoted makes any distinction between the nature of government in the two halves of the Empire.

Yet, as will be shown in the chapters that follow, the senatorial aristocracy had considerable political power in the fourth century West, though not in the East. This aristocratic political power in the West was new to the fourth century, dating from the reign of Constantine the Great, who changed the system of appointments to high state office.

In the three centuries before Constantine the senatorial aristocracy had in fact steadily been losing political power. Conscious

---

[1] C. Diehl, *History of the Byzantine Empire*, 4.
[2] *Cambridge Ancient History*, xii. 367.
[3] M. Rostovtzeff, *The Social and Economic History of the Roman Empire*, 509.
[4] A. H. M. Jones, *The Later Roman Empire*, i, 321.

that imperial power and senatorial power were at opposite ends of a political see-saw, emperor after emperor encroached upon the power of the Senate from the early Principate onwards until it was left with only ceremonial functions. But though the Senate as an institution was of no account, the men who comprised it continued to have a monopoly of most of the high state posts, notably provincial governorships. At first emperors worked through the Senate, subverting the position of the older families by introducing their own nominees into the Senate and then appointing them to governorships, and thus keeping within the traditional constitutional framework. But the third century saw a change. Particularly in the latter half of the century emperors tended to by-pass the Senate, advancing non-senators directly to high office without bothering to make them senators first. This tendency was systematized by Diocletian, in whose reign senators were debarred from all but a few high state offices and the senatorial career became a cul-de-sac. A low-born military man who cultivated an aloof manner and kept an ostentatious court, Diocletian had achieved the aim of more than one of his predecessors. He was indeed an autocrat.

Instead of seeing the reign of Constantine as a continuation of that of Diocletian, which is the normal view, I see a sharp break between the two. Diocletian is the culmination of anti-aristocratic trends that can be traced back to the earliest days of the Principate. But Constantine reversed these trends by appointing nobles to high office. Of course this did not make Constantine a cipher in government. But he had set centrifugal forces in motion—forces which were the very reverse of those which had been dominant under his immediate predecessors. With Constantine and his successors we are still a long way from the insignificant king of the Middle Ages, but we are certainly moving in that direction. For we already have a rich, close-knit aristocracy living on self-contained large estates controlling the lives of a large number of peasants— and the same people gaining increasing control over the imperial government in the West.

But how is the change to be explained ? To explain it in terms of an idiosyncratic predilection on Constantine's part for aristocrats is inadequate—unless we are to suppose that this predilection was hereditarily transmitted not only to successors of his own blood but also to others not related to him at all, such as the emperors of the Theodosian house. For it must be emphasized that Constantine's policy was continued by his successors for as long as there was an emperor in the West—and even beyond that time. Even an emperor like Valentinian I, who made no secret of his dislike of the aristocracy and who had genuine sympathy for the man at the bottom of the social and economic pyramid, conformed to the Constantinian pattern, giving a free hand in the West to a noble— and corrupt—praetorian prefect. The appointment of members of the aristocracy to imperial posts by Constantine and his successors may best be understood as an attempt on the part of these Christian emperors to placate and win over an ardently pagan class which already had considerable landed wealth and local influence in the West.

The East gives us a very different picture. There were some old Greek-speaking families of notables in the cities, but they lacked the wealth and influence of the Western senatorial aristocracy. Being a much more urban society as a whole, the Eastern half of the Empire was much less susceptible to the centrifugal influence of an aristocracy, and the old Roman senatorial families were heavily concentrated in the West. Hence the very small number of senatorial aristocrats in government posts in the East. There was simply no need for the emperor to woo the senatorial aristocracy with Eastern posts in the way that Constantine and his successors found it necessary to do in the West. So the East continued to be governed by non-nobles on the whole, on the Diocletianic model, and it was here that the sons of sausage-makers or manual workers were the founders of new noble lines. It was to take several centuries before the Eastern emperor was threatened by a strong aristocracy. Here the Dominate was a reality.

The emperor had given the aristocracy a share in the ruling of the Western Empire—a share which was to increase at the emperor's expense. Office-holders could use their position as a lever to enhance their wealth and local influence, and noble office-holders in general had two main advantages over most of their non-noble colleagues. First, they tended to be better endowed with wealth and land, and circumstances favoured the large landowner. The barbarian incursions in the latter half of the fourth century forced many a free peasant smallholder to barter his land in return for the protection of a neighbouring estate-owner. In this way large estates could be consolidated and on each of them, with its walls and self-sufficient economy, the estate-owner was an autocrat. Secondly, being a close-knit intricate network of interrelated families, the aristocracy had ready-made channels for the conduction and distribution of favours and influence within their exclusive group. For, though now part of the imperial administrative machine, nobles utilized their position for the benefit of their families in the localities. The aristocracy was essentially a centrifugal force, which helped to undermine the position of the imperial administration from within while war and invasion threatened it from the outside.

This brings us back to the question of 'decline and fall', a topic dearer than ever not only to scholars but to the general public as well. In his introduction to a collection of essays on our period, Arnaldo Momigliano writes: 'In this year 1959 it can still be considered an historical truth that the Roman empire declined and fell. Nobody as yet is prepared to deny that the Roman empire has disappeared.'[1] Perhaps not; but a realization that the Roman Empire has ceased to exist is hardly the same as an admission that it declined and fell. After all, who will deny that Classical Greek is no longer a living language—and yet who will claim that it declined and fell? The essential difference between the standard images of the Roman Empire and the Western Middle Ages is surely that the former was a centralized unit, tightly organized with power radiating from the emperor, while the latter was a time when power was diffused among the landed aristocracy and central authority was weak. This is of course a gross simplification of the societies concerned, but it is not a falsification. How can we account for the transition from the one type of society to the other? The normal reply is in terms of 'decline and fall': the Roman Empire fell and a new society was born from the rubble. The evidence presented in

[1] A. Momigliano (ed.), *The Conflict between Paganism and Christianity in the Fourth Century*, 1. For a discussion of theories of 'decline and fall' see S. Mazzarino, *La Fine del Mondo Antico;* W. C. Bark, *Origins of the Medieval World*, especially 41 ff. Cf. F. Lot, *La Fin du Monde Antique et le début du Moyen Age.'*

this study gives us a different picture—a gradual change, in which, it should be noted, the Germanic invaders do not play a very major role. From the reign of Constantine, fully a century before Alaric's capture of Rome, centrifugal aristocratic forces were in the ascendant. What the Germanic invasions did was to strengthen these forces still further at the emperor's expense. There is no parallel in the writings of aristocratic authors such as Symmachus or Apollinaris Sidonius to Salvian's *cri de coeur* on behalf of the peasantry. The explanation is simple: the senatorial aristocracy fared well under their new masters, and in addition to their self-contained domains the nobles were coming to control the Church, as we can see in the writings of Gregory of Tours: Land and Church, the two bases of the Middle Ages.

In eliminating the emperor, therefore, the invasions only strengthened the underlying amalgam of economic, social, and political forces, centrifugal in tendency and aristocratic in tone, which had been prominent since the reign of Constantine and which were to continue to dominate Western Europe for close on a thousand years.

ii. *Nobles, Clarissimi, and Senators*

In this study the terms 'noble' and 'member of the (senatorial) aristocracy' are used synonymously to refer to someone of senatorial birth or senatorial origin, by which is meant someone whose father at least was a *clarissimus*. Most of the nobles dealt with were in fact, as will be seen, members of families whose senatorial rank can be traced back to the third century or before, so that a son of the first member of the family to attain senatorial rank is always referred to as a new noble or by some similar designation.

While this usage of the term 'noble' is a departure from the strict Republican use of 'nobilis' to refer to the holder of a consulate or one of his descendants, it accords with the meaning of the word as used in the fourth century by writers such as Symmachus and Ammianus.[1]

While all nobles were *clarissimi*, not all *clarissimi* were nobles. By the beginning of our period the title 'vir clarissimus' had been

---

[1] Symm. *Rel.* iii. 7; Amm. xvi. 10. 13.

in common use for well over a century to refer to a senator or a man of senatorial rank. The title was hereditary, as we know from the examples that we have of the title 'clarissimus puer'.[1] The clarissimate was not confined to men and boys, for we also find the titles 'clarissima puella' and 'clarissima femina', the latter coming to a woman either from her father or from her husband. A good example of the acquisition of the title by marriage is supplied by Vinicia Marciana, who, daughter of a *perfectissimus*, and wife of a *clarissimus*, is styled 'c(larissima) f(emina)'.[2]

The clarissimate was the late Empire's equivalent to the *laticlavium* of the Principate and, just as in that period a *novus homo* could be awarded this by the emperor or be adlected 'in amplissimum ordinem', so in the late Empire individuals could be given the clarissimate by imperial 'codicilli clarissimatus', and the title could be extended to the holders of an ever-increasing number of hitherto equestrian state posts.[3]

Clarissimi became senators proper in the traditional way, namely by holding one or other of the republican magistracies, and it was still normal practice for young nobles to become senators unless too poor to be able to afford the expenditure which the tenure of a republican magistracy now entailed. Entry to the Senate without the expense of games could be had by two avenues, one being the ordinary consulship and the other adlection 'inter consulares', the only type of adlection of which we have any evidence in the late Empire, and which is discussed below. Membership of the Senate was no longer of any practical significance, since the Senate as an institution was completely unimportant, and it is hardly surprising that its meetings were so unattractive to its members that the quorum had to be fixed at fifty.[4]

Under the tetrarchy of Diocletian and his colleagues the senatorial order formed a reasonably homogeneous group comprising

---

[1] The earliest example known to the present author dates from 197: D. 1143. See also D.1152, 1201, 1226, 1355.   [2] xi. 831 = D. 1218 Mutina.
[3] See *CTh*. xii. 74. 5 (371). The formula for such *codicilli* is given by Cassiodorus, *Variae* vi. 14. The kernel is contained in the words: 'Pandite curiam, suscipite candidatum: iam senatui praedestinatus est, cui nos contulimus laticlaviam dignitatem.'
[4] See Symm. *Or*. vi, a plea for an impoverished noble to enter the Senate. On the praetorship and quaestorship see *CTh*. vi. 4.

men of senatorial birth, since, in the latter part of the third century
praetorian prefects were evidently the only *novi homines* to join
its ranks.[1] When, however, the senatorial *cursus*, which Diocletian
had turned into a *cul-de-sac*, became once again the main avenue
of political advancement under Constantine and his successors, this
homogeneity came to an end. For now, in addition to men of
senatorial birth, the order was flooded with office holders whose
positions had given them the clarissimate automatically, and, as
the fourth century passed, more and more offices came to carry
senatorial rank with them.[2]

This influx of new men into the clarissimate eventually reduced
its significance and, as a result, office-holders in the upper echelons
of power began to differentiate themselves from ordinary *clarissimi*
by adding to their titles 'spectabilis' in the case of vicars and
proconsuls and those equated with them in rank in the military and
court hierarchies, and 'illustris' in the case of the praetorian and
urban prefects, *magistri militum*, and the major palatine officials.
These new titles were not hereditary, and the son of an *illustris*
would be a mere *clarissimus* until he earned a higher title through
office.[3]

In the pre-Constantinian era, therefore, titles are much more
precise indices to a man's social background than they are in the
period from Constantine onwards. The equestrian titles 'egregius'
and 'perfectissimus' are of course always signs of non-senatorial
birth, but the gradual increase during the fourth century in the
number of posts carrying with them an automatic clarissimate made
the equestrian titles obsolete and gave many men of non-senatorial

---

[1] See Chapter ii, p. 47 f., below.
[2] See Chapters VI and VII, pp. 143 ff., below.
[3] See *CTh.* xvi. 5. 52 (412), where the distinction between the four senatorial
classes comes out from a graduated list of fines payable by Donatists of differing
ranks: '... inl(ustres) singillatim poenae nomine fisco nostro auri pondo
quinquaginta cogantur inferre, spectabiles auri pondo quadraginta, senatores
auri pondo triginta, clarissimi auri pondo viginti. . . .'
At some time between 437 and the reign of Justinian the Senate as a body was
limited to *illustres*, as can be seen from an interpolation in a text which is otherwise
the same in the *Theodosianus* and *Justinianus*. *CTh.* vi. 23. 4, *CJ.* xii. 16. 3. See
also *CJ.* xii. 1. 10 = *CTh.* ix. 35. 3; *Dig.* i. 9. 12. 1. See Jones, *Later Roman Empire*,
iii, 152, n. 16. That the titles *spectabilis* and *illustris* were not themselves hereditary
can be seen from *CJ.* xii. 1. 11 (377), x. 32. 63 (471-4).

origin the same title as that of the nobles. Thus, while under the
tetrarchy the clarissimate alone is sufficient evidence of nobility—
except in the case of praetorian prefects[1]—later, especially in the
post-Constantinian period, it usually throws no light on a man's
origins, and other criteria of nobility must be employed.

In the case of low-ranking governors such as *praesides*, however,
the title 'clarissimus' is a pointer to senatorial origin. Up to at least
379 the normal title for a *praeses* was 'perfectissimus', and all
praesides who were *clarissimi* may be assumed to have been of
senatorial origin, since it is inconceivable that the emperor would
elevate a *novus homo* to senatorial rank just to appoint him a *praeses*,
a position which he could and indeed should hold as an equestrian.[2]

In fact the only datable cases known of *praesides* with the clarissimate, in addition to three Diocletianic *praesides* of Syria, were under
Constantine. The spread of consular governorships in provinces
favoured by nobles accounts for the absence of senatorial *praesides*
under Constantine.[3]

Though Eusebius' description of Constantine as lavish in his
awards of honours is no doubt correct, there is a strong indication
in the passage concerned that the award of senatorial titles was
reserved for a select few. Indeed, Eusebius contrasts the number of
Constantine's awards of lesser honours with the number of his
grants of senatorial titles: οἱ δὲ συγκλήτου τιμῆς· οἱ δὲ τῶν ὑπάτων·
πλείους δ᾽ἡγεμόνες ἐχρημάτιζον· κομήτων δ᾽οἱ μὲν, πρώτου τάγματος
ἠξιοῦντο· οἱ δὲ, δευτέρου· οἱ δὲ τρίτου· διασημοτάτων δ᾽ὡσαύτως καὶ
ἑτέρων πλείστων ἀξιωμάτων, μυρίοι ἄλλοι μετεῖχον· εἰς γὰρ τὸ
πλείονας τιμεῖν, διαφόρους ἐπενόει βασιλεὺς ἀξίας.[4]

Furthermore, there are only two known examples of adlection
in our period. Julius Rufinianus Ablabius Tatianus, who was
adlected 'inter consulares' 'iudicio divi Constantini', presumably

[1] See Chapter II, p. 47 f., below.
[2] 'Perfectissimus' evidently remained the normal title for *praesides* into the
last quarter of the fourth century, the last datable examples being Pontius
Asclepiodotus, *praeses* of the Poenine Alps in 377 (xii. 138 Seduni) and Fl. Felix
Gentilis, *praeses* of Mauretania Sitifensis under Gratian (379/83) viii. 20266.
[3] See Chapters II and III, below.
[4] Eus. *V. Const.* iv. 1. This passage will not bear the interpretation placed
upon it by Jones to the effect that Constantine was 'liberal in granting senatorial
rank'. *Later Roman Empire*, i, 106.

in recognition of his father's panegyrics on the Emperor, was given the position of legate of the proconsul of Asia as his first appointment after his adlection. Though a low post, it was nevertheless one which could not be filled by an equestrian. Caelius Saturninus, also adlected 'inter consulares' in Constantine's reign, had held three vicariates when he entered the Senate, and his adlection must be seen as a reward for a successful equestrian career.[1]

In view of our evidence, it seems highly unlikely that a Constantinian 'v.c. praeses' would be anything but a man of senatorial origin, but in the case of all other office-holders after the time of the tetrarchy the clarissimate is of no use as an index to social background.

Since the criterion of nobility is birth and lineage, direct evidence of this is of prime importance. Where it is found, however, it must often be viewed with a fair degree of scepticism. When St. Jerome tells us that St. Paula's father Rogatus was descended from Agamemnon we cannot help giving an incredulous smile. But the statement is not altogether meaningless. Jerome, we can be sure, had not himself invented this lineage for Rogatus, but was probably expressing a current view, an exaggerated popular way of saying that Rogatus came of old noble stock.[2]

In the absence of direct evidence of nobility we must rely on nomenclature. In the late Empire a child would normally be given names from both sides of the family, the *nomen* frequently coming from one side and the *cognomen* from the other, though there was no limit to the number of names a person might have.

The next feature that we must consider is the tenure of republican magistracies. Our examination of these ancient offices will be directed towards discovering whether and, if so, in what circumstances the presence of a republican magistracy in a man's *cursus* is an indication of senatorial birth.

In addition to the ordinary consulship, which will not be dealt

---

[1] Jones's view that Nonius Verus was an *adlectus* is based on a misreading of the inscription concerned. (D. 1218). Verus was not the son of Caecilianus *v.p.*, but his son-in-law. Jones, loc. cit.

[2] Jerome on Rogatus: Jer. *Ep.* 108. 3. Rogatus was evidently a member of the noble *gens* and was probably also connected with the Crepereii. See stemma I, and pp. 133 ff., below.

with here, the quaestorship, praetorship, and suffect consulship are the only republican magistracies of which we have any detailed records from the late Empire.

But the absence of references to an office in the sources cannot be used as evidence that that office had died out, as we can see in the case, for example, of the positions of aedile and tribune of the plebs. Each of these is referred to once in fourth century sources. The tribunate of the plebs appears in a law in the Theodosian Code, issued in 371, surprisingly enough from Constantinople.[1] The reference to the position of aedile is in one of the Eclogues of Ausonius: 'aediles etiam plebi aedilesque curules/sacra sigillorum nomine dicta colunt'.[2] These lines occur in a poem describing the Roman religious festivals and what is referred to here is the *Sigillaria*, the feast of images, the last few days of the *Saturnalia* when people customarily exchanged gifts of miniature figures or images. But even more noteworthy is the surviving distinction in nomenclature between curule and plebeian aediles, a reminder of ancient struggles. Quaestors are recorded in inscriptions well into the fifth century, and we know from John Lydus and Boethius that the praetorship still existed in the sixth century: 'atqui praetura, magna olim potestas, nunc inane nomen est et senatorii census gravis sarcina'.[3] The 'gravis sarcina' to which Boethius refers is the providing of games, a burden attached to both the quaestorship and the praetorship, as is testified by numerous laws in the Theodosian Code specifying how much money should be spent on the games by the holders of the magistracies, what the fines were for defaulters, and who was exempted from such punishment.[4] At least, in the reign of Constantine games were also attached to the suffect consulship.[5] Whether this continued to be the case later on as well is unknown, but the suffect consul who had an accident while riding in a ceremonial chariot in 401 may well have been on his way to the games.[6]

Of the eighteen certain or almost-certain suffect consuls of the fourth century eight are known to have held both the quaestorship

---

[1] *CTh.* xii. 1. 74.   [2] Aus. *Ecl.* xxiii; *de Feriis Romanis*, 31–2.
[3] Boethius, *de Philosophiae Consolatione*, iii. 4. See also Joh. Lydus, *de Magistratibus Populi Romani*, II. 30.
[4] *CTh.* vi. 4. 11; vi. 4. 1, 7; vi. 4. 13, 14.
[5] *CTh.* vi. 4. 1.   [6] Symm. *Ep.* vi. 40.

and the praetorship before their consulships, and a further two to have held the praetorship. Though the remaining eight suffect consuls are not recorded as having held either of the other republican magistracies, they are very likely to have held at least one of them. For, in all cases where we know of the suffect consulship from a detailed *cursus* the holder of it is also recorded as praetor or quaestor, or, more usually, as both, and the suffect consulships of those who are not recorded as quaestors or praetors are known to us from epithets such as 'vir consularis' or from some other casual reference.[1]

On the other hand, however, the great majority of men recorded as quaestors, praetors or both in detailed sources are not recorded as suffect consuls. That the praetorship could take the place of the quaestorship as a qualification for membership of the Senate can be seen from a law in the Theodosian Code enjoining proconsuls and vicars to follow the example of two of their number in holding the praetorship: 'Meministis profecto, patres conscripti, nec ullius temporis avellet oblivio, quod Facundus ex proconsule et Arsenius ex vicariis praetorum insignibus splenduerunt, nec quisquam horum putavit esse praeturam intra propriam dignitatem. Quid autem inlustrius his repperitur examplis?'[2] A similar injunction is applied to *duces* when they became *clarissimi* at the end of the century.[3]

We come now to a most important question: who held the suffect consulship and how do they compare with those who held only the praetorship, quaestorship or both? A passage in a letter of Symmachus to Theodosius and Arcadius may be interpreted to mean that a man's wealth would determine how many of the republican magistracies he would hold: 'nullo enim dissentiente decretum est, quis modus censuum semel aut saepius fungendis (muneribus obnoxius sit)'.[4] If we accept the inclusion of the suffect consulship in this vague statement, we have to attribute games to it, which seems likely, as has been remarked above.

Most of those recorded as quaestors and praetors were men of senatorial birth, but among the praetors are found some men of a very different background, men like Facundus and Arsenius men-

<hr>

[1] See list of noble holders of republican magistracies, p. 224 ff., below.
[2] *CTh.* vi. 4. 15 (359).   [3] *CTh.* vi. 4. 28 (396).   [4] Symm. *Rel.* viii. 3.

tioned in a law of Constantine who were not of senatorial birth but who reached positions in the imperial service entitling them to the style 'clarissimus'.[1] Such men appear to have taken the praetorship rather than the quaestorship to enter the Senate. It is not difficult to distinguish the two types of praetor, the noble and the non-noble, since a man of senatorial birth would become praetor very early in his career before holding any governorship, whereas the non-noble praetor would of course already have an established career behind him. Where the quaestorship or praetorship appear early in a career or alone, the holder must be considered as of senatorial birth.

So much for quaestors and praetors. But what of the suffect consuls? Chastagnol has expressed the view that the suffect consulship was no longer to be found 'dans le *cursus* des grandes familles urbaines; il paraît attribué à de récents *allecti* ou à des clarissimes de familles moins connues . . .'[2] According to Chastagnol, therefore, the suffect consuls came from two groups: the lesser nobility and men of non-senatorial birth who were adlected to the Senate 'inter quaestorios' or 'inter praetorios' but 'qui n'ont pas bénéficié de la faveur d'une *allectio inter consulares*'.[3] The evidence, however, points in the opposite direction. There are, as has been noted above, several men about whom we know nothing more than that they were suffect consuls. But, those whose careers we know in any detail tend to have held the quaestorship and praetorship before becoming suffect consuls. This gives the lie to Chastagnol's idea that *adlecti* became suffect consuls, and in any case there are no examples of *adlecti* in the fourth century other than 'inter consulares', and men so adlected were of course exempt from the duty of holding the praetorship or quaestorship. The suffect consuls of the fourth century, it will be seen, were men of senatorial birth, some of newer and others of older families.

Chastagnol's claim that the barbarians appointed consul by Constantine (according to Julian in Ammianus) were suffect

[1] *CTh.* vi. 4. 15 (359), quoted above.
[2] A. Chastagnol, 'Observations sur le consulat suffect et la préture du Bas-Empire', *Revue Historique* 219 (1958) 233.
[3] Ibid., n. 1.

consuls must be rejected.¹ The relevant passage in Ammianus is as follows: 'Tunc (sc. Iulianus) et memoriam Constantini, ut novatoris turbatorisque priscarum legum et moris antiquitus recepti, vexavit, eum aperte incusans, quod barbaros omnium primus ad usque fasces auxerat et trabeas consulares.' It is worth noting, however, that the passage continues: 'insulse nimirum et leviter: qui cum vitare deberet id quod infestius obiurgavit, brevi postea Mamertino in consulatu iunxit Nevittam, nec splendore, nec usu, nec gloria horum similem, quibus magistratum amplissimum detulerat Constantinus: contra inconsummatum et subagrestem, et quod minus erat ferendum celsa in potestate crudelem'.² Julian's attack on Constantine for making barbarians consuls was nullified by his own appointment of Nevitta. Now, Nevitta, of Frankish origin, was consul in 362—*consul ordinarius*. We should therefore expect the reference to Constantine's appointments to be likewise to ordinary consuls. But no obviously barbarian names are to be found among Constantine's ordinary consuls, though Seeck has tried to cast Symmachus' grandfather, ordinary consul in 330, in the role of a barbarian elevated to high station by imperial favour.³

That Ammianus wrote 'Constantinus' and not 'Constantius' is clear from the context, though Constantine appointed Arbitio as *consul ordinarius* in 355. The true explanation probably lies elsewhere. In his bitter attack on the memory or a relative whom he despised as the instigator of a new religious order Julian attributed to Constantine any innovation of which he could think. This blanket condemnation of his uncle as a dangerous revolutionary is well conveyed by the words 'novator turbatorque priscarum legum et moris antiquitus recepti', and it is quite possible that Julian genuinely believed at the time that the promotion of barbarians to the ordinary consulship had been one of Constantine's innovations. In any case, there is no known case of a military leader

¹ Chastagnol, op. cit., 233. A. Cameron, 'The Roman friends of Ammianus', *JRS* 54 (1964), rejects the identification.
² Amm. xxi. 10. 8.
³ O. Seeck, P-W IVA, 1141 (cf. Ensslin, P-W VIIA, 998), and O. Seeck, *Hermes*, 41 (1906), 533. A. Alföldi, *Conversion of Constantine*, 119, n. 2, is doubtful about the identification and A. Cameron rejects it. A. Cameron, 'The Roman friends of Ammianus', *JRS* 54 (1964) 21–2.

being honoured with the suffect consulship, whereas the ordinary consulship was frequently extended to such men.[1] A list of all known suffect consuls in our period will be found at the end of this volume. All of them were noble, as I have demonstrated elsewhere.[2] Within the complex skein of interconnected noble families some relationships were, needless to say, more important than others. A fifth cousin twice removed would no doubt tend to be a less valuable connection than a brother or first cousin. But there is no sign of the division of the aristocracy into hostile factions in our period as there was in the days of the Republic. Nor should we expect to find such a division. The whole ethos of political life in our period was totally different from that of the Republic. The beginnings of aristocratic oligarchy belonged to a period known even to men of the Republic only through legends. Only fifteen new men appeared in the consular *fasti* in the three centuries before Cicero's consulship.[3] Political office was the prerogative of the senatorial aristocracy. So much so that the word for 'state' was the same as that for 'senatorial oligarchy': *respublica*. In the third century of the Principate the senatorial aristocracy is politically impotent. With Constantine they return to office, but they never again have the monopoly of politics that they had in the days of the middle Republic. In these circumstances, the taste for internal dissension seems to have been lost.

If there was any issue which divided men in the fourth century it was religion. Yet it does not appear to have divided the aristocracy. The *gens* Ceionia, for example, was noted for its devotion to the ancient gods.[4] Caeionius Rufius Albinus was of the circle of Symmachus, if we can believe Macrobius.[5] His brother Publilius

---

[1] Cameron (loc. cit.), identifying the consul of 330 with the Symmachus who was vicar of Moesia in 319, argues that a military man (which is what a barbarian would most likely be) would not be appointed to a vicariate, which was a civil office. But cf. the case of Verinus, p. 42 f., below.

[2] See M. T. W. Arnheim, 'Suffect consuls in the Later Roman Empire', *Latomus* (forthcoming). See also M. T. W. Arnheim, 'The Influence of the Senatorial Aristocracy on the Imperial Government in the late third and fourth centuries A.D.', unpublished Cambridge Ph.D. dissertation, 1969, 13 ff.

[3] M. Gelzer, *The Roman Nobility*, 50 ff.

[4] See p. 50 f.   [5] Macrob. *Sat.* iii. 4. 12; vi. 1. 1.

Caeionius Caecina Albinus was a *pontifex*.[1] But both married Christians, and their daughters, Albina and Laeta respectively, and granddaughters, Melania the Younger and Paula,[2] were imbued with a rigid and ascetic Christianity through the influence of St. Jerome. Christians and pagans coexisted peacefully in the same family.[3] 'Quis hoc crederet', writes Jerome to Paula's mother, Laeta, 'ut Albini pontificis neptis de repromissione matris nasceretur, ut praesente et gaudente avo parvulae adhuc lingua balbutiens alleluia resonaret et virginem Christi in suo gremio nutriret et senex?'[4]

As will be seen in Chapter V, the aristocracy formed a very close-knit and exclusive circle and tended to marry within their own ranks. Noble birth was one of the most highly prized qualities in our period as in so many others. More important, coupled with office, landed wealth, and local influence, family connections gave the senatorial aristocracy an independence that could not have been shared by non-noble office-holders. Office, nevertheless, even on its own, was a very valuable commercial tool, as we shall see in Chapter VII, and with its help a non-noble official could transcend humble origins. Flavius Ablabius, for instance, praetorian prefect in the East under Constantine, was a Christian who began his career as an *officialis* of the governor of Crete,[5] and Domitianus, another Eastern praetorian prefect, but this time under Constantius II, was the son of a manual worker.[6] With the aid of their offices such men no doubt soon left their background far behind them. We should not be surprised to find a reference in Eunapius to an estate of Ablabius in Bithynia.[7] Though a *clarissimus* by virtue of his office and probably a rich man, Ablabius never became part of the senatorial aristocracy. In fact, he is known to have been hostile to it. For, as we read in the entry for the year 338 in Jerome's Chronicle: 'Ablabius praefectus praetorio et multi nobilium occisi'.[8]

Some non-noble office-holders were, admittedly, on good terms with members of the senatorial aristocracy, but that is not the same

[1] Jer. *Ep.* 107. 1.   [2] See stemma I.
[3] This point is forcefully made in a most illuminating article: P. R. L. Brown, 'Aspects of the Christianization of the Roman aristocracy', *JRS* 51 (1961) 1–11.
[4] Jer. loc. cit.   [5] Lib. *Or.* xlii. 23; Eun. vi. 2–3; Zos. ii. 40–3.
[6] Lib. *Or.* xlii. 24–5.   [7] Eun. vi. 3. 10.   [8] Jer. *Chron.* s.a. 338.

thing as being part of it themselves. The only real exception is Ausonius, who was praetorian prefect under Gratian and who also secured the elevation of his son and aged father to the same rank. In his case it was his literary reputation and court connections as the Emperor's teacher which enabled him to mix on equal terms with a noble literateur such as Symmachus, who could write to him that 'neminem esse mortalium, quem prae te diligam; sic vadatum me honorabili amore tenuisti'.[1]

Though noble and non-noble office-holders shared the same titles and posts, there is no sign of 'fusion' between them. But, since the clarissimate was hereditary, the sons and grandsons of an original non-noble office-holder would be unobtrusively absorbed into the ranks of the aristocracy. Symmachus himself seems to have belonged to only the second or third generation of senatorial Symmachi.[2]

---

[1] Symm. *Ep.* i. 31. 1.   [2] See p. 83 f., below.

3

I

EMPEROR AND SENATE IN THE PRINCIPATE

THE 'dyarchy' which Mommsen discerned in the Augustan Principate has now been relegated by scholarly consensus to the history of historiography.[1] Far from being a genuine compromise with the Republic, it is now generally held, the Principate was an undiluted monarchy. All Augustus' laborious attempts to persuade his contemporaries that this was not so are of no avail. His 'restored Republic' is roundly denounced as a sham and a pretence.[2]

That the power of the emperor was formidable cannot be denied—nor was it, of course, Mommsen's intention to do so.[3] Even if we concentrate our attention upon those areas in which the power of the Senate was enhanced under the Principate, we shall see that it was not at the expense of the emperor.

If the Senate gained some judicial authority, namely the right to try criminal cases—and, it must be admitted, that it tried some of the most important political cases in the early Principate—the emperor was recognized from the very beginning as the fountainhead of all justice.

Augustus, according to Suetonius, was in the habit of trying cases in person day and night and did not spare himself even when indisposed but would then recline on a litter in the court-room or even in his bed at home.[4] In Dio we find Augustus thronged about by crowds in court while Maecenas was trying to push his way through to the emperor to get him to give fewer death sentences

---

[1] Mommsen, *Röm. Staatsrecht* iii. 2, 1252 ff.
[2] See R. Syme, *The Roman Revolution*, especially 313 ff.; Jones, 'The Imperium of Augustus', *JRS* 41 (1951) 112–19. E. T. Salmon, 'The evolution of Augustus' Principate', *Historia* 6 (1956) 456–78. But cf. T. Rice Holmes, *The Architect of the Roman Empire*, i. 179 ff.; F. B. Marsh, *The Founding of the Roman Empire*, 212 ff.; M. Hammond, *The Augustan Principate*, 121 ff.
[3] See *Staatsrecht* ii. 2, passim.
[4] Suet. *Aug.* 23.

than he seemed inclined to.[1] As we can see from this incident, the emperor had the right of capital sentence—as the Senate also now had. This was a new departure in both cases, since under the Republic only the jury courts had had this right.[2] Though evidence of primary civil jurisdiction by the emperor is scanty, it does seem to have existed, but it was probably exercised, as Jones suggests, only when the praetor could not settle the case in the normal way by means of the *ordinarium ius*.[3]

More important in practical terms was the growth of the appellate jurisdiction of the emperor, another field into which the Senate also now moved for the first time. Though appeals from Italy and the senatorial provinces should constitutionally have gone to the Senate rather than to the emperor, the emperor seems to have been preferred.[4] Indeed, so inundated was Augustus with appeals that he had to delegate them to others, using ex-consuls for provincial cases.[5]

In the second century A.D., according to the jurist Gaius, a *senatus consultum* 'legis vicem obtinet'.[6] Speaking constitutionally and theoretically, this too extended the bounds of senatorial competence beyond their limits in the time of the Republic— when, after all, they had never been equivalent to *leges*.[7] The senate passed numerous decrees in the Principate, some of them on important matters.[8] But here again, of course, the position of the emperor was supreme. Two clauses in the so-called *Lex de Imperio* of Vespasian are relevant here:

Utique quaecunque ex usu reipublicae maiestate divinarum hum[an]-
arum publicarum privatarumque rerum esse censebit, ei agere facere ius

---

[1] Dio 55. 7. 2.

[2] See Jones, 'Imperial and Senatorial Jurisdiction in the early Principate', *Studies in Roman Government and Law*, 86 ff.; Jones, 'I Appeal unto Caesar', ibid., 51–65; P. Garnsey, 'The Lex Julia and appeal under the Empire', *JRS* 56 (1966) 167–89.

[3] Jones, 'Imperial and Senatorial Jurisdiction', *Studies in Roman Government and Law*, 83 ff. Suetonius relates a charming incident in a case of parricide tried by Augustus to illustrate the Emperor's humanitarianism. Suet. *Aug.* 23. 1.

[4] Jones, op. cit., 77 ff. F. Millar, 'The Emperor, the Senate and the Provinces', *JRS* 56 (1966) 162 ff.

[5] Suet. *Aug.* 33. 3.   [6] Gaius: *Inst.* i. 4.

[7] See Mommsen, *Staatsrecht* iii. 2, 1032 ff.; P. F. Girard, *Manuel Elémentaire de Droit Romain*, Paris, 1924, 59 ff.

[8] For examples see C. G. Bruns, *Fontes Iuris Romani Antiqui*, nos. 46 ff., p. 191 ff.

potestasque sit, ita uti divo Aug., Tiberioque Iulio Caesari Aug., Tiberioque Claudio Caesari Aug. Germanico fuit.

Utique quae ante hanc legem rogatam acta gesta decreta imperata ab imperatore Caesare Vespasiano Aug., iussu mandatuve eius a quoque sunt, ea perinde iusta rataq. sint ac si populi plebisve iussu acta essent.[1]

The first of these clauses is vague and broad enough to cover almost any legislation. The term *decreta*, which appears in the second clause, refers, strictly speaking, only to judicial decisions but was often used in a broader sense. In practice imperial *constitutiones* of all types were accorded full recognition as law, be they *decreta, mandata, edicta* or *rescripta*. Augustus' Cyrene edicts are perhaps a good example of the early recognition of imperial *edicta*—and, notably enough, in this case in a public province.[2] The words in the first Cyrene edict, ἄχρι ἂν ἡ σύνκλητος βουλεύσεται περὶ τούτου ἢ ἐγὼ αὐτὸς ἄμεινον εὕρω τι, would appear to indicate that such edicts did not lapse upon the death of their authors but continued to be valid until and unless expressly revoked.[3] In any case, edicts would be included among an emperor's *acta*, and as such appear to have been sworn to by the Senate—or by one senator for all—each year.[4]

The emperor's all-embracing legislative power had long been recognized in practice by the time Ulpian penned his oft-quoted terse statement, 'quod principi placuit legis habet vigorem'.[5] From the letters of Pliny the Younger, for example, we can get some idea of the finality of the emperor's word in legislative matters[6] and Dio Chrysostom, a contemporary of Pliny's, could write ὁ δὲ νόμος βασιλέως δόγμα.[7]

In addition to the power to make laws himself, the emperor was exempted from the provisions of some laws. The wording of the *lex de imperio* of Vespasian makes it quite plain that Vespasian was 'solutus' only from those laws from which he or one of his predecessors had been explicitly exempted.[8] But by the third century

---

[1] D. 244.   [2] Cyrene Edicts: *SEG* ix. 8.
[3] For other examples of general imperial edicts see Millar, op. cit., 160 ff. The words quoted are from lines 12–13 of Edict I, *SEG* ix. 8.
[4] See Dio 58, 17. 2; 57. 8. 4; Tac. *Ann.* I. 72. 2; Dio 51. 20. 1; 53. 28. 1.
[5] *Dig.* i. 4. 1.   [6] See for example Plin. *Ep.* x. 79–80.
[7] Dio Chrys. *Or.* iii. 43.   [8] D. 244.

Ulpian can baldly say: 'Princeps legibus solutus est'[1]—a constitutional state of affairs which Cassius Dio regarded, probably erroneously, as going back to the earliest days of the Principate.[2] Another right which the Senate gained for the first time under the Principate was that of electing the magistrates, a right which was transferred to it from the comitia by Tiberius at the beginning of his reign.[3] Yet, imperial *commendatio* of candidates for election to magistracies was normal from the time of Augustus onwards, such candidates being known as *candidati Caesaris* or *candidati Augusti*.[4]

Only two of the twenty quaestors and four of the twelve praetors elected each year could be designated in this way, but in the case of the consulship both were regularly named by the emperor, thus reducing the election to a mockery. This right was, straightforwardly enough, known as *nominatio*,[5] and before long consuls appear to have been directly appointed by the emperor.[6] But the quaestorship itself, which, since the time of Sulla, swung the wide bronze portals of the curia open to the young seeker after a public career, was itself open to only a select few. An appointment as *tribunus militum* or to a position on the vigintivirate was a necessary preliminary to election as quaestor, and for those of non-senatorial families this step had to be preceded by yet another, namely the attaining of senatorial rank. The emperor, needless to say, had the right of granting senatorial rank, a rank symbolized by the *tunica laticlavia*.[7] This was one way in which the emperor controlled recruitment to the Senate from outside. The other was by *adlectio*, which can be considered as a development from the power of censors under the Republic to admit new members to the Senate. Among the people adlected by Augustus were Germanicus and Drusus, but the practice of adlection only became frequent in the second century.[8]

---

[1] *Dig.* i. 3. 31.
[2] Dio 53.18.1. For discussion of this see Mommsen, *Staatsrecht* ii. 2, 728; Hammond, op. cit., 114–16.
[3] Tac. *Ann.* i. 15. 1.   [4] See Dio 55. 34. 2.
[5] Quaestors: Tac. *Ann.* ii. 2299. Praetors: ibid. i. 15. 2. Consuls: ibid. i. 14. 6. Cf. Plin. *Pan.* 69.
[6] Tac. *Hist.* i. 77. 2; ii. 71. 3.
[7] Plin. *Ep.* ii. 9; Suet. *Vesp.* 2. 2; Suet. *Claud.* 24. 1.
[8] Germanicus and Drusus, Dio 56. 17.

In the three areas of government discussed above, then, in each of which the authority of the Senate was purportedly expanded, that of the emperor was in fact supreme. The third century Dio Cassius sums up very neatly and directly the powers of the emperor:

Οὕτω μὲν δὴ τό τε τοῦ δήμου καὶ τὸ τῆς γερουσίας κράτος πᾶν ἐς τὸν Αὔγουστον μετέστη, καὶ ἀπ' αὐτοῦ καὶ ἀκριβὴς μοναρχία κατέστη . . . λέλυνται γὰρ δὴ τῶν νόμων, ὡς αὐτὰ τὰ Λατῖνα ῥήματα λέγει· τοῦτ' ἔστιν ἐλεύθεροι ἀπὸ πάσης ἀναγκαίας νομίσεώς εἰσι καὶ οὐδενὶ τῶν γεγραμμένων ἐνέχονται.[1]

In this Dio agrees with Ulpian: 'Princeps legibus solutus est.' Together with this constitutional and political development was a tendency to revere the emperor in a religious sense. Deification of the emperors right from the time of Augustus and even the worship of emperors as gods in their own lifetime, particularly in the eastern provinces, are examples of this.[2]

Divine protection of the emperor was a constant theme. Pliny the Younger used it in his *Panegyric* on Trajan: 'ad te imperii summam et cum omnium rerum, tum etiam tui potestatem di transtulerunt'.[3] The legend 'Providentia Deorum' on coins is another example of this, as Nock has pointed out.[4] Another sign of this development is the use of the radiate crown in imperial coin portraits. This is the emblem of Apollo as the god of the sun (Phoebus). There are coins with Augustus wearing it, but these coins were issued only after his death, and the radiate crown signified the deification of the emperor. Nero, however, was shown on *dupondii* minted during his lifetime wearing a radiate crown.[5] The significance of this is obvious. In the third century the radiate crown was a regular feature on *antoniniani*, which soon took the place of *denarii*. Here is a blatant symbol of the divinity of the living emperor.[6] In the late third century the radiate crown gave way to the jewelled diadem of the sun-god. Gallienus was the first to be

[1] Dio 53. 17. 1, 18. 1.
[2] See L. R. Taylor, *Divinity of the Roman Emperor*.
[3] Plin. *Pan.* 56. 3.
[4] A. D. Nock, *Harvard Theol. Rev.* 23 (1930) 266 ff.
[5] Mattingly-Sydenham, *Roman Imperial Coinage*, iii, 178–9, and Plate xi.
[6] Rostovtzeff, *JRS* 13 (1923) 91–109.

portrayed wearing this, and was followed by Aurelian: 'Iste primus apud Romanos diadema capiti innexuit.'[1] This emblem became more common later on. While the emperor thus became identified with the sun, so the empress became identified with the moon. From the time of the Severi empresses are shown on coins together with a crescent moon. An ever-closer link was forged between emperors and gods. Commodus linked himself with Hercules. Thus reverse legends on his coins read 'Herculi Comiti'[2] and even go so far as to identify the emperor and the god. For example:

Obv.: L. AEL. AUREL. COMM. AUG. P. FEL.
Rev.: HERCULI ROMANO AUGUSTO.[3]

Julia Domna, wife of Septimius Severus and 'Mater Augustorum',[4] went further than this in appearing on coins as Cybele.[5] Aurelian Carus and Diocletian continued this. We have for example, an inscription reading: 'Deo et domino Caro invic(to) Aug(usto)'.[6] We also have inscriptions such as: 'Herculi Aug., consorti d. n. Aureliani invicti Augus[t] . . .'.[7]

What is notable here is both the link with the god, and the use of the term 'dominus noster', which became general in the third century. It is already in evidence in the reign of Septimius Severus. For example: 'Diane Auguste pro salute dd. nn. Severi et Antonini Augg. et Getae Caes. totiusq. d(omus) d(ivinae) . . .'.[8] This inscription dates from the year 204. Diocletian continued to use this title: 'dd. nn. impp. Caes. Gaius Aurel. Valerius Diocletianus p. p. invictus Augustus et imp. Caesar Marcus Aurel. Valerius Maximianus Pius Felix invictus Aug.'.[9]

An oath by the emperor's genius was now considered more binding than one by the gods: 'providentissimo principi, rectori

[1] Aur. Vict. *Epit.* 35. 3.
[2] Mattingly-Sydenham iii, 438, no. 634.
[3] Mattingly, *Roman Coins*, 439, nos. 637–40, 643, 644.   [4] D. 324.
[5] H. Cohen, *Description historique des monnaies frappées sous l'Empire Romaine*, iv, p. 114, nos. 110 ff.
[6] Mattingly-Sydenham V.ii, 146, no. 99.
[7] D. 583.   [8] D. 428; D. 430 = iii. 427.
[9] xii. 2229 = D. 620. See also viii. 814, cf. p. 979 = D. 508, *Not. Scav.* 1884, p. 422 = D. 549.

orbis ac domino, fundatori pacis aeternae Diocletiano P.F. invicto Aug. . . .'.[1]

Titles such as 'rector orbis',[2] 'pacator orbis',[3] 'restitutor generis humani',[4] 'restitutor orbis',[5] and 'restitutor saeculi'[6] are to be found on coins.

'Invictus' makes its first appearance as an imperial epithet under Commodus. It too must be connected with the sun-god.[7] 'Aeternitas Augusti' first appears under Gordian III and 'perpetuitas' under Alexander Severus[8]—even though the latter is often considered a 'senatorial' emperor.[9] These terms can probably be interpreted not only as indicating the deification of the emperor after death but even during his lifetime. This is manifest in Aurelian's coin legend:

'deo et domino nato Aureliano',

and

Obv: 'Imperatori deo et domino Aureliano'
Rev: 'restitutor orbis'.[10]

Probus and Carus kept these epithets.[11] Diocletian followed suit: 'diis genitis et deorum creatoribus dd. nn. Diocletiano et (Maximiano invict)is Augg.'.[12]

Similarly, everything connected with the emperor was given the adjective 'sacrum'.[13] This appears in Greek inscriptions as well as in Latin ones. For example, an edict of Septimius Severus and Caracalla is described as ἱερὰ γράμματα.[14] In addition, the custom of standing in the presence of the emperor may be seen in coin-types showing the emperor seated, surrounded by standing figures. Such types originate from the time of Alexander Severus.[15]

---

[1] *Dig.* xii. 2, 13, 6. iii. 5810 = D. 618.
[2] Cohen, op. cit. iv, 63, no. 596.
[3] Mattingly-Sydenham V.i, 55 and 91, nos. 218 and 294.
[4] Ibid.   [5] Ibid., 412.   [6] Ibid., 290, no. 235.
[7] Alföldi, *Röm. Mitt.* 1934, 3 ff.
[8] Cohen, op. cit., iv. 421, nos. 190 ff.; v. 26, nos. 36 ff.
[9] See Baynes, *Historia Augusta*, App.; Sir R. Syme, *Ammianus and the Historia Augusta*, 45 ff.
[10] Mattingly-Sydenham, v. i, 264, 299, nos. 305 ff.
[11] Ibid. V.ii, 19 and 109, no. 841; 114, no. 885; 135 and 145, no. 96.
[12] iii. 710 = D. 629.   [13] vi. 1531–2 = D. 1190–1.
[14] Dittenberger, *Sylloge* ii, No. 881.
[15] Cohen, op. cit., iv, p. 442, no. 406; p. 481, nos. 5–6; p. 491, no. 15.

Emperors wore the *toga praetexta* right up to the late third century, but they are often shown wearing triumphal costume for more special occasions. The right to wear the purple *paludamentum* had long been the sole prerogative of the Imperator. Tacitus saw in this the seeds of autocracy.[1] Purple gradually became the imperial colour.[2] At the same time the sceptre, long associated with Jupiter Optimus Maximus, became an adjunct to imperial costume from the time of the Severi. The globe, symbol of rulership of the world, is to be seen on coins of Caracalla and Philip the Arab.[3]

As befitted a supernatural being, the emperor was addressed in very revered terms. Here is an example from the early third century: 'Hoc anno cenatum est in diebus singulis . . . et adclamaverunt: fe[*li*]cissime! felicissime! te salvo et victore felicissime! o nos felices qui te imp. videmus! . . . d(i) t(e) s(ervent) in perpetuo, Augu(sta), Aug(uste)!.'[4]

Under Diocletian the imperial court was well and truly decked out in Oriental trappings, and an aura of cool aloofness on the one hand and abject self-abasement on the other pervaded everything. Diocletian adopted the name 'Jovius', and Maximian, his partner, was called 'Herculius'. Diocletian and Jupiter were thus linked together, though it is difficult to say whether there was exact identification or whether, as Baynes believes,[5] the emperor was simply the god's agent. Such religious links were designed to inculcate greater respect for, and indeed, awe of, the emperor on the part of the populace. Also by linking himself with Jupiter, 'father of gods and men', and Maximian only with Hercules, Diocletian proclaimed himself the supreme ruler of the Roman Empire, even though in theory Maximian was his equal. To go with all this, the emperor was now sometimes portrayed with a nimbus, an idea borrowed from Persia, as Keyssner has pointed out.[6]

Diocletian was not the originator of the new ceremonial, as Aurelius Victor, Eutropius and Ammianus Marcellinus believe,[7] yet he it was who turned these tendencies into an obligatory

---

[1] Tac. *Ann.* xii. 56.   [2] Herod. ii. 8. 6; v. 3. 12; vi. 8. 5. Aur. Vict. *Caes.* 23. 28.
[3] Cohen, op. cit., iv, p. 186, nos. 411–2; v, p. 165, no. 46.
[4] vi. 2086 = D. 451.   [5] Baynes, *JRS* 25 (1935) 81–7.
[6] Keyssner in P-W, s.v. 'Nimbus'. See also Ensslin in P-W, s.v. 'Maximianus Herculius'.   [7] Eutr. ix. 26; Aur. Vict. *Caes.* 39. 2–4; Amm. xv. 5. 8.

system, and it is by no means unlikely that he was influenced by the Sassanian court.[1] The act of *adoratio* is another sign of the same feature: 'Adorari se iussit, cum ante eum cuncti salutarentur'.[2] Such obeisance was obligatory even for members of the imperial family.[3] Diocletian also adopted the bejewelled garb which Aurelian had affected: '(Aurelianus) . . . gemmisque et aurata omni veste, quod adhuc fere incognitum Romanis moribus visebatur, usus est.' '(Diocletianus) ornamenta gemmarum vestibus calceamentis indidit: nam prius imperii insigne in chlamyde purpurea tantum erat; reliqua communia.' Diocletian lived a secluded life, showing himself to the public only on very rare occasions, which for that reason took on an added dignity.[4]

As imperial power was on the ascendant, so the power of the Senate was on the wane. A good example is the gradual elimination of the Senate's financial control. It was probably Vespasian who established branches in Rome of the imperial provincial fisci of Asia and Egypt, which probably produced bigger surpluses than any other provinces. In this way the emperor deprived the Aerarium Saturni of a major source of revenue. So impoverished was the Aerarium even in the early principate that it had to be subsidized by the emperor.

'Quater pecunia mea iuvi aerarium, ita ut sestertium milliens et quingentiens ad eos qui praeerant aerario detulerim,' Augustus could write in his *Res Gestae*. Similarly, Nero could rebuke his predecessors for their ruinous public spending and could point out that he had given the state sixty million sesterces a year.[5] But the distinction between Fiscus and Aerarium, between, that is, the emperor's private funds and the state treasury was artificial, and, as Cassius Dio says of Augustus in one of his parenthetical asides. λόγῳ μὲν γὰρ τὰ δημόσια ἀπὸ τῶν ἐκείνου ἀπεκέκριτο, ἔργῳ δὲ καὶ ταῦτα πρὸς τὴν γνώμην αὐτοῦ ἀνηλίσκετο.[6] So, when an emperor with a legalistic turn of mind, like Marcus Aurelius, makes a

---

[1] There is some difference of opinion about this. See *CAH* xii, Ch. xi.
[2] Eutr. ix. 26.   [3] Lact. *de Mort. Pers.* 18. 9.
[4] Aurelian: (Aur. Vict.) *Epit.* 35. 5. Diocletian: Eutr. ix. 26; Aur. Vict. *Caes.* 39. 2. The one custom in this connection that Diocletian apparently did not adopt was the diadem. On his coins he is most often shown wearing the laurea.
[5] Augustus: *Res Gestae* 17. 1; Nero: Tac. *Ann.* xv. 18.   [6] Dio 53. 16. 1.

point of asking the senate's permission to withdraw funds from the Aerarium, Dio's comment is apt: οὐχ ὅτι μὴ ἔκειντο ἐπὶ τῇ τοῦ κρατοῦντος ἐξουσίᾳ, ἀλλ' ὅτι ὁ Μᾶρκος πάντα τῆς βουλῆς καὶ τοῦ δήμου καὶ αὐτὰ καὶ τἆλλα ἔλεγεν εἶναι.[1]

As the emperor was travelling ever upwards on his end of the political see-saw, so the Senate's end was constantly dropping. As an institution the Senate was a mere cipher, happy to humour the emperor's every whim. But the same does not apply to senators as individuals. For, though some important posts were now held by equestrians or even by freedmen, the great majority of high imperial appointments continued to be reserved for senators until the second half of the third century.

As the demands upon the emperor increased, so did his means of satisfying them. Above all, the principate saw the development for the first time in Roman history of a professional bureaucratic machine. Since the men who staffed this civil service were technically the private servants of the emperor they were recruited initially from among freedmen and later on from the equestrian order. It is easy to see how the *a libellis*, *ab epistulis* and *a rationibus*, each of which was to become a great department of state, began as humble secretarial appointments. The considerable power which their proximity to the emperor gave some freedmen favourites becomes a *locus classicus* in the pages of senatorial writings.[2] Under Claudius all three posts were occupied by freedmen, Narcissus, Pallas, and Callistus, to whose wishes the emperor was thought to have been unduly subservient. So much so that Claudius is himself represented in the *Apocolocyntosis* as a freedman's slave.[3] Even Seneca, probably the author of the *Apocolocyntosis*, was not above winning the favour of a freedman *a libellis* by gross flattery.[4] Of Claudius Etruscus, a freedman and *a rationibus* under Nero, Statius could write:

> . . . Uni parent commissa ministro,
> quae Boreas quaeque Eurus atrox, quae
> nubilus Auster invehit.[5]

---

[1] Dio 72. 33. See Brunt *JRS* 56 (1966) 75–91; Millar *JRS* 53 (1963) 29 ff.; Jones, op. cit., 99–114.   [2] See Plin. *Ep.* vii. 29, viii. 6, vi. 31. 9–11.   [3] *Apocol.* 15.
[4] Seneca, *Cons. ad Polyb.* 6. 5. Cf. Momigliano, *Claudius*, 119, n. 3.
[5] Statius, *Silvae* iii. 3. 95–7.

The rise of a man of servile origin to a powerful post could always be guaranteed to make the blood of an *ingenuus* boil with fury.[1] But as the civil service posts originally held by freedmen gradually lost their stigma and came to be imbued with the esteem which their importance merited, equestrians were appointed to them.[2]

Otho and Vitellius were the first emperors to appoint *equites* to posts previously reserved for freedmen.[3] But it was not until the reign of Hadrian that freedmen were finally replaced by equestrians in the three important secretariates.[4] The change marks the final transition of these posts from the realm of private service to that of public administration.

Though, as we have seen, the emperor controlled recruitment to the Senate, the continued ascendancy of senators in government and the hereditary nature of senatorial rank perpetuated the old Republican ethos. Once a man became a senator he was marked off by title, dress, and office alike from lesser mortals and from his own past life. Despite, therefore, the impotence of the Senate as a body, there was an imperial senatorial aristocracy with an *esprit de corps*. This aristocracy was very different, of course, from the exclusive, self-perpetuating, inbred aristocracy of the Republic. Indeed, the huge bronze portals of the curia were continually welcoming new members from an ever-widening circle of provinces. New men rubbed shoulders with the scions of ancient families and gradually became assimilated to the senatorial ethos. It is perhaps worth noting, for example, that Thrasea Paetus, Helvidius Priscus, and other members of the senatorial 'philosophic' opposition to Nero and the Flavians came from the *municipia et coloniae*, and Tacitus himself was far from being of ancient noble stock.[5]

Yet at no time would the newcomers have outnumbered the more established elements, and not a few office-holders even in the third century were members of families whose senatorial rank can

[1] See Tac. *Ann.* xii. 60. 6; xii. 26–7; Plin. *Ep.* vii. 29; viii. 6.

[2] See Jones, 'The Roman Civil Service', *Studies in Roman Government and Law*, 153–75. A. M. Duff, *Freedmen in the Early Roman Empire*, 158 ff. A. Stein, *Ritterstand*. Momigliano, op. cit., 39 ff.

[3] Plutarch, *Otho*, 9; Tac. *Hist.* i. 58. See Duff, loc. cit.

[4] See also Duff, op. cit., 159, and R. H. Lacey, *Equestrian officials of Trajan and Hadrian*.

[5] See R. Syme, *Tacitus*, ii. 585 ff.

be traced back a century and more. C. Caecina Largus, for example, legate of Thrace under Septimius Severus, was a descendant of his namesake, consul in 42.[1] L. Saevinius Proculus, a Severan legate of Asia and Sicily, and father of a *quindecimvir*, is thought by Barbieri to have been descended from the Saevinius Proculus who is recorded as a senator in 69.[2] The Pomponii Bassi, one a late second-century proconsul of Lycia-Pamphylia, another governor of Moesia at about the same time, a third a *legatus legionis* in Moesia, another ordinary consul in 271 and yet another suffect consul in 283 seem all to have been descendants of the T. Pomponius Bassus who was legate of Asia in 79–80 and suffect consul in 94.[3] The mid-second-century Desticius Sallustius Juba, 'c(larissimus) i(uvenis)', was similarly doubtless an ancestor of Valerian's legate of Britain recorded simply as Desticius Juba.[4] Among the surviving senatorial families in the third century were some ancient Republican lines such as the Acilii Glabriones, Valerii Messallae, and Cornelii Scipiones, all of whom also survived into the fourth century, as will be seen later on.

By the third century the Senate as an institution had no power worth mentioning. Yet it was from this body, whose *esprit de corps* stemmed from a combination of heredity and assimilation, that the chief office-holders of the Empire continued to be drawn.

In the course of the third century, however, this traditional framework was gradually abandoned, until by the end of the century only very few posts of importance were open to senators. Emperors, it is true, had always been able to appoint men of non-senatorial origin to high posts by introducing them into the Senate beforehand. But in the third century the tendency was to bypass the Senate by appointing non-senators directly to governorships without bothering to make them senators.[5]

There already were precendents in the early Principate for the appointment of non-senators to high state posts. The positions of praetorian prefect and prefect of Egypt, *praefectus annonae* and

---

[1] Barbieri, *Albo Senatorio*, no. 98; see also p. 493.
[2] Ibid., nos. 846 and 457; see also p. 493.
[3] Ibid., 495.   [4] Ibid., 503.
[5] See H. Petersen, 'Senatorial and Equestrian governors in the third century A.D.', *JRS* 45 (1955) 47–57.

praefectus vigilum are cases in point, as are the governorships of Mauretania, Thrace, Judaea, Raetia and Noricum, and smaller areas such as the Cottian and Maritime Alps and the Balearic Islands.[1]

All these examples of posts occupied by non-senators, it should be noted, were new offices, and it took a long time before posts exclusively reserved for senators were occupied by equestrians— and even then always under a different title. There was an attempt under Commodus to entrust the British legions to equestrian commanders instead of senatorial *legati legionum*, but it seems to have been unsuccessful.[2] Septimius Severus appointed equestrian prefects to the command of his three new Parthian legions, and the newly conquered province of Mesopotamia was similarly entrusted to a governor of the same rank.[3] In some established provinces Severus appointed equestrians as acting governors with titles such as *procurator agens vices praesidis* or *procurator vice defuncti proconsulis*. There are only five examples of temporary governors in the first two centuries of the Principate, three of them being in Syria, where one of the *legati legionum* was acting governor, and only two cases where the acting governor was an equestrian procurator. One was in Judaea, of unknown date, and the other in Asia, probably under Domitian. In the first half of the third century alone, however, there are a dozen cases of temporary governors, nine of whom were equestrians. This would lead us to believe that the titles purporting to show that these men were just stop-gaps were a legal fiction.[4] The tendency to appoint equestrians directly to governorships is particularly marked in the latter half of the third century.[5]

---

[1] See G. H. Stevenson, *Roman Provincial Administration*, 110 ff. For regions such as 'Moesia et Treballia' and Asturia and Gallaecia temporarily under equestrians see Jones, op. cit., 117–25. For *praefecti civitatum* see P-W, xxii, 1290–4. Judaea, it should be noted, was placed under a senatorial legate by Vespasian after the revolt and, similarly, when Marcus Aurelius introduced legions into Raetia he placed that province under a legate. See P-W, iA, 54.

[2] Dio 72. 9 (cf. 13. 1); Herod. i. 9; SHA V. *Comm.* 6. 2. See Stein, *Ritterstand*, 450.

[3] Parthian legions: iii. 99, cf. p. 969 = D. 2771; D. 1356; viii. 20996. Mesopotamia: viii. 9760, cf. 9757; vi. 1642.

[4] See the list in C. W. Keyes, *The Rise of the Equites*, 3 ff.

[5] See Keyes, op. cit., 8 ff.

By the end of the century not only were most governorships open to equestrians; they were also closed to senators.

A passage in Aurelius Victor has given rise to the belief that it was an edict issued by the Emperor Gallienus that was instrumental in depriving senators of military commands. Because of the somewhat ambiguous phrasing of the passage in question, it has become the plaything of scholars:

Et patres quidem praeter commune Romani malum orbis stimulabat proprii ordinis contumelia, quia primus ipse metu socordiae suae, ne imperium ad optimos nobilium transferretur, senatum militia vetuit et adire exercitum.[1]

Abhinc militaris potentia convaluit ac senatui imperium creandique ius principis ereptum ad nostram memoriam, incertum an ipso cupiente per desidiam an metu seu dissensionum odio. Quippe amisso Gallieni edicto refici militia potuit concedentibus modeste legionibus Tacito regnante, neque Florianus temere invasisset, aut iudicio manipularium cuiquam bono licet, imperium daretur amplissimo ac tanto ordine in castris degente.[2]

Homo's interpretation is that the edict was enforced by Gallienus, repealed by Tacitus, but enforced again by Carus and Carinus.[3] He believes that Gallienus thus replaced senatorial with non-senatorial governors in the imperial provinces (the only provinces which had military forces) as a general principle. He finds some cases in which senatorial governors remain in charge of imperial provinces, but he simply shrugs them aside as being 'exceptions'. Yet, clearly, such a treatment of the problem only begs the question.

In fact, contrary to what one would expect from the enforcement of an edict, the date of the change from senatorial to non-senatorial governors varied considerably from one province to another. The changes took place at different times throughout the latter half of the third century.[4]

---

[1] Aur. Vict. Caes. 33-4.

[2] Ibid. 37. 5-6. See discussion in Homo, Rev. Hist. 138 (1921) 161-203 and 138 (1921) 1-52. See also N. H. Baynes, 'Three Notes on the reforms of Diocletian and Constantine', JRS 15 (1925) 195-208; J. G. C. Anderson, 'The genesis of Diocletian's provincial reorganisation', JRS 22 (1932) 224-32.

[3] L. Homo, 'Les privilèges administratifs du sénat romain sous l'Empire et leur disparition graduelle au cours du IIIe siècle', Revue Historique 137 (1921) 193 and 138 (1921) 6.

[4] Petersen, art. cit., 47 ff.

The only way of accounting for the continuance in office of senatorial governors in imperial provinces while the edict was supposedly in force is to show that such governors were merely civil governors. It must be shown, in other words, that the separation of civil and military functions in the provinces was the work of Gallienus rather than of Diocletian. This postulate has been forthcoming from Keyes, Baynes, and Anderson.[1] Keyes has put forward the view that the senatorial *legatus legionis* was replaced as legionary commander by the *praefectus legionus*, but is at a loss when it comes to explaining who took over from the *legatus Augusti pro praetore* as provincial commander-in-chief.[2] Baynes has to admit that 'there is no undoubted reference to the later provincial military commander—the *dux*—until the year 289.' He concludes: 'In the present state of the evidence I see no direct means of demonstrating this (i.e. Keyes's) general theory of the effect of the edict of Gallienus.'[3]

Indeed, if evidence is forthcoming of senatorial governors exercising specifically military functions during this period, then the theory will be shattered. In fact there are two inscriptions which may be seen as providing such evidence.[4] They concern one M. Aurelius Valentinianus, governor of Hispania Citerior, and both are dated 283, one being dedicated to Carus and the other to Carinus. What is striking in both these inscriptions is the description of Valentinianus as 'v(ir) c(larissimus) praeses prov(inciae) Hisp-(aniae) Cit(erioris) leg(atus) Aug(ustorum) p(ro) p(raetore)'.[5] What are we to make of this curious designation? Why is Valentinianus described both as *praeses* and as *legatus*? Valentinianus in our two inscriptions is clearly distinguishing himself from a mere *praeses*—but in which respect? There are two views here. One, Mommsen's, is that the addition of *legatus* to *praeses* indicates that Valentinianus was a military governor.[6] Baynes, on the other hand, believes that *legatus* is only meant to inform the reader that Valentinianus was a senatorial governor, unlike the normal *praeses*

---

[1] Keyes, op. cit., 49 ff. Baynes op. cit. Anderson, op. cit.
[2] Keyes, op. cit., 18 ff.
[3] Baynes, op. cit. 200.   [4] ii. 4102–3 Tarraco.
[5] ii. 4103. The text of 4102 is the same except that 'Praeses prov(inciae)' is abbreviated to 'p.p.'   [6] Mommsen, ad ii. 4102.

4

of his day.[1] Of the two views Mommsen's is the more plausible, since the fact that Valentinianus was a senatorial governor is indicated by the clarissimate. If Mommsen is right in seeing Valentinianus as a military governor, is he also right to see him as an exceptional case?.[2] No one else is known with the same curious combination of titles. But we know that the reign of Gallienus did not bring an end to senatorial legates, since several provinces where legions were stationed are recorded under senatorial legates after his reign.[3] Moesia Inferior was evidently still under such governors in the reign of Aurelian (270-5).[4] In Britannia Superior a legate, either the governor of the province or merely *legatus legionis*, is recorded shortly before 271. In either case the governor must have been a senator, since a *legatus legionis* would not be placed under an equestrian governor.[5] The first known equestrian governor in Britain dates from the tetrarchy.[6] Though Pannonia Inferior was governed by a 'vir egregius agens vices praesidis' in 267, this seems to have been a genuinely temporary equestrian governorship, since the province is under our legate of Tarraconensis, M. Aurelius Valentinianus, probably in the late 270s or early 280s.[7] L. Artorius Pius Maximus was senatorial legate of Syria Phoenice as late as the first decade of the tetrarchy, the earliest known equestrian governors of the province dating from 293/305.[8] As for Syria Coele, it did not go equestrian at all.[9] There is no reason to doubt that these legates were traditional *legati Augusti pro praetore*, at the head of both civil and military affairs in their provinces, especially when we recall the late appearance of the equestrian *dux* in our sources.

---

[1] Baynes, op. cit., 200 ff.

[2] 'Observa hic . . . ut munus civile cum militari videatur coniunctum esse extra ordinem.' (Mommsen ad ii. 4102).

[3] See Petersen, art. cit.

[4] iii. 7586, iii. 14460, A. Stein, *Legaten von Moesien*, 106-7. M. Aurelius Sebastianus, thought by Stein to have been an equestrian, seems more likely to have been a senatorial governor, as Petersen argues, op. cit., 56. *IGR* i. 591. *Rev. Arch.* 12 (1908) 36, no. 31.

[5] vii. 95 Isca.

[6] *AE* 1930, 114 = *JRS* 21 (1931) pl. v.

[7] Vir Egregius: iii. 3424, 10424 Aquincum. Valentinianus: iii. 3418 Aquincum.

[8] Maximus: *AE* 1939, 58 Heliopolis, Syria. Equestrians: *AE* 1907, 145 prope Paneam; iii. 6661 Palmyra.

[9] See p. 40 ff., below.

Gallienus's 'edict' was most likely never issued, and it must probably be seen as a neat and handy device whereby Aurelius Victor could explain a protracted development in a brief and memorable way. In any case the change from one class of military leader to another would not normally have been a matter for an edict.

It is thought by some scholars that the imperial offensive against senatorial governors was prompted by the inefficiency of senators in comparison to *equites*, who had in many cases risen from the ranks.[1] 'En réalité', declares Homo, 'les dernières privilèges sénatoriaux ont succombé devant les nécessités de la défense nationale'.[2] But there appears to have been more to the imperial attack upon senators than the loss of military commands. Indeed, between the middle of the third century and the reign of Diocletian, in addition to some provinces with legions, the provinces of Cilicia, Lycia-Pamphylia, Pontus et Bithynia, Macedonia, and Dalmatia, none of which had any legions, experienced a change from senatorial to equestrian governors.[3] But while equestrians moved into the erstwhile preserves of senators, there was no movement the other way to produce Lambrechts's fabled 'fusion' of the two orders.[4]

The only certain example in the third century of a senator being appointed to an equestrian post is Elagabalus' anonymous praetorian prefect, who reached his high office via an equestrian career followed by the legateship of a legion.[5] This hybrid career is the product of a period of transition from one system of appointments to another. The republican system demanded that all high posts be reserved for senators, and so imperial favourites duly became senators. But the growing force of imperial power gave equestrians more and more powerful positions, until an equestrian office, the praetorian prefecture, became the most important position in the Empire, second only to that of the emperor himself. Hence the

---

[1] Homo, op. cit., 51.   [2] Ibid.
[3] Petersen, art. cit., 49–51, 55.
[4] Lambrechts, *La composition du sénat romain de Septime Sévère à Dioclétien*, 107 ff.
[5] vi. 3839 = D. 1329. See Howe, *Pretorian Prefect*, 74; M. T. W. Arnheim, 'Third century praetorian prefects of senatorial origin: fact or fiction ?', *Athenaeum* (forthcoming).

strange situation in which an equestrian is first promoted to the Senate and then given an equestrian appointment. The legal fictions used by Septimius Severus and his successors avoided this complication and gave senatorial positions to equestrians as such on the ground that they were just stop-gap appointees. From this it was not a long step to appointing equestrians directly, and in the second half of the third century such appointments spread until they became the standard type.

II

DIOCLETIAN, HAMMER OF THE ARISTOCRACY

F O R three centuries emperors had whittled away the power of the Senate and of senators, and this process culminated at the end of the third century in the reign of Diocletian. It is hardly surprising that the elimination of men of senatorial origin should have reached its furthest development under this Emperor, for of all those who donned the imperial purple Diocletian had probably risen to it from the humblest origins: '(Exercitus) Diocletianum imperatorem creavit, Dalmatia oriundum, virum obscurissime natum: adeo ut a plerisque scribae filius, a nonnullis Anulini senatoris libertinus fuisse credatur.'[1] Lactantius describes Diocletian's administrative reforms as follows: 'Et ut omnia terrore complerentur, provinciae quoque in frusta concisae, multi praesides et plura officia singulis regionibus ac pene iam civitatibus incubare, item rationales multi et magistri et vicarii praefectorum . . .'[2] The provinces which suffered the greatest reductions were, again predictably enough, the old proconsular provinces of Africa and Asia. The former was divided into three provinces: Africa, Byzacena, and Tripolitana; the latter was even more finely fragmented, into six provinces: Asia, Hellespontus, Lydia, Caria, Phrygia I and Phrygia II.[3] The truncated provinces of Africa and Asia were the only pro-consular provinces under the tetrarchy, and as such exempt from the authority of praetorian prefects and vicars. All the new African and Asian provinces, like all the other provinces everywhere else except for those of Italy and Achaea, were praesidial.

Among the proconsuls of Africa are to be found some of the noblest names of the age: T. Flavius Postumius Titianus, Amnius

---

[1] Eutrop. ix. 19.   [2] Lact. *de Mort. Pers.* vii. 4–5.
[3] Cod. Veron.

Anicius Iulianus, C. Annius Anullinus, Ceionius Rufius Volusianus.[1] The origins of these men contrast rather markedly with those of the governors, all *praesides*, of the new African and Asian provinces. The only *praeses* of Byzacena of known origin under the tetrarchy, . . . cius Flavianus, was a *perfectissimus*.[2] In Tripolitana two such *praesides* are known, C. Valerius Vibianus Obsequius and Aurelius Quintianus, and both of these were also non-senatorial.[3] There are only three *praesides* of the various components of the old province of Asia under the tetrarchy whose origins are known: Fulvius Asticus and Aurelius Marcellus being governors of Caria, and a Phrygian governor of whose name the only legible letters are Ju . . . All of these were *perfectissimi*.[4]

This pattern of equestrian appointments was repeated in praesidial posts all over the Empire, with the single exception of Syria. For, though styled *praesides*, the three Syrian governors under the tetrarchy whose origins are known, namely L. Aelius Helvius Dionysius, Latinius Primosus, and Verinus, were men of senatorial origin.

L. Aelius Helvius Dionysius had an ordinary senatorial caerer, two urban *curatelae* and the correctorship of Italy, before becoming *praeses* of Syria Coele, which post he evidently held together with appellate jurisdiction throughout the diocese of Oriens—'iudex sacrarum cognitionum totius Orien(tis)'.[5] This combination of the governorship with diocesan appellate jurisdiction is also found in the pre-Diocletianic case of [*Vi*]rius Lupus, urban prefect from 278 to 280, who appears in an inscription as 'iudex sacrarum cognitionum [*per Asiam*] et per Ori[*e*]ntem, praes(es) [*Syriae*] Coeles et Arabiae'.[6] Dionysius was probably the same man as the Aelius Dionysius who was proconsul of Africa in 298, and he certainly was urban prefect in 301–0.[7]

Of all Dionysius' offices the only one which might be thought to be out of keeping with a senatorial career as it now was under

---

[1] *PLRE*—Fasti.   [2] *ILAlg*. I. 3832.

[3] Vibianus: *AE*. 1929, 4 Lepcis Magna. Vibianus and Quintianus: viii. 22763 = D. 9352 Centenarium Tibubuci.

[4] *PLRE*—Fasti.

[5] vi. 1675 = D. 1211.   [6] vi. 31775 = D. 1210.

[7] Proconsul of Africa: Frag. Vat. 41.

Diocletian was the appointment as *praeses* of Syria Coele. Perhaps we gain a clue to this puzzle from another inscription:

PALLADI
PRVDENTISSIMO
ET
BENIGNISSIMO
PATRI
P. AELIO DIONYSIO
P.V. RATIONALI
VETTENIA SABINILLA V.V.[1]

That P. Aelius Dionysius was related to our L. Aelius Helvius Dionysius is indisputable. Perhaps they were father and son or uncle and nephew. What is of the utmost importance is the difference in rank between them: Publius was an equestrian while Lucius was a *clarissimus*. Publius's inscription was dedicated to him by his daughter Vettenia Sabinilla *v(irgo)* *v(estalis)*, but Vestal virgins had to be of senatorial stock. Another problem is that, though Sabinilla specifically refers to P. Aelius Dionysius as her father, she shares no names in common with him whatsoever. Arthur Stein believes that Lucius was the son of Publius Aelius Dionysius and that the Vestal virgin was Publius' natural daughter.[2] But this in itself does not explain why the son was a senator while the father was an equestrian. Since Vestal virgins had to be senatorial, the brother's adlection to the senate would not account for the sister's being a Vestal virgin. The most likely explanation would appear to be that the Vestal virgin and L. Aelius Helvius Dionysius were brother and sister, the children of P. Aelius Dionysius, and that both of them were adopted by the senatorial family of the Vettenii. Of course, the usual practice in adoptions in Roman times as in the present day was for the adoptive children to take the names of their adoptive parents, but there are some precedents for Dionysius' retention of his original name, the case, for example, of Cornelia Cethegilla, who calls herself the daughter of M. Gavius Squilla Gallicanus and his wife Pompeia Agrippinilla in the mid-second century.[3]

---

[1] vi. 1587 = D. 1446.   [2] A. Stein, *Ritterstand*, p. 344.   [3] D. 8825 Lesbos.

If this explanation is correct, our *praeses* was of equestrian origin and became a senator later. Even so, he was a senatorial *praeses*, a very rare animal indeed for the tetrarchy. But perhaps it is pertinent to point out that Syria seems to have had at least one senatorial *praeses* under Constantine, and was one of the few Eastern provinces to change over to consulars under that emperor. The corrector of Campania, P. Helvius Aelius Dionysius, was no doubt a son of our *praeses*.

Locrius Verinus, who, like Dionysius, governed Syria under the tetrarchy, seems also to have had appellate jurisdiction at the same time over the diocese as a whole.[1] In addition Verinus was evidently a military governor of Syria, commanding an expedition against the Armenians: 'Virtutem, Verine, tuam plus mirer in armis, Eoos dux Armenios cum caede domares.'[2] Verinus, who is probably to be identified with the Lucrius Verinus who was vicar of Africa between 318 and 321 and urban prefect from 323 to 325, is considered by Chastagnol to have been an equestrian. Since Chastagnol argues from Verinus's vicariate, held under Constantine my counter-arguments will be found in the next chapter.

Of Latinius Primosus much less is known than is the case with either Dionysius or Verinus. A man referred to only as Primosus received a law under the tetrarchy. The full name Latinius Primosus occurs in a list of donors to some unknown fund, most of whom were members of well-known noble families. Among them are to be found the names Iulius Festus, Annius Anullinus, Nummius Tuscus, Caecina Sabinus, Caecina Tacitus and Acilius Glabrio. Though Primosus' appearance in this list is by no means conclusive proof of his nobility, it makes it a strong likelihood, especially in view of the background of the two other governors of Syria known under the tetrarchy.[3]

These three cases leave Syria as the only province traditionally governed by legates not to have been transferred to equestrian governors. This governorship was also to give birth, through the diocesan appellate jurisdiction attached to it, to the Constantinian post of *Comes Orientis*, as will be seen in the next chapter.

---

[1] For Verinus's career see Symm. *Ep.* i. 2. 7. Appellate jurisdiction: *CJ* iii. 12. 1.
[2] Symm. *Ep.* i. 2. 7.   [3] Primosus: *CJ* vii. 33. 6. Latinius Primosus: vi. 37118.

In addition to the governors of Syria there are several other cases of *praesides* under the tetrarchy who have been claimed as noble, but none of these can be substantiated. Agricola, presumably *praeses* of Byzacena, and Castrius Constans, *praeses* of Phrygia, were *clarissimi* but are more likely to be Constantinian than tetrarchic governors, and Priscus is more likely to have been proconsul of undivided Asia than *praeses* of Phrygia. Though there was a senatorial and probably noble Acilius Clarus as corrector of Italy in 286 there is no reason to identify him with his namesake *praeses* of Numidia, whose inscription points to a Constantinian date. M. Aurelius Julius, *praeses* of Dalmatia, on the other hand, seems to have been a pre-Diocletianic governor. Perhaps the most puzzling case is that of Bassus the 'legatos' recorded as presiding at a trial in Durostorum in 303. But the fact that Moesia Inferior, the province in which Durostorum was situated, is recorded as early as 270 under an equestrian *praeses* casts a heavy shadow of doubt upon Bassus' claim, which is based in any case on a record of a martyrdom, not on the whole a very reliable type of document, to say the least. Of the 37 Western *praesides* dateable to the tetrarchy, 27 are known to have been non-senatorial and the origins of the remaining 10 are unknown. So much for Diocletianic *praesides*.[1]

In addition to the drastically pared proconsular provinces of Africa and Asia and that curious relic of a former age, Syria, the only offices left to the senatorial aristocracy under the tetrarchy were the Italian and Achaean correctorships, the urban prefecture and the entirely ornamental ordinary consulate.

There has been some dispute as to how many correctorships there were in Italy in the tetrarchy. Men such as Paetus Honoratus, Acilius Clarus, T. Aelius Marcianus, and C. Ceionius Rufius Volusianus are each described as 'corrector Italiae', which may lead us to believe that the whole of Italy comprised one correctorship.[2] But what does 'corrector Italiae' mean? It is possible that the

---

[1] Agricola: *AE* 1946, 45. Castrius Constans: D. 8881, *MAMA*, vi., p. 35. Priscus: iii. 1419². Acilius Clarus: App. 1. M. Aurelius Julius: iii. 1938 = 8568 = D. 3710. Bassus: *Anal. Bull.* 16 (1897) 11 ff. Praeses 270: *IGR* i.591, 1432 Nicepalis.

[2] Paetus Honoratus: v. 2817 = D. 614 Patavium; Acilius Clarus: v. 8205 Aquileia; T. Aelius Marcianus: xi. 1594 Florentia; C. Ceionius Rufius Volusianus: D. 1213.

genitive is being used here in a loose sense, to mean 'Italian corrector' or 'corrector in Italy' rather than 'corrector of Italy'. The
inscription describing C. Ceionius Rufius Volusianus as 'corrector
Campaniae' instead of the designation used in his other inscriptions,
namely 'corrector Italiae', might be a pointer to this looser usage
of the genitive. But the authenticity of this inscription has long
been in doubt.[1] Another puzzling designation is that of L. Aelius
Helvius Dionysius as 'corrector utriusque Italiae'.[2] Does this mean
that Italy was normally divided into two correctorships which were
united under a single governor in this particular case? Or does it
mean that Dionysius was a governor of each of the two regions in
turn? Or was there only one Italian correctorship, which just
happened to include Gallia Cisalpina? The duplication in the dates
of Italian correctors is strong evidence for two correctorships, and
the provenance of one of the northern correctors' inscriptions from
Florentia indicates that this region was larger than the old Cisalpina,
which is what Chastagnol sees it as.[3] It was more likely to have been
the whole of what came later on to be called Italia Annonaria.
Among correctors are some of the noblest names in the period.
The family background of a C. Ceionius Rufius Volusianus, an
Acilius Clarus, or a T. Flavius Postumius Titianus presents a
sharp contrast to that of the more usual type of governor under the
tetrarchy.

Titianus is described in the same inscription as 'corr(ector)
Italiae Transpadanae' and 'corr(ector) Campaniae', in that chronological order. This may mark the beginning of a further division of
Italy into smaller regions, 'Italia Transpadana' probably corres-
ponding to the region of Aemilia et Liguria, first recorded under that
name in 321.[4] This is not the only evidence of the further division
of Italy under the tetrarchy. Venetia and Histria appear as a single
region for the first time under the rule of the noble corrector
Attius Insteius Tertullus,[5] and an equestrian corrector, Ulpius
Alenus, is recorded as governing Apulia and Calabria between
305 and 307.[6] If we omit Ceionius Rufius Volusianus, the first

---

[1] x. 304.   [2] vi. 1675 = D. 1211.
[3] Chastagnol, *Fastes*, p. 53.
[4] Titianus: vi. 1418 = D. 2941. Aemilia et Liguria: *CTh.* iv. 13. 1 (321).
[5] v. 2818 Patavium.   [6] ix. 687.

Campanian governors known to us are T. Flavius Postumius Titianus and Pompeius Appius Faustinus, both nobles, who held office in the 290s. Aurelius Victor informs us that Tetricus, the Gallic usurper, whose full name as C. Pius Esuvius Tetricus, became corrector of Lucania after his surrender to Aurelian, in other words in 274 or 275.[1] But how accurate is Victor's description of the post to which Tetricus was appointed ? As late as 268/9 there is a record of one Pomponius Bassus as 'corrector totius Italiae', before, that is, Italy was even divided into the two administrative regions that we encounter in the first part of the tetrarchy.[2] It is possible, therefore that Aurelius Victor was mistaken in his designation of Tetricus's post. Another of the fourth-century provinces which may have come into existence under the tetrarchy was that of Tuscia and Umbria. But here again the evidence is not very reliable, coming as it does from the *Acta Sanctorum*. Three men are mentioned as governing either Tuscia or Umbria, with various titles. Olympiades is described as a 'consularis' or 'augustalis' in Umbria, this latter title also being applied to his successor Megetius,[3] while Pancratius appears as 'proconsul Tusciae', all under the tetrarchy.[4] Though long the popular term of reference for a legate of consular rank, the title 'consularis' is not to be found in Italy until the reign of Constantine, who made it the official title of some Italian governorships. The governor of Tuscia and Umbria was not in fact promoted from corrector to consular until 366 at the earliest.[5]

Of all areas in the Empire Italy as a whole will be found to have undergone the least degree of change between the end of the tetrarchy and the death of Constantine a generation later. The familiar Italian regions of the fourth century, or some of them, were already established, and nobles were to be found at their heads together with non-nobles.

In Achaea the nobles suffered a temporary set-back. L. Turranius Gratianus, a noble who was to become urban prefect in 290, was

---

[1] Aurel. Vict. *Caes.* 35. 5; *Epit.* 35. 7.
[2] vi. 3836 = 31747 = *IGR* i. 137.
[3] *Acta S. Firminae* in A. Dufourcq, *Etudes*, iii, pp. 129–32.
[4] *Acta S. Cassiani*: AASS Aug. iii, p. 27.
[5] Maximinus, the last corrector of Tuscia and Umbria, is recorded in office in 366, *CTh.* ix. 1. 8.

corrector of Achaea probably in the first years of the tetrarchy.[1] The only other governor of this province under the tetrarchy whose origins are known dates from the latter half of it, was styled 'praeses', and was only a *perfectissimus*.

Among the urban prefects under the tetrarchy were such men as Ceionius Varus, L. Caesonius Ovinius Manlius Rufinianus Bassus, L. Turranius Gratianus, Anicius Faustus, Nummius Tuscus, Aradius Rufinus and T. Flavius Postumius Titianus. Two of these, Nummius Tuscus and Postumius Titianus, also were ordinary consuls under the tetrarchy and a third, A. Annius Anullinus, ordinary consul in 295, was to become urban prefect under Maxentius in 306–7. A member of the Anician house, Anicius Faustus, is known only as ordinary consul in 298, having already been a suffect consul, as is indicated by the 'II' after his name in the *fasti*. These noble consuls and urban prefects were representatives of families which, though now excluded from most positions of real importance, were within a generation to make their appearance in the *fasti* of a greatly enlarged and more significant range of posts.

The contrast between them and the Diocletianic vicars could hardly have been greater than it was, for, not surprisingly, Diocletian appointed to these new posts of his own creation men whom he could trust, men of humble origin who owed their rise to imperial goodwill. Though only six Diocletianic vicars can be traced, it is significant that four of these are known to have been of non-senatorial origins, the origins of the remaining two being unknown.[2]

Similarly, of the five praetorian prefects whose names are known for the tetrarchy, three were of non-senatorial origin and the remaining two of unknown origin. Afranius Hannibalianus, whom Lambrechts claims as of senatorial birth, and his colleague Iulius Asclepiodotus, pose an awkward problem. Basing himself largely upon these two praetorian prefects, Lambrechts sees the period as one of 'fusion' between the equestrian and senatorial orders.

Bien entendu, aux deux premiers siècles de l'Empire, ce dernier ordre (l'ordre sénatorial) recrutait dans son sein de nombreuses personnes de rang équestre par le système de l'adlectio Imperiale. Mais il semble que

---

[1] iii. 6103. Cf. vi. 1128 and p. 845 = vi. 31241.
[2] Lambrechts ii. 110 ff.

le passage d'un ordre a l'autre se fait beaucoup plus facilement main-
tenant.

Il semble avéré que des sénateurs . . . furent admis a de hautes fonctions
équestres qui leur avaient été jalousement refusées jusqu'ici.[1]

Several points must be borne in mind, however, in connection with
the cases of Hannibalianus and Asclepiodotus. First, though of
senatorial rank from 292, neither appears to have been of senatorial
birth. Secondly, neither was appointed to an equestrian post while
holding senatorial rank; the two men were already praetorian
prefects when they became consuls in 292 and they appear to have
continued as such through their consulships and beyond. Thirdly,
and most significantly, Hannibalianus and Asclepiodotus are the
only men of senatorial rank known to have held equestrian posts
in the tetrarchy. At the same time, however, this period saw almost
all the provincial governorships—hitherto the preserve of the
nobles—concentrated in the hands of equestrians. What sort of
fusion is this? While equestrians gain access to—and, indeed,
a monopoly of—senatorial posts, senators are for the most part
condemned to political impotence. There was no fusion between the
two social groups, the nobles and equestrians, nor was there fusion
between equestrian and senatorial titles, except in the cases of our
two praetorian prefects. Though it was unusual to give a praetorian
prefect an ordinary consulship while in office, the effect, namely the
elevation of the prefect concerned to senatorial rank, was no different from that achieved by the lesser honour of the *ornamenta
consularia*, which had long been traditionally conferred upon
praetorian prefects in office.

The two careers, the senatorial and equestrian, were quite
separate under the tetrarchy, converging only at the ordinary
consulate. A man of noble birth would begin his career with one or
more of the traditional republican magistracies, after which the
only positions open to him were the urban *curatelae*, the correctorships, the governorship of Syria, the proconsulates of Africa and
Asia, the urban prefecture and the ordinary consulate.

From the limited range of offices open to nobles it is clear that the
senatorial *cursus* under the tetrarchy was a *cul-de-sac*. But, if so,

[1] Lambrechts ii. 110 ff.

why were praetorian prefects so ready to exchange their title 'vir eminentissimus' for the clarissimate, as they did in assuming the ordinary consulate, which was still regarded as the crown of a man's career? The consulate was, as it had been for three centuries, merely a title of honour imbued with the aura of antiquity. Though the equestrian career was now the path to positions of importance in the imperial service, Roman traditionalism continued to rank the senatorial order above the equestrian order and to regard the ordinary consulship as a precious prize. A praetorian prefect would escape the disabilities of senatorial rank which affected the nobles, since he could rise no higher. The fact that a praetorian prefect could be a *clarissimus* while in office should mean that, theoretically speaking, the praetorian prefecture was open to nobles. But this is meaningless in view of the actual situation. The anomaly was, of course, the result of a conflict between ceremonial tradition and practical affairs. In theory a praetorian prefect with the title *eminentissimus* was of lower rank that any *clarissimus*; in fact he was more important than anyone except the emperor. To reconcile theory and practice praetorian prefects were given senatorial rank, thus producing another anomaly, which has played havoc with historians.

III

CONSTANTINE THE REFORMER

His religious leanings and his different emphasis on military affairs are not the only important matters of policy in which Constantine must be seen to contrast with Diocletian. For Constantine was responsible for initiating a major reform which has not been recognized as such and which represents a reversal of the trends noted in the last two chapters and a return to an earlier dispensation.

From the time of Constantine nobles are once again prominent in public affairs, though the new development is already foreshadowed in Maxentius's appointment of Ceionius Rufius Volusianus as praetorian prefect. But Maxentius's misconduct with senators' wives and his execution of some senators probably left the nobles in general less than enthusiastic about him.[1] In any case, Volusianus' prefecture is the only known departure on the part of Maxentius from the pattern of appointments under the tetrarchy, whereas under Constantine this pattern was discarded for another.

What were Constantine's motives for turning his back upon a policy no doubt designed to enhance imperial power and strengthen the hand of the central government generally? In the absence of sufficiently detailed sources, we do not know what was thought or said about this matter at the time. But, whatever the Emperor's motive, the fact remains that he was making a major concession to the nobles in admitting them once again to the citadels of power. It is perhaps not altogether inappropriate to recall at this point that it was Constantine who introduced the tax on senators known as the *collatio glebalis* or *follis*.[2] His Christianity, or pro-Christian leanings, were also not calculated to endear the Emperor to the senatorial aristocracy, nor indeed to the majority of his subjects in the early part of his reign. For until 324, when he wrenched the

[1] Volusianus: Zos. ii. 14. 2; Aurel. Vict. *Caes.* xl. 18.   [2] Zos. ii. 38.

East from Licinius and united the whole Roman world under his sway, Constantine ruled over a purely Western Empire. But the West was still largely pagan, and the nobles fervently and ostentatiously so, as evidenced in the numerous priesthoods and pagan religious dedications lavishly displayed by the proud scions of noble houses. The fourth-century history of the *gens Ceionia*, for example, which, together with the Anicii, was the most important noble family in the late Empire, combines the two facets of high state appointments and devotion to paganism. Maxentius's praetorian prefect Ceionius Rufius Volusianus was a *quindecimvir sacris faciundis*, as was his grandson, Constantius' praetorian prefect Lampadius, who was also a *pontifex maior* and *tauroboliatus*.[1] The same combination is found in the case of the vicar of Africa of 381, Alfenius Ceionius Julianus Kamenius, who added to this collection the ancient priesthood of *septemvir epulonum*.[2] Lampadius's son Volusianus, vicar of Asia, had the *taurobolium* twice, the second time apparently together with his sister Rufia Volusiana and her husband Petronius Apollodorus.[3] Lampadius's wife Caecinia Lolliana was also engaged in pagan religious practices and is recorded as a priestess of Isis.[4] The paganism of the fourth century was synecretist, combining the ancient state religion of Numa Pompilius with cults from Egypt and the East. For a long time a *quindecimvir* had presided over the *taurobolium* ceremony, when the blood of the slaughtered animal would cleanse and purify the worshipper upon whom it poured from above; and in the shrines of Mithras one could see not only representations of the Persian deity in his Phrygian cap in friendly or hostile encounters with a bull, but also statues of Jupiter, Venus, or even of Hecate.[5] But now with the spread of a religion which demanded sole allegiance or none, claiming for itself the whole truth, the bonds between the religions of Mithras, Cybele, Isis, Hecate, and the Olympian and Italian gods were strengthened.

---

[1] Volusianus: vi. 2153. Lampadius: vi. 512 = D. 4154.
[2] D. 1264.
[3] Volusianus (vicar): vi. 512 = D. 4154. Volusiana: vi. 509 = *IG* xiv. 1018 (370), cf. vi. 30966 = xiv. 1019 (377), both at the Phrygianum in the Vatican.
[4] vi. 512 = D. 4154. See list of holders of pagan priesthoods.
[5] See Dill i. 555–7; Cumont: *Intr.* 334.

It should hardly surprise us if an emperor favourably inclined to Christianity and prepared to impose a special land-tax on the guardians of paganism should find it necessary to reconcile this ardently pagan aristocracy by means of state appointments. For, though deprived of office by the centralizing military emperors of the third century, the senatorial aristocracy was still a force to be reckoned with. Indeed, as a landed class their local power can only have been enhanced by the disruptions of the third century, in which emperor after emperor fell by the wayside and the grip of the central government on the provinces was loosened as defence against marauding invaders claimed the attention of the authorities. Though our evidence of social history in this period of crisis is minimal, it seems likely that the tendency of peasants to seek protection and security as *coloni* on the estates of landed magnates— of which we read in the pages of Salvian of Marseilles written during a later spate of invasions—had its origin in the third century.[1] The extensive estates in the hands of fourth-century nobles had not grown up overnight. From the time of the Punic Wars *latifundia* had spread, and in the first century of the Principate Pliny the elder could blame them for ruining Italy.[2]

Constantine seems to have been a man of antiquarian tastes and the revival of the term 'patricius' as a title of honour and the introduction of the title 'consularis' for certain provincial governors are examples of this. Another such antiquarian innovation was the creation of the post of *quaestor sacri palatii*, which is attributed by Zosimus to Constantine, though the first known holder of the post, one Montius, is recorded only in 353.[3] The ancient republican quaestorship still existed, though it had become merely a financial burden. The new quaestorship was reminiscent of the position in the Principate of the 'quaestor Augusti', who was charged with reading the emperor's speeches to the Senate. But Constantine was essentially an eminently practical man of affairs, and, in any case, such

[1] Salvianus: *de Gubernatione Dei* v. 38 ff.
[2] Plin. *H.N.* xviii. 7. 35. This well-known statement has been much discussed and rejected by some as unreliable. See K. D. White, 'Latifundia', *University of London Institute of Classical Studies Bulletin* 14 (1967) 77 f.
[3] Patricius: See Ath. *Apol. c. Ar.* 76 (Julius Constantius); Zos. ii. 40 (Optatus). *Quaestor sacri palatii:* Zos. v. 32. Montius: Amm. xiv. 7. 12.

5

a sentimental attachment to old titles is not sufficient in itself to account for the continuance of noble prominence in government under Constantine's successors.[1]

As we have seen, the only noble *praesides* known under the tetrarchy were governors of Syria, which did not undergo the change experienced by all other provinces under imperial legates from senatorial to equestrian governors.[2] Under Constantine the majority of *praesides* remain equestrian but a significant minority are men of senatorial birth.[3] The provinces to which noble *praesides* were appointed were not chosen at random. First, all of them were Western provinces—and provinces in which large estates abounded: Byzacena and Numidia in Africa, and Gallaecia and Lusitania in the diocese of the Spains. In addition we have examples of senatorial *praesides* of Lugdunensis Prima, Sardinia, and a possible one in Britain.[4] It is not insignificant that more than a third of all known Western Constantinian *praesides* were nobles, and that forty per cent of all Western Constantinian *praesides* of known origin were noble. This is particularly noteworthy by comparison with the figures for the tetrarchy, none of whose Western *praesides* are known to have been noble.[5] It would be interesting and instructive to compare the proportion of noble *praesides* in the East and West, but the paucity of references to Eastern Constantinian *praesides* makes this impossible, though we should expect the nobles to be concentrated in the West, and all our cases of noble *praesides* are indeed in that half of the Empire.

Among the most interesting Constantinian *praesides* were the two brothers, L. Aradius Valerius Proculus Populonius and Q. Aradius Rufinus Valerius Proculus Populonius, both *praesides* of Byzacena. 'Clara quidem sed miserabilis domus' is the way Symmachus describes the family.[6] The earliest fourth-century Aradius of whom we know is Aradius Rufinus, consul in 311 and

---

[1] The same argument also applies against the theory that attributes the revival of noble fortunes in politics to Ausonius' favour with Gratian. e.g. J. Matthews, *Historia* xvi (1967) 484–509.

[2] See previous chapter.   [3] See statistical Table I.

[4] For details see Arnheim, *The Influence of the Senatorial Aristocracy on the Imperial Government in the late third and fourth centuries A.D.*, 23–40.

[5] See statistical Table 1.   [6] Symm. *Ep.* vii. 126.

urban prefect under Maxentius in 312 and then again under
Constantine in 312–13. He was probably a very close relative of
our L. Aradius Proculus, perhaps his father or uncle, and his
namesake the urban prefect of 376 is very likely to have been his
grandson. An Aradius Rufinus, possibly the same man as the
prefect 312–13, was urban prefect in 304–5. In a letter of Libanius
to the prefect of 376 we are told than an ancestor of the Aradii
called Rufinus had been governor of Syria: ἐγὼ τοίνυν ἐνθυμούμενος
ὡς ἡδέως μοι διηγοῦ περὶ τῆς εἰκόνος ᾗ σε ἐδίδαξεν ὡς ὁ σὸς
πρόγονος ἄρξειεν ἡμῶν—θύειν γὰρ ἔφησθα τὸν ἄνδρα ἐκεῖνον τῇ ἡμᾶς
ἐχούσῃ καλλιόπῃ.[1] This ancestor of Rufinus's, then, was a governor
in Antioch, presumably therefore legate of Syria, and may have
been identical to the Rufinus who was responsible for the death of
Odenathus under Gallienus, thought to have been governor of
Syria Phoenice.[2]

The family goes back yet further. In 219 Q. Aradius Rufinus
was co-opted as *sodalis Augustalis Claudialis*, as a member, that is,
of the fellowship which was instituted on the death of Augustus
to attend to the cult of the deified emperor, and which later also
took on the cult of Claudius. From the beginning it was open only
to senators. Another or the same Q. Aradius Rufinus was suffect
consul, probably, as Groag believes, in the early third century.[3]
Another namesake has left us a seal with his name together with
that of his wife, Junia Aiacia Modesta,[4] presumably daughter of
Q. Aiacius Modestus, ordinary consul in 228. We know of two men
called Aradius Roscius Rufinus Saturninus Tiberianus, one with
the *praenomen* Lucius and the other Publius—unless they were the
same person, as Groag believes. Both were *clarissimi*, Lucius being
described as 'triumvir (sic) stlitibus iudicandis, sevir equestrium
turmarum, [*quaestor*] kandidatus, augur, curio'. He was also patron
of Privernum.[5] The position of *curio* is most interesting, since it
indicates that the family was noble. Publius appears in an inscription from Bulla Regia in Africa together with his daughter, [*Aradia*]

[1] Lib. *Ep.* 825 (Teub.).   [2] Petr. Patr. *FHG.* iv, p. 195, Frag. 7.
[3] viii. 14688 = D. 3937; viii. 10602 = 14689 = D. 3938 Thuburbo. On the
Aradii see *CIL* vi, p. 367 and viii. ad loc. Groag: *PIR*² A. 1017.
[4] xv. 8088.
[5] x. 6439; vi. 1578; vi. 1695; vi. 30553. Cf. *CIL* vi, p. 855.

Ros[*cia*], . . . ne . . . e . . . Calpurnia Purgilla.[1] Other members of the family also had African connections. One Aradia Roscia and an early third century suffect consul Q. Aradius Rufinus Optatus Aelianus are recorded as patrons of Bulla Regia, and another or the same Q. Aradius Rufinus, also described as a suffect consul, set up dedications to the sun and moon at Thuburbo.[2] In the fourth century the family's ties with Africa are no less manifest. Before becoming *praeses* of Byzacena L. Aradius Proculus had been legate of the proconsul of Africa and was to become proconsul himself later on together with the powers of a vicar over all the other African provinces.[3] In addition the proconsuls of Africa of 319 and 340, each recorded simply as Proculus, were probably also Aradii.[4] The family's long-standing African connections cannot but be a pointer to landed possessions there. Office therefore enabled the family to attend to their ancestral lands and probably also to add to them.

The position of corrector could be occupied by senators and non-senators alike, and it is hardly surprising that the known noble correctors under Constantine outnumber those who are known to have been non-noble by almost three to one. Among the Constantinian correctors were several relatives of our Aradii. Brittius Praesens, corrector of Lucania and Bruttium, who is probably to be identified with a namesake *pontifex maior*, was related to the Aradii through the Valerii Maximi, and the Brittii themselves were an old family whose nobility can be traced back to the first century, as will be shown below. Another noble house, the Turcii, who were related to the Brittii by marriage, are well represented in the *fasti* of correctors. L. Turcius Apronianus the elder was apparently corrector of Lucania and Bruttium in 323,[5] and his two sons, L. Turcius Apronianus Asterius and L. Turcius Secundus Asterius, were also correctors of Italian provinces, the former of Tuscia and Umbria and the latter of Picenum and Flaminia.[6] The Turcii were an old noble family, as we learn from Paulinus of Nola, who was friendly with a later member of the family, also called Turcius

---

[1] viii. 14470 Bulla Regia. On *curiones* see Kübler, P-W iv. 2. 1836–8.
[2] viii. 14688 = D. 3937, viii. 10602 = 14689 = D. 3938. Aradia Roscia: viii. 14470.
[3] vi. 1690 = D. 1240.   [4] 319: *CJ* viii. 52. 2; 340: *CTh* xi. 30. 21.
[5] x. 407.   [6] vi. 1768 = D. 1229; Secundus: vi. 1772 = D. 1230.

Apronianus, who, converted to Christianity by Melania the elder, is described as 'aetate puerum, sensibus carnis senem, veteri togarum nobilem prosapia sed clariorem Christiano nomine, qui mixta veteris et novi ortus gloria vetus est senator curiae, Christo novus'.[1] The elder Apronianus was urban prefect in 339 and his father Secundus was a consul (probably suffect) in the late third century.[2] We also have a record of a third-century man called L. Turcius Faesasius Apronianus 'cos' (i.e. 'consularis') who was married to Aemilia Callista c.f.[3] In addition to their noble ancestry the Turcii had a mansion on the Esquiline in which a rich find of silver has been excavated.[4]

Both the Brittii and Turcii were connected with the large family complex of the Ceionii. But the other main noble family group, that centred about the Anicii, is equally in evidence in the *Fasti*. Perhaps the most interesting Constantinian corrector in this clan was Clodius Celsinus Adelphius, described in a Beneventan inscription as 'corr(ector) regionum duarum'.[5] This description poses two problems. The first is whether the 'two regions' must be taken to mean regions governed by Adelphius consecutively or at the same time. Secondly, which province or provinces did he govern? It is unlikely that the 'duae regiones' could refer to combined regions like Apulia and Calabria, and even less to 'Campania cum Samnio'. The word 'regio' is the technical term for an Italian province, and, the descriptions 'Apulia et Calabria'. 'Venetia et Histria' or 'Tuscia et Umbria' each refer to one *regio*. The case of Campania ad Samnium is even more clear-cut, for there is no reference to Samnium before it became a separate province, except in the case of Julius Festus Hymetius, who is described as 'consulari Campaniae cum Samnio',[6] shortly before it appears as a separate province under its own *praesides* in the 350s.[7] The inscription was set up at Beneventum by the townspeople to their patron, who was clearly also governor of the province. But in what province was Beneventum? There are a good number of references showing that

---

[1] Paulin. Nol. *Carm.* 210 ff.—CSEL xxx. 165; Pall. *Hist. Laus.* xli, liv.
[2] vi. 1768. [3] ix. 2801; ix. 6078 164–5.
[4] See *Röm. Mitt.* xlv (1930) 124–36.
[5] ix. 1576 = D. 1239.
[6] vi. 1736. [7] Rudi Thomsen, *The Italic Regions*, 213–14.

it was in Campania,[1] but there is an undated fragmentary Beneventan inscription which has caused some doubts to arise.[2] Both Thomsen and Chastagnol argue that Beneventum was, at least for a time, in the region of Apulia and Calabria.[3] But the positive evidence that Beneventum was in Campania spans a period of a century.[4] The evidence is diverse, ranging from the records of the Council of Sardica in 342[5] to a fifth century inscription showing that Beneventum still fell under the jurisdiction of the Campanian governor,[6] though much later, after the Lombard invasion, Beneventum became the centre of a separate duchy, as we know from the Ravenna geographer,[7] and Paul the Deacon.[8] Adelphius was, therefore, corrector of Campania, after holding another corrector-ship elsewhere. He must have governed Campania before 324, when the province is first recorded under a consular M. Ceionius Julianus.

Coming in practice to designate, as it did, an equestrian governor, the title 'praeses', it may be surmised, could not have been greatly alluring to the aristocracy. It was probably at least partly to give provincial governorships greater dignity that Constantine invented the title 'consularis'. The title itself was far from new, and its use in the original sense of 'ex-consul' survived side by side with the new. Though it had never before been used as the official designation for a position in the imperial government, 'consularis' had been for a long time the informal popular term of reference for

[1] Beneventum: ix. 1563, 1566, 1568–9, 1575, 1580, 1589, 1591, 1597.

[2] ix. 1579 Beneventum. Fl. Cornelius Marcellinus, the governor whose name appears here, seems to have been governor of Apulia and Calabria and also to have shown devotion to his 'patria', presumably Beneventum. This is the only 'evidence' of Beneventum's being in Apulia and Calabria. If Marcellinus was a native of Beneventum and governor of Apulia and Calabria, we cannot conclude that Beneventum was even at that time in Apulia and Calabria, though this is what Thomsen argues, followed by Chastagnol.

[3] Thomsen, *The Italic Regions*, 207–9, 251 ff. Chastagnol, *Fastes*, 132–3. Indeed Chastagnol goes so far as to make Adelphius corrector of Apulia and Calabria, finding in this not only the solution to the Beneventan problem but also the interpretation of the term 'regiones duae'.

[4] See Thomsen, loc. cit.

[5] J. D. Mansi, *Sacrorum Conciliorum nova et amplissima collectio*, 1901. iii. 42.

[6] ix. 1563 Beneventum.

[7] Ravenna Geographer (ed. Parthey and Pinder) iv. 29 (p. 248, 12 ff.); see Thomsen, 251; Mommsen, *Kosmographia*, 318, 309 n. 4.

[8] Paulus Diaconus: Lang. iv. 44, 46. vi. 1, 39. Thomsen, 251.

consular legates.[1] The new type of governorship likewise seems to have developed from senatorial *praesides* or correctors of some Western provinces who were in fact *consulares* in the sense of ex-suffect consuls. P. Helvius Aelius Dionysius, 'cons(ularis) vir. corr(ector) Camp(aniae)' and Acilius Clarus, 'v(ir) co(n)s(ularis) praes(es) Num(idiae)' are good examples of the transition to the new type of governorship.[2] Clarus was probably the last *praeses* of Numidia and Dionysius was probably one of the last correctors of Campania.[3] These were two of the provinces where the governorship is known to have been upgraded to a consular post under Constantine, the others being Aemilia and Liguria, Sicily, Syria Coele, Phoenice, probably Byzacena and temporarily Pontus and Bithynia and 'Europa et Thracia'. It is hardly surprising that all Constantinian consulars whose origins are known were noble.[4]

The first known consular of Campania, in office in 324, was a member of the *gens* Ceionia, M. Ceionius Julianus Kamenius,[5] who then went on to become proconsul of Africa (between 326 and 333) and finally urban prefect, in 333–4.[6] Another member of the family, Ceionius Italicus, was consular of Numidia, also probably under Constantine.[7]

[1] Legates referred to as 'consulares': D. 8824a—Britannia (Greek); D. 8841—Britannia and Dacia (Greek); D. 9179a—Germania Superior, 231, 'co(n)s(ularis)'. D. 1146—duae Pannoniae. D. 2456—Pannonia. D. 8830—Pannonia Inferior et Superior. D. 8836—Pontus et Bithynia (Greek). D. 2927—Pontus et Bithynia (C. Plinius Caecilius Secundus).

[2] P. Helvius Aelius Dionysius: x. 6084 = D. 6310 Capua. Acilius Glarus: viii. 2729 Lambaesis, Numidia.

[3] In the *Fasti* of the *PLRE* Clarus appears as *praeses* of Numidia before 286, as a result of identifying him with the Italian corrector, also called Acilius Clarus, recorded in that year. It is argued by the present author, however, that the *praeses* of Numidia was not the same person as the corrector though no doubt related to him.

[4] Aemilia et Liguria: No correctors are known here at all, the first recorded governor being Iunius Rufus, 'consularis Aemiliae'. (*CTh.* IV. 13. 1–321) Sicily: The first known consular was Domitius Zenophilus in 320. Syria Coele: One Fl. Dionysius is the first known consular, recorded in office at some time between 329 and 335. (Eus. *V. Const.* iv. 42. 3; Soc. i. 28; Lib. *Or.* i. 36) Phoenice: Here the earliest recorded consular was Archelaus, in office in 335 and later to become *Comes Orientis*. (Soc. i. 29. 2; Rufinus *H.E.* x. 17) Byzacena: Whether Cezeus Largus Maternianus, the first known consular, who was legate to the proconsul of Africa at some time between 326 and 333, held his governorship of Byzacena during Constantine's reign or not is not known. For figures see statistical table II.

[5] *AE* 1939, 151, near Abellinum, Campania; *Not. Scav.*, 1938, pp. 75–81.

[6] viii. 14436 = D. 5518, Hr el-Fouar, nr. Vaga; viii. 25525 Bulla Regia.

[7] viii. 7012–3 Constantina, Numidia.

The Constantinian consular who was to enjoy the most successful career was probably Q. Flavius Maesius Egnatius Lollianus Mavortius, who, beginning his public life as *quaestor candidatus* and urban praetor, went on to hold three of the urban *curatelae* traditionally set aside for senators, and then became consular of Campania, *comes intra palatium*, *comes Orientis*, proconsul of Africa, urban prefect (in 342), praetorian prefect and finally ordinary consul (in 355). Mavortius's family can be traced back well into the second century, and it was related through the Fabii to the important noble complex of the Memmii/Maecii/Furii and Scipiones/Gracchi.[1]

Pontus and Bithynia were united temporarily under Lucius Crepereius Madalianus, who, described as 'consularis Ponti et Bithyniae', was in office at some time between Constantine's winning of the East in 324, after which date Madalianus' legation of Asia must be placed, and 341, when he became vicar of Italy.[2] In the case of both Pontus and Bithynia Madalianus succeeded *praesides*, and after his governorship these two provinces were separated again and appear to have returned to praesidial governors. We know of two *praesides* of Bithynia at the end of the tetrarchy.[3] For the period after Madalianus' governorship, though a good number of Bithynian governors are known, we are not given their exact designations in the sources. In one case, that of Apellio, however, we know that the governorship of Bithynia, held in 355, was followed by a governorship of Cilicia, in 358.[4] Though Libanius, one source in this case, never tells us whether Apellio was a *praeses* or a consular in either post, we know that Cilicia was under *praesides* at least until 367, the earliest date for the last recorded *praeses*, Domitius Eutropius.[5] Since Apellio was governor (i.e. *praeses*) of

---

[1] vi. 37112—vi. 1723 and vi. 1757. For the family see p. 122 ff., below.

[2] The province called 'Pontus et Bithynia' in the Principate appears to have comprised the whole of the Diocletianic province of Bithynia together with the coastal strip of Paphlagonia and part of the coastal area of the later Pontus, Diospontus or Helenopontus. Both Diospontus and Pontus Polemoniacus had been part of the huge Severan province of Cappadocia. See Jones, *The Later Roman Empire*, Map I and Appendix 3.

[3] Praesides: Lact. *Mort. Pers.* 16. 4.

[4] Bithynia: Lib. *Epp.* 394–7, Cilicia: Lib. *Ep.* 372.

[5] *CIG* 4427 Tarsus.

Cilicia after his governorship of Bithynia, his Bithynian governorship could hardly have been anything more than a praesidial post. In Pontus what little we know points in much the same direction. Between 317 and 324 one Valerius Ciipus . . . ur, an equestrian *praeses*, is recorded in office, and at some time between 333 and 337, in other words either just before or shortly after Madalianus' governorship, another equestrian *praeses* is recorded.[1] In addition we know of one Jovinus, a *praeses*, who is referred to in an undated inscription found in the province and so therefore presumably *praeses* of Pontus. Madalianus is most likely to date from the first years of Constantine's rule over the East, when we should most expect Westerners to make an appearance in Eastern posts. But why should two provinces be temporarily reunited just for the duration of his governorship, and why should he enjoy a more elevated position than was accorded to governors of those provinces both before and after his tenure of office ? Madalianus, whose career was altogether most distinguished, differed from all other governors of Pontus or Bithynia whose origins are known in being a noble, as is shown elsewhere.[2] It was felt, no doubt, that to offer him a praesidial governorship of Pontus or Bithynia or even perhaps of both would not sufficiently attract him, so the two provinces were united under him as a *consularis*, and then separated again and returned to *praesides*—a good pointer to the rationale of Constantine's creation of the new type of governorship.

Another similarly unique position was held by another noble, L. Aradius Valerius Proculus Populonius, whom we have already met as *praeses* of Byzacena and who also appears as 'consularis provinciae Europae at Thraciae' soon after 324.[3] As pointed out by Jones, the provinces of Europa and Thrace were not adjacent, and, since 'Thracia' was not only the name of a province but also of the diocese in which both that province and Europa were situated, Jones believes that Proculus was in control of Europe and also of the other provinces of the diocese of Thrace.[4] If this is correct,

[1] Ciipus: III. 14184[31] = *AE* 1900, 152. Between 333 and 337 (Fl. Iulius Leontius): III. 14184[17], X 14184[37]; *AE* 19;8, 1.
[2] See Chapter V, page 133, below.
[3] vi. 1690 = D. 1240.
[4] Jones, *The Later Roman Empire*, i. 83, iii. 11, n. 13.

Proculus must be seen as a precursor of the proconsul of Constantinople, who appears to have governed not only the city but also surrounding provinces. Whether the proconsulate of Constantinople was actually created by Constantine or by Constantine II is not known, the first reference to a holder of the post being in 343.[1]

Another case of a proconsul governing more than just his own province is that of Amnius Manius Caesonius Nicomachus Anicius Paulinus Junior Honorius. After being legate of Carthage to his father the proconsul of Africa Anicius Julianus, Paulinus became '(pr)oconsul prov. Asiae et Hellesponti vice sacra iudicans'.[2] This must have been at some time between 324, when Constantine gained the East, and 334, when Paulinus became Prefect of Rome. Hellespontus had formed part of pre-Diocletianic Asia but is recorded under a separate equestrian *praeses* at some time btween 293 and 305.[3] Its reunion with Asia was temporary, for we find it again under its own governor in the middle of the century.[4] It is more than likely that the brief restoration of Hellespontus to the proconsulate of Asia was motivated by the same considerations as those governing the shortlived reunification of Pontus and Bithynia: the gratification of a proud aristocrat.

The promotion of the governorship of Achaea to a proconsulate was probably also the work of Constantine, and the two men known to have been appointed by him to this post, namely Vettius Cossinius Rufinus and Publilius Optatianus Porphyrius, were both nobles.[5] Vettius Cossinius Rufinus is the earliest known proconsul of Achaea, being in office probably in 314–15.[6] An inscription dedicated to him as patron by the people of Atina gives his career as:

---

[1] Athanasius: *Apol. de fuga*, 3.

[2] vi. 1682 = D. 1220. Also vi. 1683 = D. 1221.

[3] Iulius Cassius: *BSA* 1962, p. 183, n. 106 Chersonese.

[4] Fl. Eusebius: Lib. *Epp.* 457–8. See the Nicene list of Eastern provinces. Gelzer, *Patrum Nicaenorum Nomina* (Teubner).

[5] Rufinus: x. 5061 = D. 1217 Atina. See Groag, *Die Reichsbeamten von Achaia in spätröm. Zeit*, 16–20. Chastagnol, *Fastes*, 65. Porphyrius: *SEG* xi. 810 = *AE* 1931, 6, Sparta. Jer. *Chron.* s.a. 328 (ed. Helm, p. 232). Groag, *Wien. Stud.* 45 (1926/7) 103 f. and *Reichsbeamten von Achaia*, 25. Chastagnol, *Fastes*, 80–2.

[6] The last datable corrector is L. Turranius Gratianus, who was in office under the tetrarchy and before his urban prefecture in 290. (iii. 6103 Athens). As the proconsulate of Achaea was Rufinus's last post before his urban prefecture in 315, and since all the rest of his appointments were in the West, it is safe to place his proconsulate between that year and Constantine's acquisition of Moesia in 314.

corrector of Campania under Maxentius, corrector of Tuscia and Umbria, corrector of Venetia and Histria, 'curator alvei Tiberis et cloacarum', curator of the Via Flaminia, proconsul of Achaea, and finally urban prefect in 315.[1] He is thought by Seeck to have been the father of Vettius Agorius Praetextatus, praetorian prefect under Theodosius. For, in addition to the name Vettius, their careers, both civil and religious, show many parallels.[2] Despite an attempt on the part of Groag and Chastagnol to identify our man with the unnamed subject of a horoscope who 'paternum ostendit ignobile',[3] there is evidence to show that Rufinus was a noble. Vettius Agorius Praetextatus, who, as we have seen, was probably Rufinus's son, is described as 'superbo qui creatus germine',[4] and we know of a third century proconsul of Asia called Cossinius Rufinus, probably an ancestor of our proconsul.[5]

The other side of the family was probably the old family of the Vettii Grati Sabiniani, which can be traced back to C. Vettius

---

[1] x. 5061 = D. 1217 Atina, Campania.

[2] Seeck, *Symm.* p. lxxxvi.

[3] Groag, *Reichsbeamten von Achaia*, 16–20. Chastagnol, *Fastes*, 65. The horoscope (Firmicus Maternus, *Mathesis* ii. 29, 10—Teub. vol. i, 81) reads as follows: Is, in cuius genitura Sol fuit in Piscibus, Luna in Cancro, Saturnus in Virgine, Iuppiter in Piscibus in eadem parte in qua Sol, Mars in Aquario, Venus in Tauro, Mercurius in Aquario isdem cum Marte partibus, horoscopus in Scorpione, eius geniturae pater post geminum ordinarium consulatum in exilium datus est, sed et ipse ob adulterii crimen in exilium datus et de exilio raptus in administrationem Campaniae primum destinatus est, deinde Achaiae proconsulatum, post vero ad Asiae proconsulatum et praefecturam urbi Romae.

A little further down (ii. 29. 12) we are told: 'Paternum ostendit ignobile', which Chastagnol takes to mean 'il serait donc un récent *allectus*' (op. cit. 66). According to the horoscope, the governorship of Campania was followed by the proconsulship of Achaia, a proconsulship of Asia and the prefecture of Rome. Yet in the inscription describing Rufinus's career there is no sign of a proconsulship of Asia at all. Chastagnol, however, is far from daunted: 'Il s'agit donc d'un oubli sur le texte d'Atina, soit négligence de lapicide, soit omission dé libérée' (loc. cit.). And sure enough, there is an inscription from Nacrasa containing a reference to a proconsul of Asia called Cossinius Rufinus (*IGR* iv. 1162).

Two points must be noted here. First, the man is called ἀνθύπατος (proconsul). Secondly, the inscription was set up at Nacrasa. Now, Nacrasa was part of Asia *proconsularis* until the time of Diocletian, when it became part of Lydia instead, which was under *praesides* from the time of Diocletian until late in the fourth century, and was then governed by consulars. Our Nacrasa inscription therefore dates from before the time of Diocletian and cannot come to Chastagnol's rescue after all. In short, there is no basis upon which to rest the identification of the urban prefect of 315–16 with the unnamed subject of the horoscope quoted above.

[4] vi. 1779ᵈ.   [5] *IGR* iv. 1162.

Sabinianus Julius Hospes, who apparently started life as an equestrian, was adopted by the Vettii Sabini and went on to become an imperial legate and consul.[1] His son, C. Vettius Gratus Sabinianus, was ordinary consul in 221 and his grandson, C. Vettius Gratus Atticus Sabinianus, was ordinary consul in 242.[2] The ordinary consul of 250, Vettius Gratus, was perhaps a brother of the consul of 242.

Gratus is the name of a proconsul of Africa under Valerian and Gallienus,[3] and also of an ordinary consul of 280 thought by Groag to be a member of the Vettian family.[4] The Vettii Sabini, the family into which Hospes was adopted, may have been descended from the Ravennate equestrian probably of the early principate, P. Vettius Sabinus.[5] A later member of the family, was C. Vettius Sabinus Granianus, quaestor in Achaea in the first or second century A.D.[6] In addition to Vettius Rufinus and his son, Vettius Agorius Praetextatus, the family was represented in the late Empire by Q. Sattius Fl. Vettius Gratus, corrector, presumably of Lucania and Brittium,[7] Vettius Justus, ordinary consul in 328, and Gabinius Vettius Probianus, urban prefect in 377. In addition there was C. Vettia Grata, of unknown date, who died in Amalfi at the age of two.[8]

Though the only man in the fourth century undoubtedly descended from the Vettii Grati Sabiniani of the principate was Q. Sattius Fl. Vettius Gratus, Rufinus's nobility is indicated in the first place by his relationship to the Asian proconsul, and his son's marriage into the Aconii makes it more than likely that he was related to the old family of Vettii Grati, since noble families tended to marry within their own stratum.

Unlike Rufinus, Publilius Optatianus Porphyrius is known to have held only two posts, the proconsulate of Achaea and the prefecture of Rome, which he held for a month in 329 and again for a month in 333. St. Jerome tells us that Porphyrius, whose name is best known as a poet, was recalled from exile by Constantine in

[1] *ILAfr.* 83 No. 281.   [2] viii. 823 (P-W Nos. 31 and 32).
[3] *ILAfr.* 356.   [4] *PIR*², P-W s.v.
[5] xi. 863 = D. 6665 Mutina.   [6] *AE* 1947, 87 Athens.
[7] *AE* 1923, 61. See Barbieri, *Albo*, 314, No. 1750.
[8] x. 648.

325,[1] and his proconsulship is more likely to be after that date than before his exile, especially since both East and West were under Constantine from 324. The poet's name also appears in a list of senators, possibly the members of some priestly college:

TVRRANIV	
CREPEREIVS	RO
PVBLILIVS	OPTATIA
CEIONIVS RVFIVS	VOLVSI
N ANICIVS	P
CILIVS[2]	

This, together with some of the words and phrases in a Spartan inscription in which Porphyrius is described as a v.c. and proconsul of Achaea, indicates that he was probably a pagan, though Groag believes that he later converted to Christianity.[3]

More important, the list points to Porphyrius's nobility. The first name must be that of L. Turranius Gratianus, Prefect of Rome in 290-1, and the second is a member of the old family of the Creperii. As Groag points out, the Ceionius is probably the ordinary consul of 311 and 314 and the Prefect of Rome of 310-11 and 313-15. The Anicius must be Junius Anicius Paulinus, who probably was M. Junius Caesonius Nicomachus Anicius Faustus Paulinus, suffect consul at an unknown date, ordinary consul in 298 and Prefect of Rome in 299. This is a more likely identification than the one Groag puts forward with Sex. Anicius Paulinus, the suffect consul, among whose names Iunius is never recorded. The next name on the list is probably a member of the *gens Acilia*, one of the noblest houses in the Empire.

The post of vicar originated, as we have seen, under the tetrarchy, and no vicars in that period are known to have been noble.[4] But

---

[1] The exile was imposed by Constantine in the first place, though the reason is not known. See Groag, *Wien. Stud.* 45 (1926/7) 103 f. and *Reichsbeamten von Achaia*, 25. See also Chastagnol, *Fastes*, 80-2. Constantine's pardon: Hieron. *Chron.* ad a. 328 (ed. Helm, p. 232). For the date 325 see Groag, *Wien. Stud.*, loc. cit.

[2] *Not. Scav.* 1917, 22, Rome.

[3] *SEG* xi. 810 = 1931, 6 Sparta, *Wien. Stud.* 45 (1926/7) 107, Groag, *Reichsbeamten von Achaia*, 26.

[4] See page 46.

here too Constantine was prepared to break with the past, and just under half his vicars whose origins are known were nobles. Again the dioceses chosen are significant, Africa and Spain, the same areas as those where the senatorial *praesides* were concentrated.

Lucrius Verinus is recorded as vicar of Africa from 318 to 321 and as urban prefect from 323 to 325. He also received a law with the senatorial greeting, 'Have, Locri Verine, carissime nobis',[1] dated 314 in the MS., but redated by Seeck to 320 to fall into Verinus's vicariate. Was this Constantinian vicar and urban prefect the same man as our tetrarchic *praeses* of that exceptional province, Syria Coele ? Neither Chastagnol nor the *PLRE* makes this identification, but nothing stands in its way: the name Verinus was very rare and the dates are not too widely separated. Moreover this identification provides the best explanation for the urban prefect's military exploits celebrated in verses written by the elder Symmachus:

Virtutem, Verine, tuam plus mirer in armis,/Eoos dux Armenios cum caede domares,/An magis eloquium morum vitaeque leporem,/Et—nisi in officiis, quotiens tibi publicae curae—/Quod vitam innocuis tenuisti laetus in agris ?/Nullam ultra est virtutis opus, quam si esset, haberes.[2]

Moreover, if we recall Verinus' appellate jurisdiction as governor of Syria, it becomes clear to us that he was no ordinary *praeses*.

Chastagnol's argument to show that Verinus was an equestrian cannot be accepted:

La préfecture urbaine est, on le sait, une haute fonction clarissime; par contre, le vicariat est a cette date—et jusque vers la fin du règne de Constantin—une charge reservée aux perfectissimes. Nous pensons donc que Verinus était un chevalier et qu'il a été promu au clarissimat, par une *allectio inter consulares*, entre 321 et 323 . . . Sans doute avons-nous là un homme de main de Constantin, énergique et autoritaire, mis en place comme préfet pour mater le Sénat pendant le conflit entre l'assemblée et l'empereur.[3]

First, it is by no means true to say that vicariates under Constantine were reserved for equestrians. As is shown in Statistical Table 3, seven of the thirteen Constantinian vicars whose origins are known were nobles. On the other hand, not even Chastagnol himself claims non-senatorial origins for any Constantinian urban prefect other than Verinus. Indeed, there is no proven case of a non-noble

---

[1] *Cy* iii. 12. 1.   [2] Symm. *Ep.* i. 2. 7.   [3] Chastagnol, *Fastes*, 75–6.

prefect of Rome until the reign of Valentinian. Was Constantine's 'conflict' with the Senate then decided in the space of Verinus's fifteen-month urban prefecture ? Or is the whole idea a figment of Chastagnol's imagination ? If the identification of the vicar with the Syrian governor is accepted, that is another reason for seeing Verinus as a noble. In any case, as was shown in Chapter II, new men did not tend to enter the Senate under the tetrarchy except in the case of praetorian prefects entering as such. For it appears to have been the deliberate policy of Diocletian to turn senatorial rank into a *cul-de-sac*.

L. Aradius Valerius Proculus Populonius, who has already been mentioned in connection with his appointments as *praeses* of Byzacena and consular of 'Europa and Thrace', went on to be consular of Sicily and then 'proconsul provinciae Africae vice sacra iudicans idemq. iudicio sacro per provincias proconsularem et Numidiam Byzacium ac Tripolim itemque Mauretaniam Sitifensem et Caesariensem perfunctus officio praefecturae praetorio'.[1] Proculus was therefore not quite a praetorian prefect but was, so to speak, acting praetorian prefect or, in other words, vicar over the whole diocese. It is interesting to find that Proculus had authority over proconsular Africa in two capacities, as proconsul and as acting prefect—the more so since proconsular provinces were normally considered to fall outside the jurisdiction of imperial officials. Proculus was the product of two noble lines, that of the Aradii and that of the Valerii, and his career did honour to them both. At the end of Constantine's reign the emperor dedicated a statue to his noble acting praetorian prefect, describing his lineage as 'insignem nobilitate prosapiam'.[2]

A more normal kind of vicar than Aradius Proculus was C. Annius Tiberianus, who became a praetorian prefect at the end of Constantine's reign. Between 325 and 327 he is recorded as *comes Africae* and between 332 and 335 as *comes* or vicar of the Spains.[3]

[1] vi. 1690 = D. 1240.
[2] *AE* 1934, 158. On acting praetorian prefects see M. T. W. Arnheim, 'Vicars in the later Roman Empire', *Historia* 19 (1970) 593–606.
[3] *CTh.* xii. 5. 1—MSS. 326, Seeck 325; *CTh.* xii. 1. 15—327; *CJ* VI. 1. 6 'ad Tiberianum comitem Hispaniarum'—332; *CTh.* III. 5. 6 'ad Tiberianum vicarium Hispaniarum—335.

Under the year 336 Jerome includes a reference to him as praetorian prefect in Gaul and a man of culture: 'Tiberianus vir disertus praefectus praetorio per Gallias'.[1] Like many another noble of his day Tiberianus had literary leanings. He was the author of 'versus Platonis de Graeco in Latinum translati' and 'versus Socratis philosophi'.[2] His nobility is indicated partly by his *nomen*, and partly, paradoxically perhaps, by his absence from the consular *fasti*. Tiberianus appears in the well-known Tubernuc inscription of 337 together with three other praetorian prefects, Fl. Ablabius, Papius Pacatianus, and Nestorius Timonianus, all four being described as 'viri clarissimi praefecti praetorio'.[3]

In itself the title *clarissimus* tells us nothing about the birth of the man concerned. As it happens, both Ablabius and Pacatianus are known to have been of humble birth. In the case of Ablabius we know this from Eunapius and Libanius. Eunapius deals with Ablabius's humble origins and recounts the portents at the time of his birth.[4] Libanius informs us that Ablabius began his public career as an *officialis* of the governor of Crete, hardly a post for a noble. Ablabius himself evidently had no love for the aristocracy, as may be inferred from the passage in Jerome's *Chronicle*: 'Ablabius praefectus praetorio et multi nobilium occisi'.[5] Pacatianus began his career as 'v(ir) p(erfectissimus) pr(a)es(es) prov(inciae) Sard(iniae)' under Domitius Alexander in 308–9.[6] Both Ablabius and Pacatianus owed their clarissimates to their consulships, held by Ablabius in 331 and by Pacatianus in the following year. Nestorius Timonianus, the last of the four prefects named in the Tubernuc inscription, is otherwise unknown, but it seems likely that he was the praetorian prefect of the Caesar Delmatius, for the order probably reflects seniority. If so, he was probably killed together with his master shortly after the erection of the inscription, which would explain his absence from the consular *fasti*. The case of Tiberianus is very different. We know a fair amount about his career, and we should naturally expect his name to appear among

---

[1] Jer. *Chron.* s.a. 336.   [2] *Anth. Lat.* 490, 719B, 809.

[3] *ILT* 814 Tubernuc, Africa Proconsularis. See the discussion of it in P-W xxii. 2 s.v. *Praefectus Praetorio*, col. 2430 by W. Ensslin.

[4] Eunap. *V.S.* vi. 3. 1–7.   [5] Lib. *Or.* xlii. 23 Jer. *Chron.* s.a. 338.

[6] i. 372 Sotgiu, Sardinia.

the ordinary consuls, but in vain. Adding to this fact the evidence of his *nomen* Annius we can be in little doubt that his clarissimate came to him from birth. For the Annii were a well-known noble family in the late Empire, related to the Anicii and Petronii. Tiberianus was therefore not the first member of his family to be a Constantinian praetorian prefect. This distinction must go to Petronius Annianus, who was ordinary consul together with Ceionius Rufius Volusianus in 314 and praetorian prefect together with Iulius Julianus from at least April 315 to March 317.[1]

Two inscriptions bear the names of the two prefects, one dating from before and the other after Crispus was named Caesar in March 317, and both inscriptions display a most interesting and unusual feature: in each Annianus appears as 'vir clarissimus' while Julianus is described as 'vir eminentissimus'.[2] That Julianus was of non-senatorial origin is clear from his designation in 314 as an equestrian prefect of Egypt.[3] But what about Annianus? His clarissimate could have come to him in adult life, through his consulship or by some other means—or he could have inherited it from his father. But, lacking a precise date as it does, the earlier inscription itself can throw no light on this problem. However, though nothing more is known of Annianus's career, his name is not without significance. The Petronii were a noble family connected by marriage in the fourth century with the Anicii and also, perhaps earlier on, with the Ceionii. The Anicii in turn were connected with the Annii.[4] The Petronii were connected with the Anicii by marriage in the fourth century, and Petronius Probus, Valentinian's famous praetorian prefect, was head of the Anician house in his day.[5] That Petronius Annianus was related to Petronius Probus can hardly be doubted, both by reason of the *nomen* which they

---

[1] These *termini* are given us on the one hand by a letter from Annianus and Julianus to Domitius Celsus, vicar of Africa, dated April 315 (Opt. *App.* viii) and on the other by an inscription referring to the prefecture of Annianus and Iulianus which mentions the Caesar Crispus, who was raised to that dignity only in March 317. *AE* 1938, 85, Ephesus.

[2] Before Crispus became Caesar: iii. 13734 = D. 8938 Propaeum Traiani, Moesia Inferior. After Crispus became Caesar: *AE* 1938, 85 Ephesus.

[3] P. Isid. 73.   [4] See p. 110, below.

[5] vi. 1753, vi. 1748; Aus. *Ep.* xvi. 1. 32.

6

shared and the connection between the Petronii and the Anicii/ Annii.

Annianus was also therefore related to Petronius Probus' grand-father, Petronius Probianus, who was contemporary with himself. Probianus is first recorded in 315 and 316 as proconsul of Africa.[1] In 321 he seems to have been praetorian prefect. For though never referred to as such, in 321 he received a law about the property of proscribed and condemned persons, a general sort of law which would normally go to a praetorian prefect but could conceivably also go to a lesser functionary. Sent by Constantine from Serdica, the constitution is addressed simply 'Petronio Probiano suo salutem'.[2] The best reason for believing that the unnamed office was a praetorian prefecture is the fact that Probianus is recorded as ordinary consul together with Anicius Iulianus in the following year, and then as prefect of Rome between 329 and 331. If the law of 321 is correctly dated, Probianus can have been nothing but praetorian prefect in that year, since that is the only position in the order of honour to fall between a proconsulate and an ordinary consulate—other than the prefecture of Rome, which Probianus was in any case to hold several years later and which is not marked in the *Chronography* of 354 as a second appointment. Probianus was a worthy scion of a noble house, and received a flattering tribute from the elder Symmachus.[3]

The connection of the Annii with the Ceionii can be seen in the name M. Nummius Ceionius Annius Albinus, who may have been the urban prefect of 256 listed simply as Nummius Albinus or the Albinus who was ordinary consul in 263.[4] The family can be traced back at least to the time of Trajan, as is shown in the discussion on the Ceionii in Chapter V where the Annii and Petronii are also dealt with. Like the Annii the Petronii, as will be seen, were related to the Ceionii as well as to the Anicii.[5]

The family with the longest pedigree of nobility in the late Empire was probably the Acilii Glabriones, tracing their ancestry as they did from the consul of 191 B.C., victor over King Antiochus III of

---

[1] *CTh*. xi. 30. 3; *CTh*. xi. 30. 5–6.   [2] *CTh*. ix. 42. 1.

[3] Symm. *Ep.* i. 2. 6.   [4] vi. 3146. *Vita Aureliani* 9. 8.

[5] See pp. 130 f., 111, below.

Syria. Representing this ancient line in the time of Constantine was the Acilius Severus who was ordinary consul in 323 and urban prefect two years later. In addition we have three laws dating from between 322 and 324 addressed to a man called simply Severus, two of these laws lacking any designation and the other describing Severus as urban prefect. The dating and designation make it difficult to avoid identifying this Severus with Acilius Severus. But what office could he have had at the same time as an ordinary consulship and just before the urban prefecture ? Here the consulship is the best clue, for it was unusual for it to coincide with any post other than a praetorian prefecture. So Acilius Severus was probably praetorian prefect between 322 and 324.[1]

Though evidently not as yet connected, by the early fifth century the Acilii and Anicii were related by marriage. A roll-call of noble Constantinian praetorian prefects reveals the significant fact that only two of them belonged to neither the *gens Anicia* nor the *gens Ceionia*. Acilius Severus, as we have seen, was one. The other was Valerius Maximus, recorded as praetorian prefect in 327–8, 332–3 and 337.[2] He is thought by Palanque to have been prefect in Gaul for all ten years and by the *PLRE* to have been in different parts of the Empire for three short spells.[3] He was consul in 327 and was either the same person as or a close relative of the urban prefect of 319–323 recorded as Valerius Maximus Basilius.[4] It is also

[1] *CTh.* iii. 32. 1—322, no office indicated. *CJ* iii. 12. 3—323, no office indicated. *CTh* vi. 22. 1—MSS. 321, Seeck 324—'ad Severum p.u.' Severus' praetorian prefecture is rejected by the *PLRE*, s.v. but accepted by Chastagnol, *Fastes*, 77–8 and Schuurmans, *Samenstelling*, no. 673. On the dating of the laws see Seeck, *Regesten*, 62, and Palanque, *Essai*, 5 and n. 24. On the family see p. 107 f., below.

[2] *CTh.* i. 5. 2 (327), *CTh.* i. 4. 2 (327), pp. (MSS. dat. Treviris), *CTh.* i. 16. 4 (328), *CTh.* vii. 20. 5 (328) pp. (MSS. dat. Treviris), *P. Flor.* i. 1–3 (327), *CJ.* vi. 36. 7 (332), *CTh.* viii. 1. 3 (333), *CTh.* xiii. 4. 2 (337).

[3] Seeck, *Regesten*, 69, accepts the 'dat. Treveris' of the MSS., but Palanque, *Essai*, 10, 131, reads 'acc(epta)' or 'p(ro)p(osita)' instead. Hence his view that Maximus was in Gaul. The *PLRE* has assigned praetorian prefects to Constantine and his sons in accordance with imperial itineraries as worked out in an as yet unpublished article by Mr. John Martindale, who was kind enough to allow me to consult it. The result of his work is embodied in the *PLRE*'s *Fasti*.

[4] From a misreading of a papyrus (P. Fior. 53) it used to be thought that the consul's name was Ulpius Maximus (which form is still to be found in Palanque, op. cit., 10), but a second edition of the same papyrus together with two other papyri showed that it was Valerius Maximus. (*P. Soc. It.* vi, 147, n. 1; *P. Thead.* 36; *P. Soc. It.* iv. 309). See Chastagnol, *Fastes*, 73–5.

possible that the Maximus who was urban prefect in 361-2 was another member of the family. This urban prefect was certainly a noble, since we know that he was the son of a sister of Vulcacius Rufinus. From the name of Melania the elder's son Publicola one might conclude that Melania married into the Valerii Maximi.[1] So, though related to no other Constantinian praetorian prefect, Maximus was related to that distinguished Constantinian noble acting prefect, L. Aradius Valerius Proculus Populonius, who has already been discussed. In all, a third of Constantine's praetorian prefects were nobles, a fifth non-nobles, and the origins of the rest unknown.

Though the term 'comites' or emperor's companions, had long been used to refer to those who formed the imperial retinue on journeys, the title had no official standing until the time of Constantine. Those *comites* who really were attached to the person of the emperor became known as 'comites intra palatium', 'comites intra consistorium', or 'domestici' to distinguish them from those whose duties took them away from the court.[2] *Comites* were arranged in three numbered grades and could be charged with a variety of duties, either civil or religious. Those given religious tasks were invariably Christians, such as Acacius and Strategius, and they would represent the Emperor at Church synods or would be responsible for the building of churches and the stamping out of pagan worship.[3]

More important for our purpose are the *comites provinciarum*, who appear to have performed the same duties as vicars though they were of a superior rank. Sometimes however these *comites* are bracketed together with praetorian prefects to act as a direct channel between provincials and the emperor: 'Praefectis praetorio

---

[1] Maximus PUR 361-2: *Chron.* 354. Son of a sister of Vulcacius Rufinus: Amm. xxi. 12. 24. Publicola: Pall. *Hist. Laus.* 54, 58, 61. Following Cardinal Rampolla's *Santa Melania Giuniore* (pp. 111-17), which the present author has been unable to consult, Chastagnol sees our prefect, with whom he identifies the urban prefect of 319-23, as the father of the urban prefect of 361-2, whom he regards as the husband of Melania the Elder. *Fastes*, 73, 155. But unless Rampolla was using evidence which has not as yet seen the light of day, such conclusions can only be regarded as very tentative.

[2] For *comites* see Eus. *V. Const.* iv. 1; *CTh.* i. 16. 6, vi. 30. 1, vi. 30. 4; *CJ.* xii. 16. 1. See list of *comites ordinis primi intra palatium*.

[3] Amm. xv. 13. 2; Eus. *V.C.* iii. 52-3, 62; iv. 42.

et comitibus qui per provincias constituti sunt provincialium nostrorum voces ad nostrum scientiam referentibus.'[1] And again: 'Conquerendi vocem omnibus aperimus apud comites aut apud praefectos praetoria.'[2] Yet *comites* are most frequently to be found doing the work of vicars, and, while it was not possible to appeal against the decision of a praetorian prefect, it was permissible to appeal against the judgement of a proconsul, vicar or *comes*, as a law of 331 informs us.[3] Appointment as a *comes provinciarum* was always temporary (except in the case of the *comes Orientis*). Though the head of a diocese was normally a vicar, when there was a *comes* there was no vicar, and the titles are used almost interchangeably in this connection. Thus, Annius Tiberianus appears in 325 as 'comes per Africam', a position which he retained for just under two years; in 332 he is 'comes Hispaniarum', but in 335 he is referred to as 'vicarius Hispaniarum'.[4] What is particularly significant is that of these imperial roving ambassadors who enjoyed the confidence and the ready ear of the emperor a significant number were nobles. The most important *comites* were those of the first rank who were members of the imperial *consistorium* or 'cabinet', which comprised in addition the household officials, namely the *quaestor sacri palatii, magister officiorum, comes sacrarum largitionum* and *comes rerum privatarum*, who were members of this august body *ex officio*, as were probably the *praepositus sacri cubiculi* and the praetorian prefect on the spot (*praefectus praetorio praesens*) if there was one.[5] Nobles such as L. Aradius Proculus and M. Nummius Albinus are recorded among such *comites ordinis primi intra palatium*.[6]

In only one diocese did a *comes* permanently replace the vicar, and that was the diocese of Oriens. Different explanations for this anomaly have been put forward, Seeck attributing it to the religious difficulties in the diocese and Downey, relying on Malalas's

---

[1] *CTh*. i. 16. 6 (331).　　[2] *CTh*. i. 16. 7 (331).

[3] *CTh*. xi. 30. 16.

[4] *CTh*. xii. 5. 1 (MSS. 326, Seeck 325); *CJ* vi. 1. 6 (332); *CTh*. iii. 5. 6 (335).

[5] See *CTh*. xi. 29. 5 (362), vi. 30. 1 (379), vi. 30. 4 (378), vii. 8. 3 (384); Amm. xxviii. 1. 25, xvi. 8. 7, xiv. 7. 11, xv. 4. 8.

[6] Proculus: vi. 1690 = D. 1240; vi. 1693 = D. 1241; vi. 1694; vi. 1692 = D. 1242. Albinus: vi. 1748.

Chronicle, seeing the reason in military exigencies.[1] Malalas's evidence, of which Seeck appears to be ignorant, is probably to be trusted, for, though writing in the sixth century, he had access to good contemporary sources and he dates the first *comes Orientis*, one Felicianus, to 335.[2] We also have epigraphical evidence which both corroborates Malalas's view and links the new anomalous office with the old exceptional provincial governorship of Syria. Syria was, as we have seen, the only praesidial province in the Empire to have a series of senatorial governors under the tetrarchy. *Praesides* of Syria, moreover, tended to have jurisdiction not only over their own province but over the rest of the diocese as well.[3] Though not exactly vicars, Virius Lupus—whose governorship dates from before the institution of dioceses—L. Aelius Dionysius, and probably Verinus had appellate jurisdiction over Oriens. Verinus is known to have had military duties, though possibly in some other post. The *comes Orientis* was perhaps in a sense an old-style legate in addition to being a vicar, both in his military functions and in the fact that the post tended to be occupied by nobles, at least in the early days. Of the three *comites Orientis* recorded under Constantine, the origins of only one are known, and he was a noble called Q. Fl. Maesius Egnatius Lollianus, later to become praetorian prefect.[4]

Short of psychoanalysis across the barrier of time we shall never know Constantine's motives in reversing the policy of appointments built up over a long period—though it should of course always be remembered that nobles never regained access to military posts. Any motive attributed to him cannot but be conjectural. But, as was pointed out above, a purely personal reason will not explain the continuance of the new policy under Constantine's successors. Perhaps it would not be altogether unreasonable to suggest that the appointment of nobles to high office was an attempt to mollify their hostility to the advent of an emperor with pro-Christian

---

[1] Seeck, P-W iv. 631, 659–60; G. Downey, *A study of the Comites Orientis and the Consulares Syriae*, 7–10; Malalas 318. 23.

[2] Malalas loc. cit.

[3] See for example the case of Verinus: Symm. *Ep.* i. 2. 7. *CJ* iii. 12. 1. See Chastagnol, *Fastes*, 74–6.

[4] Lupus: vi. 31775 = D. 1210. Dionysius: vi. 1675 = D. 1211.

leanings. Would it be surprising if Constantine preferred to have these possessors of landed wealth and local influence on his side rather than against him?[1]

[1] If Constantine's conversion is seen as an act of political expediency, as an accommodation with a powerful new force, namely the Christian Church, his change of the system of state appointments to favour nobles in the West will appear inexplicable. But this view of Constantine's conversion must be rejected, despite the battery of eminent historians supporting it. (J. Burckhardt, *Die Zeit Constantins des Grossen*, 369 ff; E. Schwartz, *Kaiser Constantin und die Christliche Kirche, passim;* M. Rostovtzeff, *The Social and Economic History of the Roman Empire*, 2nd edn., 509; A. Alföldi, *The Conversion of Constantine and Pagan Rome*, 10 ff.). The interpretation of Constantine's conversion proffered by these scholars is based upon the belief that the Christian Church of the early fourth century was a strong organization, a force to be reckoned with. Thus Alföldi: 'The final settlement which began in A.D. 300 between the menacing power of Christianity and the forces of the state, was the unavoidable consequence of a long and slow development . . . As all know, the climax was reached with the conversion of Constantine.' ('The helmet of Constantine with the Christian monogram', *JRS* 22 (1932) 9). Similarly, Rostovtzeff: '. . . The Christians, increasing in numbers and in strength, grew tired of being outcasts and of fighting the state. The time was ripe for a reconciliation of state and Church, each of which needed the other . . . (Constantine) offered peace to the Church, provided that she would recognise the state and support the imperial power. The Church— to her detriment, as many scholars believe—accepted the offer. For the first time the imperial power became firmly established on a solid basis, but it lost almost completely, save for some irrelevant formulae, the last remnants of its constitutional character as the supreme magistrature of the people of the Empire. It now resembled the Persian monarchy of the Sassanidae and its predecessors in the East, the monarchies of Babylonia, Egypt and the rest.' (Rostovtzeff, loc. cit.) In fact, however, it is clear that the Christian Church was far from strong or well organized at the time of Constantine's accession, particularly in the West— and it should be remembered that Constantine gained the East only in 324. Baynes estimates Christians as amounting to 'perhaps one-tenth' of Constantine's subjects. *Constantine and the Christian Church*, 4). The strength of the Church was not a cause but rather a result of Constantine's conversion, which is to be seen as an act of faith. (Baynes, op. cit., 40–9; A. H. M. Jones, *Constantine and the conversion of Europe*, 251). Far from giving him a firm basis of support, Constantine's Christianity placed him in a weak position; hence the need to placate the rich, influential and very pagan senatorial aristocracy.

IV

FROM CONSTANTINE TO THEODOSIUS

SOME months after the death of Constantine in May 337, his surviving sons, the Caesars Constantine, Constantius and Constans, each assumed the title Augustus and divided the Empire among themselves. Constantine, the eldest, became ruler of Britain, Gaul and Spain, the same regions which had first come under the sway of his father; Constans, the youngest brother, who had become Caesar only four years before, received Italy, Illyricum and Africa; while Constantius was given the East as his share. But within three years fratricidal conflict delivered the whole of the West into the hands of Constans, and eleven years later, when he in turn had lost his life at the hands of a usurper and his death had been avenged by Constantius, the Empire was once again united under the rule of a single Augustus.[1]

Though not baptized until adult life, Constantine's sons were the first rulers of the Roman world to be brought up as Christians. Constans was a pious and orthodox Christian who followed the creed of Nicaea, while Constantius favoured the Arians, embroidering his religion with superstitious beliefs and having a taste for theological disputation.[2]

In 341 an imperial edict was issued reiterating the illegality of pagan sacrifice which had evidently been banned by a Constantinian law which has not survived,[3] and a later constitution demands that all temples be closed, declaring death as the penalty for performing sacrifices and even threatening confiscation of the property of governors who failed to enforce the edict.[4] After his victory over Magnentius, Constantius prohibited nocturnal sacrifices, which had been permitted by the usurper,[5] and a law of 356 lays down capital

[1] Zos. ii. 39 ff. [2] Amm. xxi. 16. 18.
[3] CTh. xvi. 10. 2.
[4] CTh. xvi. 10. 4. The date, 346, conflicts with the address Taurus, praetorian prefect, who is known to have been in office 355–61.
[5] CTh. xvi. 10. 5 (353).

punishment for the performance of sacrifices and the worship of images.[1] All these laws, it should be noted, were issued in the West. It was also Constantius who was responsible for the removal of the altar of Victory from the curia, where it had stood for three centuries.[2] Magnentius's tolerance of nocturnal sacrifices can easily be understood as an attempt to attract the support of pagans, and the strongly-worded anti-pagan legislation of Constantius and Constans should not surprise anyone. Unlike their father, Constantius and Constans did not have to fight for their position. The artificial tetrarchy of named successors invented by Diocletian had given way to the hereditary principle, always dear to the troops. The murder of all the remaining male members of the family (with the exception of Gallus and Julian) in 337 left the three Caesars the unrivalled rulers of the Empire. They were, after all, the third generation of their family to be raised to the purple, and were accorded an even longer imperial lineage, as descendants of Claudius Gothicus.[3] The security of their position is sufficient to explain the Emperors' open hostility to paganism. Yet we have a tribute to Constantius for his tolerant attitude to paganism from none other than Symmachus, whose name is a byword for paganism in the late Empire:

Nihil ille (sc. divus Constantius) decerpsit sacrarum virginum privilegiis, replevit nobilibus sacerdotia. Romanis caerimoniis non negavit inpensas, et per omnes vias aeternae urbis laetum secutus senatum vidit placido ore delubra, legit inscripta fastigiis deum nomina, percontatus templorum origines est, miratus est conditores, cumque alias religiones ipse sequeretur, has servavit imperio.[4]

Symmachus of course had an ulterior motive in portraying the pious Christian emperor as a tolerant ruler, for the passage quoted is an extract from the orator's well-known appeal for the restoration of the altar of Victory to its traditional place in the Senate-house. Yet the account of Constantius's visit to Rome in 357 which we are given by Ammianus, who had no axe to grind, is closer in spirit to Symmachus's portrayal than to the picture that emerges from the Theodosian Code.[5] Is it not perhaps possible that what Constantius

[1] CTh. xvi. 10. 6.   [2] Amb. Ep. 18. 32.
[3] Anon. Vales. 1. 2; Eurt. ix. 22.   [4] Symm. Rel. iii. 7.
[5] Amm. xvi. 13.

enacted in law he was prepared to ignore in practice? If so, the reason can only have been to avoid the complete alienation of his pagan subjects, and, not least among them, the nobles. Another pointer in this direction is the fact that, in appointments to high office, Constantine's sons continued their father's policy.

None of Constantine II's praetorian prefects are known, unless Ambrosius, St. Ambrose's father, was appointed by him. Though the bishop was of senatorial origin, nothing is known of his father's origins.

Five of the seven praetorian prefects known under Constans were noble. None of Constans's praetorian prefects is known to have been non-noble and we have no information about the background of Ulpius Limenius, Eustathius, or Hermogenes. But Limenius and Hermogenes are each recorded in the *Chronography* of 354 as simultaneously urban prefect and praetorian prefect, (Limenius in 347–9 and Hermogenes in 349–50), which is probably a sign that these men were merely stop-gaps, as may also have been the case with Eustathius, despite his unqualified description as a praetorian prefect in the *Theodosian Code*. Illyricum at least, if not Constans' whole Empire, was under noble prefects throughout the period 340–50.[1]

Probably the most notable of Constans' prefects was Vulcacius Rufinus, who served him as prefect for the last five years of his reign. He retained his post under Magnentius, and was the only envoy sent by the usurper to Constantius who was not arrested.[2] The Emperor was not afraid to scorn the ruler of the West, but took care not to offend his aristocratic prefect. Indeed, after the battle of Mursa, Rufinus continued as prefect under Constantius himself, his appointment being terminated presumably because of his relationship with the Caesar Gallus. For the unfortunate

---

[1] Ambrosius: Paulin. *V. Amb.* ii. 3–4. Limenius and Hermogenes: *Chron.* 354. Eustathius: *CTh.* ii. 1. 1 (349), xi. 7. 6 (349). For the idea that Eustathius may only have been an acting prefect see *PLRE*, Fasti. Constans' noble praetorian prefects were : Antonius Marcellinus: viii. 25534; Aco Catullinus Philomathius: *CTh.* viii. 2. 1, xii. 1. 31. M. Maecius Memmius Furius Baburius Caecilianus Placidus: x. 1700 = D. 1231; Vulcacius Rufinus: vi. 32051 = D. 1237, Amm. xxvii. 11. 1. On acting praetorian prefects see M. T. W. Arnheim, 'Vicars in the later Roman Empire', *Historia*, 19 (1970), 593–606.

[2] Petr. Patr. 16.

Caesar, who fell out with Constantius and paid for it with his life, was the son of Galla and nephew of Vulcacius Rufinus and Neratius Cerealis, important figures in the mid-fourth century. The family was an old one, and was also related, through the Betitii, to the *gens Anicia*.[1]

It is largely through an incomplete inscription found in Bulla Regia that we know of the nobility of Antonius Marcellinus, another of Constans's praetorian prefects:

> il
> LVSTRIS FAMILIAE
> CVIVS INTEGRITA
> TEM ET IVSTITIAM
> AFRICA CONPROBAVIT
> ANTONIO MARCELLI
> NO CV PROconSVLI
> P.A. SPLeNDidisSIMVS
> ORDO COL. BVL1 REG
> PATRONO POSVIT.[2]

From this we learn not only that Marcellinus was proconsul of Africa, but also that he belonged to a distinguished family. With names as common as Antonius and Marcellinus it would be impossible to forge links and construct genealogies on the basis of nomenclature alone, even if both names recurred, so it is fortunate that we have detailed evidence referring to our man specifically. In addition to what we know from the African inscription, Marcellinus is mentioned as father (by Palladius and Jerome) or grandfather (by Paulinus of Nola) of Melania the elder.[3] Though Melania was of Spanish origin, it is to be doubted whether she owed this origin to Marcellinus's side of the family, since we know of no Spanish post held by him in his rather itinerant career. Either he or a relative is recorded as *praeses* of Lugdunensis Prima in a law dated 319 in the MSS. but redated by Seeck to 313.[4] His

---

[1] See p. 113 ff., below.   [2] viii. 25525 Bulla Regia.
[3] Pall. *Hist. Laus.* 46; Jer. *Chron.* 2390 s.a. 377. Paul. Nol. *Ep.* 29. 8.
[4] *CTh.* xi. 3. 1 'ad Antonium Marcellinum praesidem Lugdunensis Primae'. Seeck, *Regesten*, 58, 80.

proconsulship of Africa was at an unknown date before 340, when he became praetorian prefect, probably of Italy.[1] In the following year he was ordinary consul together with another noble, Petronius Probinus.

Constans' next noble prefect was Aco Catullinus Philomathius, who was vicar of Africa in 338–9, praetorian prefect in 341, urban prefect in 342–4 and ordinary consul in 349.[2] Whether he was also governor of Gallaecia or whether the governor of Gallaecia is rather to be identified with his relative, Aco Catullinus the Constantinian *praeses* of Byzacena and proconsul of Africa, it is difficult to say. The Gallaecian governor's inscription, though undated, cannot be earlier than Diocletian's reign, when the province was first established:

I(ovi) O(ptimo) M(aximo)
/ / / / ACO CATVLLINVS VIR CONSVLARIS
PRAESES PROV. CALLAECIAE.[3]

We already have evidence of a likely Constantinian noble *praeses* of Gallaecia, namely Aemilius Maximus, and a Constantinian date would therefore appear more likely than a tetrarchic one. Moreover, a Constantinian date would suit the chronology of the career of either of our Acones Catullini better than a tetrarchic date. To what does 'vir consularis' refer? It does not refer to an ordinary consulship, which in any case in this period came at the end of a man's career, and Catullinus was to become ordinary consul in 349. A *consularis* in the new Constantinian sense of 'governor' would do without the word 'vir', and in any case Catullinus' designation is 'praeses'. It appears, therefore, that Aco Catullinus was a suffect consul. This could be, and probably was, the origin of the position of *consularis* as a governorship: a real ex-consul who was appointed *praeses*—a return to the consular legate of the Principate, who was

---

[1] iii. 12330 = D. 8944 Traiana, Thracia. See also *CTh*. xi. 12. 1 and vi. 22. 3.

[2] Vicar of Africa: *CTh*. xii. 1. 24, vi. 22. 2, xv. 1. 5, xii. 1. 26. PPO: *CTh*. viii. 2. 1, xii. 1. 31. The *PLRE* (s.v.) regards him as PPO of Italy, Africa and Illyricum under Constans. PUR: Chron. 354, the only source to give the *signum* as well as the *nomen* and *cognomen*. Cos. 349: *P. Amh.* 139 ('Acontius Catullinus'); *Fasti*. See also Chastagnol, *Fastes*, 121–3.

[3] ii. 2635 Asturica, Gallaecia.

always a *consularis* in the sense of being an ex-consul and was often popularly referred to as 'consularis'.[1]

The name Aco is simply a shortened form of Aconius, and in view of the rarity of the name we can safely link our Aco or Aconius with the others. The family came originally from Volsinii, where several inscriptions have been found with the names of members of the family. L. Aco(*nius*) Cal(*listus*), a local aedile in Volsinii, is probably the earliest recorded member of the family, though his dates are unknown. We have a military tribune, and therefore either a senator or an equestrian, in another L. Aconius Callistus of Volsinii. The first certain senatorial member of the family was L. Aconius Callistus Cynegius, 'c(larissimae) m(emoriae) v(ir)', husband of Oratia Marina. Cynegius is known from only one inscription, set up by his wife after his death. In it we are told that he lived 72 years, but the only title attached to his name is 'c.m.v'. It would appear therefore that he died without holding public office —a man who had inherited senatorial rank and had perhaps spent his life on his estates.[2] Catullinus's daughter's name, Fabia Aconia Paulina, indicates that Catullinus married into the Fabii, another noble house, among whom the *cognomina* Paulus and Paulinus were favourites.

This related Catullinus by marriage to Fabius Titianus and through him also to M. Maecius Memmius Furius Baburius Caecilianus Placidus and Q. Fl. Maesius Egnatius Lollianus Mavortius, all these men being, like Catullinus, noble praetorian prefects under Constans. Placidus's well-preserved career inscription from Puteoli is a good example of the type of public career now open to nobles:

M. MAECIO MEMMIO FVRIO BABVRIO
CAECILIANO PLACIDO C.V.
PONTIFICI MAIORI AVGVRI PV
BLICO P.R. QVIRITIVM QVINDECEM
VIRO SACRIS FACIVNDIS CORREC
TORI VENETIARVM ET HISTRIAE

---

[1] Aemilius Maximus: *Eph. Ep.* viii. p. 403, 117, Bracara, Gallaecia. For consular legates in the Principate see Dio 77. 8; x. 408 = D. 1117; vi. 1531–2.
[2] xi. 2699 Volsinii.

PRAEFECTO ANNONAE VRBIS
SACRAE CVM IVRE GLADII COMITI
ORDINIS PRIMI COMITI ORIENTIS
AEGYPTI ET MESOPOTAMIAE IVDI
CI SACRARVM COGNITIONVM
TERTIO IVDICI ITERVM EX DE
LEGATIONIBVS SACRIS PRAE
FECTO PRAETORIO ET IVDICI
SACRARVM COGNITIONVM
TERTIO CONSVLI ORDINARIO
PATRONO PRESTANTISSIMO
REGIO PALATINA POSVIT.[1]

As usual, the priesthoods are grouped together at the beginning for convenience, though the civil offices are themselves in chronological order. No dates are known except that of his consulship, which was in 343, and he received a law as praetorian prefect dated 28 May 344.[2] To round off this very successful career, Placidus was urban prefect in 346–7. It is worth noting the *ius gladii* which Placidus had as *praefectus annonae*, a most uncommon combination indeed. Another unusual feature in his civil career is the position described as 'iudex ex delegationibus sacris', in which he presumably tried cases delegated to him by the emperor.

Placidus was not one for keeping his religious affiliations a secret, and his three priesthoods were among the most highly regarded positions in the old state religion. His career, both civil and religious, is that of a great pagan aristocrat, and his name combines some of the noblest strains of his day.[3]

A similar, if less spectacular, career is recorded in the case of Lollianus Mavortius:

MAVORTII
FL. LOLLIANO V.C. Q.K. PRAET. VRB.
CVRAT. ALVEI TIBERIS ET OPERVM
MAXIMORVM ET AQVARVM CONS
CAMP COMITI INTRA PALatium ET
vICE SAcra iudicanti comiti ORI

[1] x. 1700 = D. 1231.   [2] *CTh.* xii. 1. 37.   [3] See p. 87 ff., below.

ENTIS V.S. IVDICANTI PROCONS.
PROV. AFRICAE ET V.S. IVDICANTI
PRAEF VRBIS ET V.S. IVDICANTI ITE
RVM COMITI ORD. PRIMI INTRA PA
LATIVM PRAEF. PRAET. CONSVLI ORD.
PLACIDVS SEVERVS V.C. FILIVS PATRI RELIGIOSO
ET ANTONIA MARCIANILLA C.F. NVRVS
SOCERO SANCTISSIMO.[1]

His tenure of the position of *consularis aquarum et Miniciae*, one of the old senatorial *curatelae*, is recorded in the year 328.[2] None of his other posts are datable, with the exception of his urban prefecture, which was in 342,[3] and his ordinary consulship, which he held together with the *Magister Militum* Arbito in 355.[4] It is important to note than Mavortius was *comes* of the first rank 'intra palatium', before becoming praetorian prefect. His religious positions are also noteworthy, for he was apparently an ardent follower of the old gods. He was 'augur publicus p(opuli) R(omani) Quiritium',[5] and the dedication to him of Firmicus Maternus's astrological writings is another sign of his religious attachment to paganism.[6]

Only the first of Constantius' Eastern prefects was noble, and that was Septimius Acindynus, who was vicar of *comes* of the Spains at some time between 317 and 326.[7] Five of Constantius' Eastern prefects were certainly non-senatorial and a further one probably non-senatorial. There could be no greater contrast than that between, for example, Vulcacius Rufinus and Flavius Philippus, whose prefectures, in the West and East respectively, were contemporaneous. Rufinus, as we have seen, could trace his ancestry back to the Republic; Philippus was the son of a sausage-maker.[8]

[1] vi. 37112 = vi. 1723 + vi. 1757.   [2] vi. 36851 = D. 8943.   [3] *Chron. 354.*
[4] *Fasti.* See also *PLRE,* s.v. and Chastagnol, *Fastes,* 114–21.
[5] x. 4752 = D. 1223 Suessa.   [6] Firm. Mat. *Math.* 8. 15.
[7] ii. 4107 Tarraco. The text is corrupt: see note ad loc. *CTh.* ii. 6. 4 (Dec. 338), viii. 5. 3 (MSS. 326, Seeck, 339), ix. 3. 3 (340). *BGU* i. 21. That Acindynus's prefecture was in the East is shown by the 'p(ro)p(osita). . . Antioch'. See also Palanque, *Essai,* 19.
[8] Philippus: Lib. *Or.* xlii. 24–5—a list of men of humble origins who had made good. His father's occupation: Lib. *Or.* xlv. 11. See Jones, 'The Career of Flavius Philippus', *Historia* 4 (1955) 229–33. Palanque, 'Les Préfets du prétoire sous les

Though Constantius appears to have been less inclined to appoint noble prefects than Constans, Constantius' appointment of nobles to Western prefectures when he was sole emperor is an indication that the explanation is to be sought in the political and social circumstances in which the brothers found themselves rather than in their personal preferences.[1] For it was in the West that the strength of the senatorial aristocracy was concentrated, and here, too, therefore, do we find the great majority of noble appointments.

Of the thirteen praetorian prefects in the West appointed by Constantine's sons, only one, Flavius Taurus, prefect of Italy and Africa for the last six years of Constantius' reign, is known to have been of non-senatorial origin. Seven of these prefects, however, are known to have been nobles, and both C. Ceionius Rufius Volusianus Lampadius and Vulcacius Rufinus had more than one spell as prefect, the latter's terms amounting to a total of ten years under the sons of Constantine and Magnentius—and he was destined to return to office as praetorian prefect of Italy, Africa, and Illyricum for another three years under Valentinian. Rufinus is the only one of Magnentius' prefects whose origin is known for certain.

It is also worth noting that the nobles Fabius Titianus, M. Maecius Memmius Caecilianus Placidus, Vulcacius Rufinus, and Egnatius Lollianus, in addition to being praetorian prefects, were all *comites ordinis primi*, the two last-named being *comites ordinis primi intra Palatium*, members, that is, of the Imperial 'cabinet'. Placidus and Vulcacius Rufinus, it might be added, were also *comites Orientis* under Constantine's sons, and are in fact the only noble vicars known to us in this period in the East.[2] In the

---

fils de Constantin', *Historia* 4 (1955) 260–1. Other similar cases are: Domitianus: Lib. *Or.* xlii. 24–5; son of a manual worker: Amm. xiv. 7. 9–11, 16. Strategius Musonianus: Amm. xv. 13. 1–2. Fl. Hermogenes: Him. *Or.* xlviii (ed. Colonna) or xiv (ed. Dübner, Didot, Paris, 1849). Helpidius: Paphlagonian of modest origins: Amm. xxi. 6. 9. Fl. Domitius Leontius: rose 'per singulorum honorum grados' (sic) iii. 167 = D. 1234, Berytus.

[1] Constantius' noble praetorian prefects: Vulcacius Rufinus: vi. 32051 = D. 1237; C. Ceionius Rufius Volusianus Lampadius: Amm. xxvii. 3. 5; vi. 512 = D. 4154. Q. Fl. Maesius Egnatius Lollianus Mavortius: vi. 37112 = vi. 1723 + vi. 1757.

[2] Fl. Taurus: Lib., loc. cit. *AE* 1934, 159. See *Fasti* of praetorian prefects, p. 213 ff. and list of *comites*, p. 221, below.

West, however, we are not short of noble vicars. Six of the eight Western vicars appointed between 337 and 361 whose origins are known were nobles.

L. Crepereius Madalianus, who is recorded as vicar of Italy in 341, evidently held his vicariate while *comes ordinis primi*, after a career comprising republican magistracies, urban *curatelae*, appointments as legate of Africa and Asia, a correctorship of Flaminia and Picenum, a comitial appointment in the second rank, —or as it is more flatteringly described elsewhere, 'comes flavialis' —the *praefectura annonae*, and the consular governorship of Pontus and Bithynia. After his vicariate he is recorded as proconsul of Africa, which was the last post he is known to have held.[1] The family goes back to the Republic and was related by marriage in the late Empire to the Ceionii, in connection with whom it will be discussed.

At some time between 337 and 364 the father of Symmachus the orator was vicar of Rome.

PHOSPHORII
LVCIO AVR. AVIANO SYMMACHO V.C.
PRAEFECTO VRBI CONSVLI PRO PRAEFECTIS
PRAETORIO IN VRBE ROMA FINITIMISQVE
PROVINCIIS PRAEFECTO ANNONAE VR
BIS ROMAE PONTIFICI MAIORI QVINDE
CEMVIRO S.F. MVLTIS LEGATIONIBVS
PRO AMPLISSIMI ORDINIS DESIDERIIS
APVD DIVOS PRINCIPES FVNCTO QVI
PRIMVS IN SENATV SENTENTIAM ROGA
RI SOLITVS.[2]

The orator himself had only one priesthood, as *pontifex maior*. His father, however, was not only *pontifex maior* but also *quindecemvir sacris faciundis*. Though never praetorian prefect proper, Symmachus the elder acted as deputy to the praetorian prefect in Rome and neighbouring provinces. His prefecture of the grain

---

[1] See p. 82, n.1 for Constantius' appointees to the praetorian prefecture who were noble. Madalianus: xiv. 4449; viii. 5348 = D. 1228; vi. 1151 = D. 707; *CTh.* xvi. 10. 2.

[2] vi. 1698 = D. 1257.

7

supply was held at some time between 337 and 350.[1] Though only one senatorial embassy in which Symmachus the elder participated is known of in any detail, it is not surprising to learn from the inscription that he was involved in many others as well.[2] The date of his urban prefecture is 364–5.[3]

The orator's father was not the only Symmachus to be a vicar. Two laws were addressed to a man called Symmachus, both dated 319 in the MSS. but redated by Seeck to 318. In only one of these is Symmachus addressed as vicar, but the other was received at Corinth, so, adding the two together, we discover that Symmachus was vicar of Moesia. The name is rare enough for us to assume that Symmachus was a member of the orator's family, perhaps to be identified with M. Aurelius Nerius Symmachus, the last equestrian member of the family.[4]

A glance at one more mid-century noble vicar: M. Aurelius Consius Quartus junior. Quartus's first post, the correctorship of Flaminia and Picenum, must have been held before 350/2, when the governor is first recorded as a consular. After another correctorship, that of Venetia and Histria, Quartus was consular of Belgica Prima, vicar of Spain and proconsul of Africa with appellate jurisdiction, all these posts probably being before 360, after which it is difficult to insert African proconsuls.[5] The career is typical of the new standard *cursus* for men of senatorial birth, and Quartus's nobility is confirmed by his religious career:

SINGVLARIS INTEGRITATIS
ET BONITATIS EXSIMIAE
M. AVR. CONSIO QVARTO
IVNIORI V.C. CORRECTORI
FLAMINIE ET PICENI
PONTIFICI MAIORI
PROMAGISTRO ITERVM

[1] vi. 36954 = D. 726.   [2] Amm. xxi. 12. 24.
[3] *CTh*. vii. 4. 10; *CTh*. i. 6. 4. Amm. xxvii. 3. 3. See Seeck, *Symm*. xl–xliv; Chastagnol, *Fastes*, 159–63.
[4] Two laws: *CTh*. ii. 4. 1 (acc. Corintho); *CTh*. ii. 15. 1 (vic.). For dating see Seeck, *Regesten*, 57. For the family see Chapter V and Stemma II.
[5] *AE* 1955, Hippo Regius. First consular of Flaminia and Picenum: Flavius Romanus, *AE* 1951, 17.

DVODECIMVIRO
ANCONITANI ET
FANESTRES CLIENTES
PATRONO.[1]

Early on, therefore, in his civil career Quartus already held two significant priesthoods. The college of *duodecimviri* is one to which there are very few references in the late Empire, the latest being in 377.[2] Quartus was patron of Ancona and Fanum, both within his first province.

The name Consius Quartus recurs in two other inscriptions, one a seal marked 'Consii Quarti c.v.'[3] and the other a fragmentary inscription from Baetica: 'Consio Quarto . . . quaestorio . . . prae-torio . . . legionis . . . ser . . . merito'.[4] Both these Consii Quarti were either ancestors or relatives of our vicar. In view of the word 'legionis', the Spanish inscription must date from before the late third century when senators lost military commands, thus giving the family at least three generations of senators by birth, since Quartus junior could not have been in office before the early fourth century, when the province of Flaminia and Picenum first came into existence.

As we saw in the last chapter, six provincial governorships were permanently upgraded from praesidial or correctorial to consular posts by Constantine, and one further province, Byzacena, probably experienced the same change under him. By 361, when Constantius II died, a further five provinces are known to have changed to consular governors: Baetica, Lusitania, Belgica Prima, Pannonia Secunda, and Flaminia et Picenum.[5] The fact that all of these were Western provinces should hardly surprise us, since the new type of governorship, as was noted in the last chapter, appears to have been designed to attract nobles. Of the twelve consular provinces that

---

[1] vi. 1700 = D. 1249. See Chastagnol, 'La carrière du proconsul d'Afrique M. Aurelius Consius Quartus', *Libyca* 7 (1959) 191–203.

[2] D. 4148, cf. D. 1198.   [3] x. 8059¹²³.

[4] ii. 1270 Sanlucar da Mayor, Baetica.

[5] The first known consulars of these provinces are as follows: Baetica: Decimius Germanianus, ii. 2206. Lusitania: Vettius Agorius Praetextatus, vi. 1779 = D. 1259. Belgica Prima: M. Aurelius Consius Quartus—see n.1 above. Pannonia Secunda: Clodius Octavianus, ix. 2566 Bovianum Undecimanorum. Flaminia et Picenum: Fl. Romanus, *AE* 1951, 17.

there were on the death of Constantius only two, Syriae Coele and Phoenice, were in the East, and Syria Coele had always been in a different category from other Eastern provinces.[1] The presence of Pannonia Secunda among Spanish and Italian provinces such as Baetica or Flaminia and Picenum which must have been much more to the taste of the aristocracy, is puzzling. But, if it was an attempt to draw nobles to a post which they would otherwise decline, it appears to have been successful. The origins of only three consulars of Pannonia Secunda are known, two of whom were noble.[2] Now that those provinces which most interested the aristocracy in the days when they had been praesidial had been converted to consular governorships, it is not surprising that we no longer find cases of noble *praesides*. In the whole of the fourth century only two consulars are known to have been of non-senatorial origins and a further two probably so, two and possibly three of these four men being in office under Valentinian and the other probably under Constans. In the case of this earliest example we are fortunate in having a detailed record of his career in a Campanian inscription:

TATIANI
C. IVLIO RVFINIANO
ABLABIO TATIANO C.V. RVFI
NIANI ORATORIS FILIO FISCI PA
TRONO RATIONVM SVMMARVM
ADLECTO INTER CONSVLARES IVDI
CIO DIVI CONSTANTINI LEGATO PRO
VINC. ASIAE CORRECTORI TVSCIAE
ET VMBRIAE CONSVLARI AE
MILIAE ET LIGVRIAE PONTIFICI
VESTAE MATRIS ET IN COLLE
GIO PONTIFICVM PROMA
GISTRO SACERDOTI HER
CVLIS CONSVLARI CAM
PANIAE HVIC ORDO SPLEN

---

[1] See p. 40 ff., above.

[2] Clodius Octavianus (see p. 85, n.5 above) and Messala, possibly to be identified with the praetorian prefect at the end of the century, Rut. Nam. *de Red. s.* 267 ff.

DIDISSIMVS ET POPVLVS
ABELLINATIVM OB INSIGNEM
ERGA SE BENEVOLENTIAM ET
RELIGIONEM ET INTEGRIT. EIVS
STATVAM CONLOCANDAM CENSVIT.[1]

Tatianus's non-noble birth is clear both from his adlection and from his first post as *patronus fisci rationum summarum*. But though of non-senatorial origin Tatianus was already a senator by the time he was appointed *consularis* of Campania. The same is the case with our other certain non-noble consular, Lucilius Constantius, consular of Tuscia and Umbria at some time after 366, when the last corrector of the province is recorded. Constantius is described in an Etrurian inscription as 'praesidi Mauretaniae et Tingitanae (sic) v.c. consulari Tusciae et Umbriae'.[2] Only one other governor of Mauretania Tingitana is known, one Clementius Valerius Marcellinus, in office from 277 to 280, who was an equestrian *praeses*.[3] Though this is of course too early to tell us anything about the post in the second half of the fourth century, we know that Lucilius Constantius was a *praeses* and we have no record of any noble *praesides* after Constantine nor any reason to expect to find any, as has been noted above. Moreover, the peculiar position of 'v.c.' in Constantius' inscription may well be a pointer to the date of his attaining the clarissimate—between his tenure of the governorship of Tingitana and his appointment as consular of Tuscia and Umbriae. What is certain is that he, like Tatianus, was a *clarissimus* before becoming a consular. Less is known of our two probably non-noble consulars, Fl. Simplicius, consular of Numidia, and Falangius, consular of Baetica, both under Valentinian. Simplicius certainly was, and Falangius appears to have been, connected with Valentinian's ally and hammer of the aristocracy, Maximinus, a pointer to a humble Illyrian background.[4] Simplicius, however, is described as a *clarissimus* in a Numidian inscription set up while he was consular of the province;[5] and if Falangius is to be identified

[1] x. 1125 = D. 2942 Abellinum, Campania.
[2] xi. 6958 = D. 1252 Luna, Etruria.
[3] *ILAfr.* 609, 610, 621 Volubilis, Mauretania Tingitana.
[4] Simplicius: Amm. xxviii. 1. 44–5. Falangius: Amm. xxviii. 1. 26.
[5] viii. 8324 = D. 5535 Cuicul, Numidia.

with the urban prefect Tanaucius Isfalangius, as seems likely, then he too was probably a *clarissimus* at some time before his prefecture.[1] What positive evidence we have, therefore, would indicate that consular appointments tended to go to men of senatorial rank, though, of course, not necessarily of senatorial birth. Of the consulars whose origins are known, in fact, the great majority were also of senatorial birth.[2]

Perhaps the most interesting of the noble consulars under the sons of Constantine was Memmius Vitrasius Orfitus, who enjoyed a most impressive career:

HONORI
MEMMIO VITRASIO ORFITO V.C.
NOBILITATE ET ACTIBVS PRAECIPVE
PRAEFECTO VRBI ET ITERVM PRAE
FECTO VRBI PROCONSVLI AFRICAE
ET TERTIO SACRARVM COGNITIONVM
IVDICI COMITI ORDINIS PRIMI ITERVM
INTRA CONSISTORIVM LEGATO SECVN
DO DIFFICILLIMIS TEMPORIBVS PETI
TV SENATVS ET P.R. COMITI ORDINIS
SECVNDI EXPEDITIONES BELLICAS
GVBERNANTI CONSVLARI PROVINCIAE
SICILIAE PONTIF. DEAE VESTAE XV
VIRO S.F. PONTIF. DEI SOLIS CONSVLI
PRAETORI Q. (k).
CORPVS PISTORVM MAGNARIORVM
ET CASTRENSARIORVM STATVAM
SVB AERE CONSTITVIT.[3]

The fact that Orfitus held all three republican magistracies at the beginning of his career is in itself an indication of senatorial birth, as we have seen. We have a curious inscription dating from between 340 and 350 in which Orfitus and one Fl. Dulcitius appear as 'vv. cc. consulares p(rovinciae) S(iciliae)',[4] the one presumably being the current governor and the other his successor. Orfitus's

---

[1] vi. 1672ª—Tanaucius Isfalangius; vi. 1672ᵇ—(*T*)anaucius Sfalangius.
[2] See Statistical Table II.
[3] vi. 1739–42. The inscription quoted is vi. 1739.
[4] x. 7200 = D. 5905.

next appointment is particularly interesting because of the military duties attached to it. His next task, that of being a member of the senatorial embassy presumably to Constantius II, is a sign of Orfitus's prominence, and his appointment as a member of the imperial *consistorium* was one of the most influential in the Empire. His proconsulship of Africa was in 352/3, as we know from other inscriptions,[1] and he ended his career as urban prefect, a post which he held twice, in 353–5 and 357–9.[2]

In addition to his civil career, Orfitus was an ardent pagan, holding three priesthoods and setting up a shrine in honour of Apollo. Chastagnol's doubts about Orfitus's nobility are unfounded, as is shown elsewhere.[3] Ammianus Marcellinus calls him 'vir quidem prudens et forensium negotiorum oppido gnarus, sed splendore liberalium doctrinarum minus quam nobilem decuerat institutus'.[4] Indeed, he was a member of one of the noblest family complexes in the Empire, made up of the Memmii, Gracchi, Cornelii, Scipiones, Furii, and Fabii, to mention only the main components.[5]

Another member of the same complex of families was Furius Maecius Gracchus, corrector of Flaminia and Picenum at some time before the province went consular (in 350–2).[6] He was either the same person as, or a close relative of, the Gracchus who was urban prefect in 376–7,[7] and whose anti-pagan activities and conversion to Christianity are highly commended by St. Jerome in a letter to Laeta, herself the daughter of the pagan priest Albinus, probably Publilius Ceionius Caecina Albinus,[8] consular of Numidia in the early years of Valentinian's reign: 'Ante paucos annos propinquus vester Gracchus, nobilitatem patriciam nomine sonans, cum praefecturam regeret urbanam, nonne specu Mithrae et omnia portentuosa simulacra, quibus corax, cryphius, miles, leo, Perses, heliodromus, pater initiantur, subvertit, fregit, exussit et his quasi obsidibus ante praemissis impetravit baptismum

---

[1] vi. 1739–42.
[2] *Chron. 354*; *CTh.* ix. 17. 3, iii. 18. 1, xiv. 6. 1.
[3] See p. 126 f., below.
[4] Amm. xiv. 6. 1.
[5] See Stemma III.
[6] xiv. 3594 = D. 5717 Tibur.
[7] *CTh.* ii. 2. 1, ix. 35. 3.
[8] See A. Chastagnol, 'La famille de Caecinia Lolliana', *Latomus* 20 (1961) 744–58.

Christi?'[1] Gracchus was probably related to Laeta's husband Toxotius rather than to Laeta herself.[2] Toxotius was the son of St. Paula, who is described by St. Jerome as: 'Gracchorum stirps, suboles Scipionum, Pauli heres, cuius vocabulum trahit, Maeciae Papiriae, matris Africani, vera et germana progenies'[3] This effectively links the Scipiones, the Gracchi, and the Maecii.[4]

An inscription of about 400 from Salernum records the name Arrius Maecius Gracchus as patron of the town,[5] and the Theodosian Code contains a law dated 397 addressed to one Gracchus, consular of Campania, upon which Salernum borders.[6] The governors and patron are likely to have been the same person, and may also be identified with the Gracchus who was urban prefect in 415.[7] From a Roman inscription we learn the name of our corrector's father: 'Cethego v.c. patri F. Maechius Gracchus v.c'.[8] A Cethegus, either Gracchus's father or a relative, described by Ammianus as 'senator', was beheaded for adultery in 371 or 372 during Maximinus's onslaught upon the aristocracy.[9] Furius Maecius Gracchus was related to three fourth century noble praetorian prefects: M. Maecius Memmius Furius Baburius Caecilianus Placidus, Q. Fl. Maesius Egnatius Lollianus Mavortius and Fabius Titianus—not to mention the praetorian prefects of the Ceionian house, with which Gracchus was linked by marriage.

Yet another member of the same family network was the only known post-Constantinian noble *praeses*, Fabius Maximus. For, with the great increase under Constantine of the range of posts open to nobles, the humble praesidial governorship, which in any case had always had equestrian overtones, was no doubt scorned by the scions of ancient lines. We have several inscriptions from Samnium recording Maximus as a *clarissimus* and 'rector provinciae'.[10] Another inscription reads: 'Fabio Maximo/ v.c. / instauratori/moenium/publicorum/ordo et populus/curante Aurelio/

---

[1] Jer. *Ep.* 107. 2.
[2] For a more detailed discussion of the family see Chapter V, below.
[3] Jer. *Ep.* 108. 1.   [4] See Stemma III.
[5] x. 520 Salernum.
[6] *CTh.* xiv. 7. 1. For a discussion as to which province Salernum was situated in see Thomsen, *Italic Regions*, 203–5.
[7] *CTh.* viii. 7. 20. dat. Rav.   [8] vi. 1709 = 31907.
[9] Amm. xxviii. 1. 16.   [10] ix. 2212, 2338, 2447, 2956 = D. 5341.

Pauliniano cura/ [*t*]ore et patrono//. [in latere] D[*ed.*] ... /VII.k ... /
D.N. Co[*nstan*]/tio Aug. V.' The date is 352, 353, 354, 356 or 357—
these being the years when Constantius held his fifth to ninth consulships—making Maximus likely to be the first governor of Samnium
as a separate province.

Though all Maximus's inscriptions are from Samnium and the
title 'rector' was not normally used of a consular, but was the normal
title of *praesides* of Samnium, Chastagnol denies that Maximus
was governor of this province alone and sees him instead as 'encore
un consulaire de Campanie antérieure à la création de la nouvelle
province'. He gives three reasons for his view, none of which will
stand up to examination. First, declares Chastagnol, the *praeses* of
Samnium was always a *perfectissimus*. That is true enough and it
may seem strange that the first governor of the new province should
be a *clarissimus* and his successors *perfectissimi*, but that is hardly
reason enough to fly in the face of the evidence. For, after all, it is
possible that the province turned out to be unattractive to senators
after Maximus. Chastagnol's second point is even less substantial:
'Julius Festus Hymetius est *Consularis Campaniae cum Samnio*,
c'est-à-dire avant le dédoublement, peu de temps avant 361.' That
Festus was governor of the undivided province is plain enough.
What cannot be accepted is Chastagnol's argument from the date.
All we know is that Festus' governorship of Campania was before
362, when he became vicar of Rome, but we do not know how long
before. Chastagnol's final point is that the province of Samnium
'ne semble pas encore exister quand est promulguée une loi de
mai-décembre 357'. The passage in question reads as follows:
'De Sardinia Sicilia Campania Calabria Brittiis et Piceno Aemilia et
Venetia et ceteris interpositas appellationes laudabilis sublimitas
tua more sollemni debebit audire conpetenti appellatione terminan-
das.' From this it is clear that the list of names is not meant to be
exhaustive: the key phrase is 'et ceteris'. In short, there is no
sufficient reason for rejecting the evidence of four inscriptions which
inform us that Fabius Maximus was governor, presumably of
Samnium.[1]

[1] Maximus's inscription: ix. 2639 = D. 1248 Aesernia. Chastagnol, 'L'Administration du diocèse Italien au Bas-Empire', *Historia* 12 (1963) 366, and

He was clearly a member of the noble house of the Fabii. A contemporary and relative of his, Fabius Fabianus, legate of the proconsul of Africa in the 360s, is described as 'v.c. et inlustris legatus Numidiae',[1] the 'inlustris' presumably reflecting the legate's nobility, since so lowly a position as a legation did not even carry with it the title 'spectabilis' let alone 'illustris'.[2]

Julian's reign was too short to have left us many examples of his policy as regards appointments, but, though nothing is known of them other than their careers. both Saturninius Secundus, Julian's praetorian prefect of the East, and Claudius Mamertinus, prefect of Italy, Africa and Illyricum, had previously held court posts, Mamertinus being *comes sacrarum largitionum* and Secundus *quaestor sacri palatii*. Though this proves nothing, our evidence of nobles in such positions dates only from considerably later in the century, and it seems unlikely, therefore, that these prefects were noble. It is not very surprising to find Julian favouring the appointment of pagans, and he himself sought out Vettius Agorius Praetextatus, a leading pagan noble who was at that time living in retirement in Constantinople, to give him the proconsulate of Achaea. There is the well-known passage in Ammianus in which Julian received four noble senatorial envoys and appointed each to a high post. In addition to the prefecture of Rome and the proconsulate of Africa, both of which were posts traditionally occupied by nobles, the appointments were to the vicariate of the Spains (Volusius Venustus) and to the position of *comes Orientis* (Aradius Rufinus). The paucity of examples makes it impossible to come to any certain conclusions about Julian's appointments, but the evidence that we have does not indicate a more pro-noble

Historia 4 (1955) 175. The passages quoted are all from the more recent article. Law of 357: *CTh*. xi. 30. 27. The *PLRE* (s.v.) also sees Maximus as governor of Samnium alone, but does not discuss the matter.

[1] *AE* 1907, 237.
[2] The titles 'illustris' and 'spectabilis' were not strictly speaking hereditary, but there are several examples of titles such as 'ill. puella' (v. 3897—532 A.D.), 'illustr. familia' (vi. 1793—394) and 'illustr. domus' (*CJ* x. 49. 2—445). It is possible therefore that Fabianus was a son of Constantine's praetorian prefect Fabius Maximus. But the precise usage of 'illustris' to refer to prefects developed gradually and was not established in formal usage until late in the century. Our example is much more likely to be an informal use of the word to refer to Fabianus's nobility.

attitude on his part than was the case with Constantius, Constans, or Constantine. His paganism must have given him greater security in the West than any of these emperors, and this may account for his appointment of Mamertinus to the great central prefecture.[1]

The effect of Jovian's short reign on the personnel of the imperial administration cannot be gauged, and so we pass on to consider his successor, Valentinian, a rough-hewn Pannonian soldier who was to preside over the destinies of the Empire for more than a decade. A man of humble origins and only a commander of a *schola* of targeteers when he was raised to the purple, Valentinian had no personal inclination to favour members of the aristocracy.[2] Indeed we are told by Ammianus that the Emperor hated 'bene vestitos, ... et eruditos et opulentes et nobiles'.[3] The historian mentions this in connection with Valentinian's vanity, but perhaps it is more relevant to our purpose to see it as a parallel to his very real and sincere feeling for 'the forgotten man at the bottom of the economic pyramid'. His institution of 'defensores plebis' is just one example of the concern felt by him and his brother Valens for the 'humiliores' and of their determination to protect them from the wiles of the 'potentiores'.[4] The burly Pannonian is described by Ammianus as 'in provinciales admodum parcus, tributorum ubique molliens sarcinas'.[5] The new emperor also brought several of his compatriots into government. An example is Viventius, who came from Siscia and who was praetorian prefect of Gaul in 368, a position which he held for almost three years. Before this prefecture Viventius, who is first recorded as *quaestor sacri palatii* and who is most unlikely to have been a noble, was prefect of Rome, a position hitherto normally occupied by nobles. Nor was he the only non-noble to have this office under Valentinian; Bappo, Principius, and

[1] Saturninius Secundus: D. 1255. Claudius Mamertinus: Amm. xxi. 10. 8, 12. 25, 8. 1; Pan. Lat. iii. *passim*. Vettius Agorius Praetextatus: Amm. xxii. 7. 6; embassy: Amm. xxiii. 1. 4. Julian's cultural and religious predilections cut across class boundaries. For example, he appointed as consular of Pannonia Secunda the historian Sex. Aurelius Victor, who in his own words was 'rure ortus, tenuique indocto patre' (*Caes.* 20. 5; Amm. xxi. 10. 6), while Praetextatus, made proconsul of Achaea by Julian, was a noble whose appointment may have come to him in appreciation of his ardent paganism. Julian brought him back to public life from retirement in Constantinople. Amm. xxii. 7. 6.

[2] Amm. xxvi. 1. 4; Amm. xxx. 7. 2 'ignobili stirpe'. [3] Amm. xxx. 8. 10.

[4] *Defensores civitatum* or *plebis: CTh.* i. 29. [5] Amm. xxx. 9. 1.

Eupraxius also appear to have been non-noble, though there is no conclusive proof. Ampelius, another of Valentinian's urban prefects, came from Antioch and began his career as *praeses* of Cappadocis—a pointer to non-noble origins.[1] After being *magister officiorum* and proconsul of Achaea under Constantius he became proconsul of Africa early in Valentinian's reign, an interesting progression.[2] Maximinus, 'obscurissime natus' in Sopianae, Valeria, is probably the most famous or notorious of Valentinian's intimates. He was governor in turn of Corsica, Sardinia, and Tuscia and Umbria before becoming *praefectus annonae*, when he became the moving force behind the spate of indictments of nobles on charges of adultery, magic, and poisoning. The obvious favour with which Valentinian viewed this fierce attack on the aristocracy is reflected in the prosecutor's promotion first to the vicariate of Rome and later to the praetorian prefecture of Gaul.[3] The Emperor's abrogation of the ancient senatorial immunity from torture and his anti-pagan edicts are further signs of his hostility to the aristocracy.[4] Another facet of the same policy is the inflation of honours which Valentinian introduced.

The status of military and court posts was enhanced at the expense of administrative posts in the provinces. So the more important *comites* and tribunes became senators on retirement if their career was commended by the emperor, and were then exempted from the expense of the praetorian games.[5] *Magistri scriniorum* were given precedence over vicars,[6] and the *quaestor sacri palatii*, *magister officiorum*, *comes sacrarum largitionum* and *comes rerum privatarum* were given a higher status than proconsulars.[7]

Constantius is commended by Ammianus as 'numquam erigens cornua militarium'. 'Nec sub eo', the historian continues, 'dux quisquam cum clarissimatu provectus est. Erant enim, ut nos quoque meminimus, perfectissimi: nec occurrebat magistro

---

[1] Viventius: Amm. xxvi. 4. 4; xxvii. 3. 11–12; *CTh.* xiii. 10. 4, 6. Bappo: *CTh.* vi. 4. 21 (372). Principius: *CTh.* xiii. 3. 10 (373). Eupraxius: Amm. xxvii. 6. 14; vi. 1177 = D. 776. Ampelius: Amm. xxviii. 4. 3; Lib. *Ep.* 315.

[2] *CTh.* xiii. 5. 10.

[3] Amm. xxviii. 1. 5 (early career), xxviii. 1. 12 ff., 41.

[4] Torture: Amm. xxviii. 1. 6. Anti-pagan law: *CTh.* ix. 16. 7 (364).

[5] *CTh.* vi. 35. 7 (367).   [6] *CTh.* vi. 11. 1 (372).   [7] *CTh.* vi. 9. 1 (372).

equitum provinciae rector nec contingi ab eo civile negotium permittebat.'[1] A law of 386 refers to *duces* by the generic title 'clarissimi'.[2] The change in titles of which Ammianus is speaking must therefore be placed between the death of Constantius (in 361) and 386. Whether this particular promotion was the work of Valentinian is not known, but he certainly did much to bring about the ethos of which Ammianus is so critical—though the historian had himself had a military career.[3] A law of 372 equates the rank of the *magistri militum* with that of the urban and praetorian prefects,[4] and another law of the same year accords *comites rei militaris* equivalent status to that of the proconsuls.[5]

Valentinian's antipathy towards the aristocracy and the inroads that he made upon traditional strongholds of their like the pro-consulate of Africa and the urban prefecture may lead us to see in him a new Diocletian. It is true that in his reign, and particularly in the latter part of it, the number of nobles in high state posts plummets to the lowest point since the accession of Constantine. But the present author cannot share Schuurmans's view of a division of the reign into 'pro-senatorial' and 'anti-senatorial' phases.[6] For Schuurmans the first anti-senatorial measure was the institution of the position of *defensor plebis*, which he, following Hoepffner, dates to 368. Yet Hoepffner's reason for redating the law in question, which is dated 364 in the MSS., is that only in 368 did relations between Valentinian and 'the Senate' deteriorate.[7] The only evidence of good relations early in the reign, however, is the promulgation in 364 of a law confirming Constantius' institution of *defensores senatus*. Even this is not very good evidence, since the sort of senator who would need protection was not very likely to be found in the ranks of the Western aristocracy, the group against which Maximinus' prosecutions appear to have been aimed. Also, the law prohibiting nocturnal sacrifices is dated September 364, and four months later Valentinian issued an edict revoking the

---

[1] Amm. xxi. 16. 2. [2] *CTh.* xii. 1. 113.
[3] Amm. xiv. 9. 1, xvi. 10. 21, xviii. 6. 20 ff., xxiii. 5. 7, xxxi. 16. 9.
[4] *CTh.* vi. 7. 1. [5] *CTh.* vi. 14. 1.
[6] Schuurmans, *Samenstelling*, 565 ff.
[7] Hoepffner, *Revue Historique* 182 (1938) 226 ff. See Chapter VII, p. 163, n. 5, below.

senatorial immunity from arrest.[1] Though until 370 his vicars of Rome were probably all noble, there appear to have been early non-senatorial inroads into noble strongholds such as the proconsulate of Africa and the governorship of Campania in addition to the urban prefecture, mentioned above.[2]

The praetorian prefecture of the Gauls gives us another example of the same trend. In 366 Petronius Probus was given this office in succession to Decimus Germanianus, one of Jovian's few appointees. But of his successors in Gaul, Viventius and Maximinus were Pannonians with no pretensions to high birth, as we have seen, and Florentius was *comes sacrarum largitionum* before becoming prefect and altogether does not appear to have been a member of the aristocracy.[3]

In contrast to Valentinian's other appointments that have been discussed, the prefecture of Italy, Africa, and Illyricum was successively in the hands of two members of the highest nobility, Petronius Probus and Vulcacius Rufinus, for the duration of his reign, with the exception of a short period early in the reign when part or all of this immense prefecture was governed by Julian's prefect Mamertinus. Vulcacius Rufinus was brought back into public life by Valentinian after a break of some eleven years, having been praetorian prefect under Constans and Constantius. Petronius Probus received his first praetorian prefecture at the hands of Valentinian, and, though neither an attractive character nor an exemplary administrator, Probus, the head of the Anician house,

---

[1] Defensores senatus: *CTh.* i. 28. 2. Immnuity from arrest: *CTh.* ix. 2. 2. It is difficult to see how Alföldi can interpret this law and ix. 40. 10 (367) as 'reinforcing a privilege' of the 'senatorial class'. (*Conflict of Ideas in the Late Roman Empire*, 55). Was submission to the emperor of accusations against senators a privilege or a device to ensure that judges were not cowed by the great? ix. 2. 2 also insists that accused persons, of whatever rank, be imprisoned, thus revoking Julian's ix. 2. 1, which exempted senators.

[2] Vicars of Rome: Magnus' origin is unknown, but the rest are noble to 370. Africa: P. Ampelius: *CTh.* xiii. 5. 10 (364). See page 93, above. Campania: Buleforus, 364–5. Nothing is known about him but the name is unlikely to belong to a noble. *CTh.* ix. 30. 2, xv. 5. 1, viii. 5. 24.

[3] Petronius Probus: vi. 1751–3. Unpublished inscription from Capua communicated to the Fifth Epigraphical Conference, Cambridge, 1967. Decimius Germanianus: Amm. xxvi. 5. 5. Viventius: Amm. xxvi. 4. 4; *CTh.* xiii. 10. 4 and 6. Maximinus: Amm. xxviii. 1. 41. Florentius: CSL: *CTh.* xiii. 1. 6; PPO: *CTh.* xiii. 10. 5 (367).

was in office as praetorian prefect for the eleven years of Valentinian's reign, with a few short breaks. After his first short spell in Illyricum he was appointed to the prefecture of Gaul, and for the last seven years of Valentinian's reign he was in control of Italy, Africa, and Illyricum. The Emperor evidently left Probus a free hand, though Illyricum was the Emperor's own native territory, and it was only late in his reign that Valentinian learnt of his prefect's oppressive regime. But even then he failed to act against him, and Probus survived the Emperor in office. If, as Ammianus tells us, Probus entered public affairs in the interests of his family, his appointment to a position of immense power by Valentinian can only be seen as an attempt on the part of the Emperor to conciliate at least the most significant of the noble families in the Empire— and he had the consolation of knowing that the Anicii, unlike the Ceionii, were Christians.

Though Probus was loth to offend Maximinus, one of the Emperor's confidants, and therefore betrayed the trust of Maximinus's noble predecessor, in the urban vicariate, Aginatius, thus delivering him to his mortal foe. Yet Maximinus and his imperial master in their turn both appear to have been not a little awed by the aristocracy. It is true that several nobles lost their lives through the vindictive prosecutions of Maximinus. But the Pannonian plotted very gingerly against the life of Aginatius, who, as Maximinus knew, had intrigued against him. Similarly, Valentinian seems to have wanted to protect another noble, Iulius Festus Hymetius, against the venom of his own agents. In addition, though not slow to give Maximinus permission to torture senators, a practice which was contrary to all tradition, he was just as quick to recant when visited by a deputation of three senators, namely Vettius Agorius Praetextatus, Volusius Venustus, and Minervius. It was the same Praetextatus whose request for the exemption of his province, Achaea, from the law against nocturnal sacrifices had been granted by Valentinian in the first year of his reign.[1]

---

[1] Aginatius: See Appendix 6, below. Hymetius: Amm. xxviii. 1. 17 ff. Senatorial deputation to complain about torture: Amm. xxviii. 1. 24. Praetextatus. Zos. iv. 3.

The difference between Valentinian's anti-aristocratic actions and those of Diocletian was one of kind rather than of degree. Valentinian may have appointed non-nobles to positions traditionally reserved for nobles and he may have introduced an inflation of honours which devalued the hereditary clarissimate, but what he did not do was to turn senatorial rank into a political *cul-de-sac*, which is what Diocletian achieved. Instead, Valentinian worked within the Constantinian mould, and nobles retained their eligibility for the highest offices in the Empire. Admittedly, this in itself would be meaningless, since an emperor could appoint whomsoever he wished to any particular post. But Valentinian's successors returned to the pattern of appointments initiated by Constantine and his sons—and even Valentinian himself, as we have seen, while favouring men of humble origins in his appointments, entrusted the position second only to the Imperial throne itself to two of the noblest men in the Empire.

On the death of Valentinian, Valens, who, though in theory an equal partner in the Empire with his brother, had always been more inclined to follow his strong lead, became senior Augustus, and the West passed to Gratian, Valentinian's seventeen-year-old son, who was very much under the influence of his tutor, Ausonius. Combining an easy affability with a taste for politics, the poet had become *quaestor sacri palatii* before the death of Valentinian, and within two years of his pupil's accession to supreme power he and his son Hesperius were joint prefects of Gaul, his father Julius Ausonius, an aged physician, being prefect of Illyricum, a post which he held until his death at the age of ninety in 378. In that year the whole of the West came under Ausonius and his son. Nor were these the only members of the family to hold high office. A nephew of the poet's, Magnus Arborius, became urban prefect; a son-in-law Thalassius seems to have been vicar of Macedonia and then proconsul of Africa, presumably succeeding Hesperius in this Office when the latter was promoted to the praetorian prefecture. The family continued to be prominent in affairs of state, even though, after only two years at the helm, Ausonius took an ordinary consulship and retired from active politics, as did his son soon after. A grandson of the poet's called Hesperius is recorded as a *comes* in

385, and Paulinus of Pella, another member of the family, tells us about his immediate family's public life in his verse autobiography.[1]

Though no praetorian prefecture is known to have been occupied by a noble under Gratian, familiar names such as Faltonius Probus Alypius and Alfenius Ceionius Julianus reappear among the vicars. A member of a locally prominent Gallic family, Ausonius was not himself a noble, but he counted among his friends literary nobles such as Symmachus and Paulinus of Nola.[2] It is true that Symmachus knew many of the high officials of the time and recommended men to Ausonius for high office. But men such as Potitus, Fl. Gorgonius, and Palladius, all of whom were given high posts, mostly at court, whether as a result of Symmachns' efforts or not, do not appear to have been nobles.[3]

It should also not be forgotten that Gratian was the first emperor not to be *Pontifex Maximus* and that, by removing the altar of Victory once again from the curia, he precipitated the well-known controversy which raged for more than a decade after his death.[4] Though Damasus and Ambrose may well have been speaking for a majority of senators in the Empire at large, or, in other words, for all those men who held posts entitling them to a seat in the assembly, the majority of those who actually attended the sessions were evidently pagans, a good number of them probably being nobles living in Rome, as they were traditionally obliged to do.[5]

[1] Decimius Magnus Ausonius: QSP: *Aus. Grat. Act.* ii. 7; *Parent.* iv. 31; Symm. *Ep.* i. 13, 23. PPO: Aus. *Lect.*, 35–6; *CTh.* viii. 5. 35; Symm. *Ep.* i. 18, 21. Decimius Hilarianus Hesperius: Aus. *Grat. Act.*, loc. cit.; *CTh.* vi. 30. 4, xii. 1. 11, xvi. 5. 5, x.20. 10. Julius Ausonius: Aus. *Epic.* 52. Hesperius junior: Symm. *Rel.* xxiii. Paulinus of Pella: Paul. *Eucharist.* 24.

[2] Symm. *Epp.* i. 13–43; Aus. *Epp.* xxiii–xxxi.

[3] Symm. *Ep.* i. 19, 378—Potitus, vic. Rom. 379–80; *Ep.* i. 39, 370/9 ix. 5897 = D. 1290.—Fl. Gorgonius, CRP 386; *Ep.* i. 15, i. 94, iii. 50, 370/80—Palladius 'rhetor', CSL 381, Mag. Off. 382–4.

[4] Pontifex Maximus: Zos. iv. 36; Altar: Amb. *Ep.* 17. See J. Wytzes, *Der Streit um dem Altar der Viktoria;* S. Dill, *Roman Society*, 3 ff.; O. Seeck, *Geschichte*, v, 217 ff.; A. Alföldi, *Festival of Isis*, 30 ff.; H. Bloch, 'A new document of the last pagan revival in the West', *Harvard Theol. Rev.* 38 (1945) 213 ff.; A. Cameron, *JRS* 58 (1968).

[5] Amb. *Epp.* 17, 18, 57. Symm. *Rell.* 2–3. It was no longer obligatory for senators to reside in Rome, as we see from a law of 383, *CTh.* vi. 2. 13. 8. A later law recognizes the right of men of senatorial rank to live wherever they wished without leave of absence. (*CJ* xii. 1. 15). The only proviso was that if a senator with country estates also had a house in Rome, he should pay his *aurum oblaticium* there. *CTh.* vi. 2. 16 (395).

8

Indeed, the Senate was still a predominantly pagan body in the fifth century.[1]

Theodosius was no more favourably inclined to the pagan appeal to restore the altar of Victory than was either Gratian or the youthful Valentinian II, and he encouraged the pagan senators to convert to Christianity,[2] yet his reign marked a new stage in the role played by nobles in the imperial government.

Schuurmans has the view that the title 'comes ordinis primi intra palatium' was used for each of the four palatine ministers before the titles 'quaestor sacri palatii', 'magister officiorum', 'comes sacrarum largitionum', and 'comes rerum privatarum' came into use.[3] This appears unlikely, however, since a *magister officiorum* is recorded as early as 320 and a *comes rei privatae* in 340,[4] while *comites ordinis primi intra palatium* such as Vulcacius Rufinus and Memmius Vitrasius Orfitus were in this position around the middle of the century and Anicius Acilius Glabrio Faustus, described simply as 'comes intra consistorium' and no doubt of the first order, had this appointment in the early fifth century.[5] The *comes ordinis primi intra consistorium* was no doubt, as has been said above and as the title itself indicates, one of the emperor's leading advisers who was actually present at court and took part in meetings of the *consistorium* as a 'minister without portfolio'. Up to the time of Theodosius no nobles are known to have had any of the specific ministerial portfolios, and it is not difficult to see why a noble would scorn to hold a position whose origin is to be sought in the work done in the early principate by the emperor's freedmen and which even in the fourth century retained a trace of its humble domestic beginnings. But time had made the palatine portfolios respectable, and under Theodosius we find Virius Nicomachus Flavianus as *quaestor sacri palatii* and (Rufius) Festus and Caecina Decius Albinus as *tribuni et notarii*, the latter destined to become *magister*

[1] Zos. iv. 59 (394); Zos. v. 41.

[2] Zos. iv. 59.

[3] C. Schuurmans, De Samenstelling van den Romeinschen senaat vanaf de troonbestijging van Diocletianus tot aan het einde van de IVe eeuw n.C.', unpublished doctoral disseration, Ghent, 1943, 434.

[4] *Magister Officiorum: CTh.* xvi. 10. 1—Heraclianus. Comes Rei Privatae: *CTh.* xii. 1. 30—Nemesianus.

[5] For Rufinus and Orfitus see above. Faustus: xiv. 2165 = D. 1283.

officiorum and probably also *quaestor sacri palatii* at the turn of the century.[1]

A Spaniard by birth, Theodosius was brought into the imperial college to rule the East in place of Valens who was killed together with the greater part of his army in the disastrous defeat of Hadrianople in the summer of 378. Like Valentinian, Theodosius brought some of his countrymen into government with him, a good example being Maternus Cynegius, who was a vicar, *comes sacrarum largitionum, quaestor sacri palatii,* and praetorian prefect of the East, all under Theodosius.[2] This last post is interesting, and indeed most of Theodosius' Eastern prefects seem to have been Westerners.[3] In fact, the first praetorian prefect appointed by Theodosius was Q. Clodius Hermogenianus Olybrius, a member of the noble Anician family, who had a combined prefecture of the East and Illyricum, part of which Gratian had given into the safekeeping of his new imperial colleague. On Gratian's assassination Theodosius became in effect the ruler of the whole Empire with the exception of the far Western provinces, which were under the usurper Magnus Maximus, and the first three Western praetorian prefects under Theodosius were all members of the aristocracy, namely Petronius Probus, Nonius Atticus Maximus, and Vettius Agorius Praetextatus.[4]

Though the West passed on the death of Theodosius into the grip of the Vandal general Stilicho acting for Theodosius' young son Honorius, the nobles did not suffer a reverse. Indeed, under Valentinian III (423–55), as Sundwall has shown, the Italian praetorian prefecture was virtually the preserve of the aristocracy, its holders including such men as Anicius Auchenius Bassus,

---

[1] Flavianus: vi. 1782–3 = D. 2947–8. Festus: vi. 32035 = xv. 7163. Albinus: Symm. *Ep.* vii. 38.

[2] Vic.: *CJ* v. 20. 1 (381); CSL: *CTh.* vi. 35. 12 (383). QSP: Lib. *Or.* xlix. 3; PPO: Ibid.

[3] See J. Matthews, 'The Connections of Florus', MS. kindly lent by the *PLRE* team.

[4] Olybrius: vi. 1714 = D. 1271. Probus: *CTh.* xi. 13. 1; Soc. v. 11. 3, vii. 13; Cf. Symm. *Ep.* i. 58. See Arnheim, unpublished Cambridge Ph.D. thesis, 207 f., for a discussion of the question of Probus's return to office under Theodosius. See also Ibid., p. 309, n. 64. Maximus: *CTh.* xiii. 1. 12. Praetextatus: vi. 1779 = D. 1259; vi. 1778. On the question as to whether he had one or two prefectures see Arnheim, op. cit., 218, n. 268.

Rufius Antonius Agrypnius Volusianus, Caecina Decius Aginatius Albinus, Anicius Acilius Glabrio Faustus, Nicomachus Flavianus, and Petronius Maximus, this last-mentioned prefect becoming Emperor in 455—a new departure for nobles, or rather a full circle to the days when the first citizen could trace his decent from noble families of the distant past.[1]

By the time of Theodosius' death nobles had had access to high state posts for almost a century. For a time, under Valentinian, whose hostility to the aristocracy was reflected in some of his appointments, it looked as though the new dispensation introduced by Constantine was threatened with destruction, but, as we have seen, even Valentinian entrusted the important central prefecture to nobles, and in general kept within the Constantinian mould. The emperor's personal preference was certainly an important factor in the selection of men for posts, but it had to be tempered by considerations of the political and social circumstances of the day. It is this which explains the meagre number of nobles appointed to posts in the Eastern half of the Empire in a period when the number of Western offices held by them was impressive. For it was in the West that their land, wealth, and family connections were concentrated.

[1] See Sundwall: *Weström. Studien*, s. vv.

V

THE ARISTOCRATIC COUSINHOOD

'STEMMATA quid faciunt?' is Juvenal's taunt. 'Quis fructus, generis tabula iactare capaci/ fumosos equitum cum dictatore magistros,/ si coram Lepidis male vivitur?' Not in pedigrees but in character is true nobility to be found. 'Nobilitas sola est atque unica virtus.' Achievement, not family background, is the measure of men as of horses. 'Nobilis hic, quocumque venit de gramine, cuius/ clara fuga ante alios et primus in aequore pulvis.'[1] The reader is then treated to a series of masterly portrayals of nobles engaged in vice. Forgery, fraud, adultery: there is nothing surprising in their appearance in a catalogue of vice. But these subjects are dismissed in the space of half a dozen lines. The vices treated with closer brush-strokes on an ampler canvas are, however, of quite a different type. Lateranus is belaboured for stooping to drive his gig himself—and feed his horses too! His frequenting of low taverns earns him another rap over the knuckles. But nothing is condemned more forcefully than the participation of nobles in dramatic performances.

Though Juvenal rates the abilities of the nobles very poorly indeed, he judges their behaviour by very different criteria from those which he employs for people of lower social rank. That acting was a pastime ill befitting the dignity of a noble was a view not confined to Juvenal. Tacitus likewise condemns the practice, and he puts this condemnation into the mouths of unnamed detractors,[2] fittingly, since he is here no doubt reflecting a common view. A noble was expected to behave in a more 'gentlemanly' fashion than a man of lesser rank, and when he failed to do so the opprobrium was all the greater. Stemmata did matter after all.

Two centuries later social values were not very different. A long and noble pedigree was certainly cause for pride in the fourth

[1] Juv. *Sat.* viii. 1, 6 ff., 20, 60 f.
[2] Tac. *Ann.* xiv. 20. Lateranus: Juv. *Sat.* viii. 146 ff., 220. Cf. i. 58 ff.

century. The nobles' pride in their birth was complemented by the respect of the lower orders.[1] Even St. Jerome is proud to trace the lineage of his noble friends, while at the same time affecting to scorn such worldly considerations:

Neque vero Marcellam tuam, immo meam et, ut verius loquar, nostram, omniumque sanctorum et proprie Romanae urbis inclitum decus, institutis rhetorum praedicabo, ut exponam illustrem familiam, alti sanguinis decus et stemmata per consules et praefectos praetorio decurrentia. Nihil in illa laudabo, nisi quod proprium est et in eo nobilius, quod opibus et nobilitate contempta facta est paupertate et humilitate nobilior.[2]

Marcella, one of Jerome's circle of devoutly Christian noble female devotees, was descended on her mother's side from the Ceionii, one of the two most important aristocratic families in the Late Empire.

The obituary notice of Fabiola, another member of this circle, is written in the same vein:

Alius forsitan scholae memor Quintum Maximum, 'Unus qui nobis cunctando restituit rem', et totam Fabiorum gentem preferret in medium, diceret pugnas, describeret proelia et per tantae nobilitatis gradus Fabiolam venisse iactaret, ut, quod in virga non poterat, in radicibus demonstraret. Ego, diversorii Bethlemitici et praesepis dominici amator, in quo virgo puerpera Deum fudit infantem, ancillam Christi non de nobilitate veteris historiae, sed de ecclesiae humilitate producam.[3]

Again it is plain from the way Jerome handles the subject that the high regard for noble descent which we can discern in his writings is a reflection of a common attitude in his time, and this is borne out by the writings of other fourth century authors. Ammianus, for example, uses the high cultural standards expected of nobles to chide Memmius Vitrasius Orfitus, an imperial *comes* and urban prefect.[4] The esteem attached to senatorial birth comes home to us particularly clearly in the letters and speeches of Symmachus, as we have seen in more detail in connection with admission to the Senate.[5] But esteem for family and lineage could also be

[1] See Ammianus xxviii. 4. 6. [2] Jer. *Ep.* 127. 1.
[3] Jer. *Ep.* 77. 2. [4] Amm. xiv. 6. 1, quoted on p. 89, above.
[5] See Introduction ii and below, p. 165 ff. Symmachus' speeches on behalf of men wishing to enter the Senate are instructive in this connection. E.g. *Or.*, vi.

translated into more practical benefits which are discussed below.[1]

Even under the Germanic invaders the esteem attaching to the old senatorial aristocracy continued. Thanks to Apollinaris Sidonius, the literary gentleman-bishop of Auvergne, and Gregory of Tours, a man not of noble birth but of aristocratic values nevertheless, we know something about the senatorial aristocracy of fifth and sixth-century Gaul. Being of senatorial stock himself Sidonius naturally enough took pride in the nobility of his friends. In a letter, written in about 470, congratulating his friend Eutropius on his appointment as praetorian prefect of Gaul, we still find that *esprit de corps*, that common identity which can trace its origin to the days of the first Brutus:

Porro autem desidiae vicinior putabatur contemptus ille militiae, ad quam iactitant lividi bonarum partium viros non posse potius quam nolle conscendere. Igitur, quod loco primore fieri par est, agimus gratias uberes Christo, qui statum celsitudinis tuae ut hactenus parentum nobilitate decorabat, ita iam nunc titulorum parilitate fastigat; simul et animorum spebus erectis fas est de cetero sperare meliora . . . Nam memor originis tuae nobilium sibi persuasit universitas, quamdiu nos Sabini familia rexerit, Sabiniani familiam non timendam.[2]

Quite who Sabinus was is not known, but he was evidently an ancestor of Eutropius's. The reference to Sabinianus is equally obscure but presumably represents a hostile faction. It is certainly interesting to see the use of the term 'bonarum partium viri' for the aristocratic 'party', for that is no doubt what it must be understood to mean.[3]

To a young noble called Syagrius and evidently related to the two Syagrii known to us as praetorian prefects in the latter half of the fourth century, Sidonius addresses some stern words of advice. Public life has a claim on a noble, which Syagrius is shirking in attending only to his estate:

parce tantum in nobilitatis individiam rusticari. . . . Nam, si ceteris nobilium studiorum artibus repudiatis sola te propagandae rei familiaris

---

[1] See Chapter VI.   [2] Sid. Ap. *Ep.* iii. 6. 2–3.
[3] The term harks back to the Ciceronian 'consensus omnium bonorum' and 'optimus quisque', either deliberately or unintentionally.

urtica sollicitat, licet tu deductum nomen a trabeis atque eboratas curules et gestatorias bratteatas et fastos recolas purpurissatos, is profecto inveniere, quem debeat sic industrium quod latentem non tam honorare censor quam censetor onerare.[1]

In a letter of congratulation to a noble friend who had had a notable public career we find that Sidonius' expectations of men of noble birth were shared by his class generally. The friend in question, Castalius Innocentius Audax, had become prefect of Rome under the Emperor Julius Nepos:

Tu vero inter haec macte, qui praefecturae titulis ampliatus, licet hactenus e prosapia inlustri computarere, peculiariter nihilo segnius elaborasti, ut a te gloriosius posteri tui numerarentur. Nil enim est illo per sententiam boni cuiusque generosius, quisquis ingenii corporis opum iunctam in hoc constans operam exercet, ut maioribus suis anteponatur.[2]

It was now 150 years since Constantine had begun readmitting nobles to high public office, and in this time noble birth had clearly become an important claim to such office. But now, with the conversion of the aristocracy to Christianity, noble birth was also becoming a claim to appointments in the Church. This is brought home very well in the speech given by Sidonius when called upon to choose a bishop for Bourges:

Si natalibus servanda reverentia est, quia et hos non omittendos euangelista monstravit (nam Lucas laudationem Iohannis aggressus praestantissimum computavit, quod de sacerdotali stirpe veniebat, et nobilitatem vitae praedicaturus prius tamen extulit familiae dignitatem): parentes ipsius aut cathedris aut tribunalibus praesederunt. Inlustris in utraque conversatione prosapia aut episcopis floruit aut praefectis: ita semper huiusce maioribus aut humanum aut divimum dictare ius usui fuit. Si vero personam suam tractatu consiliosiore pensemus, invenimus eam tenere istic inter spectabiles principem locum. Sed dicitis iure Eucherium et Pannychium inlustres haberi superiores: quod hactenus eos esto putatos, sed praesentem iam modo ad causam illi ex canone non requiruntur, qui ambo ad secundas nuptias transierunt.[3]

It is worth noting the way in which Sidonius tries to reconcile the current aristocratic values with religious considerations. Birth became a lasting criterion of ecclesiastical preferment, and is clearly

[1] Sid. Ap. *Ep.* viii. 8. 2–3.   [2] Sid. Ap. *Ep.* viii. 7. 3.
[3] Sid. Ap. *Ep.* vii. 9. 17–18.

discernible in Gregory of Tours's *History of the Franks* written under the Merovingians in the mid-sixth century. The bishop of Tours is always more than ready and glowing with pride to trace the aristocratic ancestry of his fellow bishops.[1]

In examining a society with aristocratic values, where noble birth is highly prized, one has naturally to be on one's guard against the false assumption of noble lineage. How much credence can we give to the vaunted descent of our fourth-century senators? Certainly, when Jerome traces Fabiola and the fourth-century Fabii to the Cunctator of old or when he makes Julius Festus Hymetius and his brother Toxotius descended from the family of Julius Caesar, it is difficult for us to suppress an incredulous smile.[2] But that is not to say that we are justified in rejecting out of hand the nobility of the families concerned. It is clear from Jerome that the fourth century Fabii and Iulii, for example, were considered by their contemporaries to be old families. Given this general view, it is hardly surprising that they were linked in the popular mind with illustrious figures in the annals of Rome who happen to have shared the same *nomina*. That the fourth-century families which were thought to be of ancient noble stock by their contemporaries could claim at least several generations of nobility will be shown below. That they could always trace their nobility back as far as contemporary admirers fancied is, however, doubtful.

Some fourth-century noble families nevertheless could legitimately lay claim to pedigrees stretching back to the Republic. One such family was the Acilii. The earliest Acilius to distinguish himself was M'. Acilius Glabrio, consul in 191 B.C., well known for his victories in Greece against King Antiochus III of Syria. Of the three proconsuls who commanded legions under Augustus after 28 B.C. one was M. Acilius Glabrio, who had been suffect consul in 33 B.C.[3] Juvenal gives us a somewhat disparaging account of the behaviour of M'. Acilius Glabrio, consul in 91 A.D. and his eighty-year-old father at Domitian's *consilium*.[4] Other consuls in the family were M'. Acilius Glabrio, consul in 124, M'. Acilius

---

[1] Greg. Tur. *Hist. Franc.* ii. 24.   [2] Julii: Jer. *Ep.* 108. 4. Fabii: Jer. *Ep.* 77. 2.

[3] See Syme, *Roman Revolution*, 328 n. 3.

[4] Juv. *Sat.* iv. 45.

Glabrio Cn. Cornelius Severus, consul in 152, and M'. Acilius Glabrio, consul for the second time in 186, who was offered the imperial throne by his friend Pertinax in 193 but turned it down.[1] He was the father of M'. Acilius Faustinus, consul in 210, whose daughter Acilia Manliola married Claudius Acilius Cleoboles, son of a suffect consul named Tib. Claudius Cleoboles, the product of this marriage being Acilia Gavinia Frestana 'clarissima puella'.[2] Tib. Claudius Cleoboles had evidently himself married an Acilia, as his son's name indicates. The last plain Acilius Glabrio to be recorded, though apparently with the *praenomen* Marcus rather than the usual family *praenomen* Manius, was consul in 256. In addition there are one or two undated Acilii Glabriones, one a consul with the traditional *tria nomina* of the family who was married to Arria Plaria Vera Priscilla, another a *curator riparum et alvei Tiberis* with the name M. Acilius Memmius Glabrio.[3]

Another branch of the family was formed by the Acilii Aviolae. We know that they were related to the Glabriones because they too had a predilection for the *praenomen* Manius. The earliest known Acilius Aviola was legate of Lugdunensis in 21,[4] and then we have three men all called M'. Acilius Aviola, the first consul in 54 and proconsul of Asia in 65–6, the second consul in 122 and the last consul in 239 together with the Emperor Gordian III.[5] Another member of the family appears under Diocletian and Maximian as *curator alvei Tiberis riparum et cloacarum sacrae urbis*, namely Manius Acilius Balbus Sabinus v.c. (so uncommon had the *praenomen* Manius become that it is written out in full in the inscription).[6] The corrector of Italy in 286, Acilius Clarus, was probably another member of the family,[7] as was his namesake, one of the earliest senatorial *praesides* under Constantine.[8]

Another Constantinian member of the family was the Acilius Severus who was ordinary consul in 323, urban prefect in 325–6, and

[1] Herod. ii. 3. 4; Dio 73. 3. 3.
[2] ix. 233–4 Allifae.
[3] xi. 6333 = D. 1073; vi. 31543 = D. 5893. See *PIR*[2] A. 70, 75.
[4] Tac. *Ann.* iii. 41.
[5] vi. 1331 = 31631; vi. 10048 = D. 5287; vi. 11596. *PIR*[2] A. 49–51.
[6] vi. 1242 = D. 5894.
[7] v. 8205 Aquileia.
[8] viii. 2729[1] Lambaesis. Cf. Birley *JRS* 40 (1950) 66, and *PIR*[2] A. 55.

probably praetorian prefect at least between 322 and 324.[1] Admittedly there is no positive evidence other than the *nomen gentile* of Severus' relationship to the ancient family. But, first, it should be noted that the name Acilius was a very rare name in this period. Secondly, the *cognomen* Severus was not entirely alien to the family of the Glabriones. As was noted above, the consul of 152 was called M'. Acilius Glabrio Cn. Cornelius Severus, evidently a combination of his parents' names, and in addition two young senatorial boys, clearly related to each other, are recorded as assistants to the Arval brothers in 183 and 186, their names being Acilius Aviola and Acilius Severus.[2]

The next member of the family known to us after Acilius Severus was the vicar of Gaul in the early fifth century Acilius Glabrio Sibidius Spedius, father of Anicius Acilius Glabrio Faustus, praetorian prefect in 438. So, following many another noble house, the Acilii had at last allied themselves with the Anicii; the ancient family, prominent already in the days of the wars against Carthage, shared with their new partners, a family unknown before the time of Septimius Severus, the hallowed traditions of the men who had expelled the kings of old and who had ruled the state through many changes of fortune.[3]

Though by comparison with the Acilii the Anicii were parvenus, yet from a fourth-century standpoint they were already an old noble family. The earliest known senatorial member of the family was C. Anicius Faustus, ordinary consul in 198, who had a notable career, beginning as legate of Numidia and after his consulship becoming governor of Moesia Superior (between 202 and 207) and proconsul of Asia.[4] Anicius Faustus Paulinus, legate of Moesia Inferior in 230, is thought by Groag to have been the son of the consul of 198; whether he was or not, he must certainly have been a relative.[5] Another third century member of the family, Sex.

[1] *CTh.* iii. 32. 1 (322—no office indicated); *CJ* iii. 12. 3 (323—no office indicated); *CTh.* vi. 22. 1 (MSS. 321, Seeck 324—'ad Severum p.u.'). Severus' praetorian prefecture is rejected by the *PLRE* but accepted by Chastagnol (*Fastes*, 77–8) and Schuurmans (No. 673). On the dating of the laws see Seeck, *Regesten*, p. 62 and Palanque, *Essai*, p. 5 and n. 24.
[2] vi. 2099, 2100. *PIR²* A. 48, 80.   [3] vi. 1678 = D. 1281.
[4] viii. 2553 = D. 9177; iii. 1685. Dio 79. 22. 2–4.
[5] iii. 7473. Groag: s.v. *PIR²*.

Cocceius Anicius Faustus Paulinus, proconsul of Africa probably under Gallienus, evidently married into the family of the proconsul of Asia C. Asinius Nicomachus Julianus, the (presumed) products of this marriage being: M. Junius Caesonius Nicomachus Anicius Faustus Paulinus, ordinary consul in 298 and prefect of Rome in the following year; and M. Cocceius Anicius Faustus Flavianus, described in an inscription as 'patricius, consularis'.[1] Amnius Manius Caesonius Nicomachus Anicius Paulinus Honorius, ordinary consul in 334, may well have been a son of the consul of 298 and father of Anicia Faltonia Proba, whose inscription reads as follows:

ANICIAE FALTONIAE
PROBAE AMNIOS PINCIOS
ANICIOSQVE DECORANTI
CONSVLIS VXORI
CONSVLIS FILIAE
CONSVLVM MATRI
ANICIVS PROBINVS V.C.
CONSVL ORDINARIVS
ET ANICIVS PROBVS V.C.
QVAESTOR CANDIDATVS
FILII DEVINCTI
MATERNIS MERITIS
DEDICARVNT.[2]

Nothing is known on the Pincii, and the 'Amnii' are undoubtedly the same as the Annii, a family closely connected with the Ceionii as well as with the Anicii. Proba, we are told, was the daughter of a consul, the most eligible candidate being the consul of 334 if we take dates into account. For Proba was the wife and mother of consuls whose identity is not in the slightest doubt. That Petronius Probus, as he is normally called, was Proba's husband is known from the fact that the sons who dedicated the inscription quoted above to their mother dedicated one also to their father.[3] The name of another son is also Anicius Hermogenianus Olybrius, whose consulship in 395 together with his brother Probinus has been immortalized by Claudian.[1]

Though Petronius Probus himself evidently did not have the *nomen* Anicius, he is described in an inscription as 'Anicianae domus culmen'.[2] It would seem therefore that his mother was an Anicia, since there is no sign of Anician blood on his father's side. His father was Petronius Probinus, ordinary consul in 341 and urban prefect in 344. His grandfather was Petronius Probianus, proconsul of Africa, ordinary consul, urban prefect and probably also praetorian prefect under Constantine.[3] The family goes back a bit further and was evidently connected with the Ceionii as well as with the Anicii. This can be seen in the name of the first member of the family to rise from equestrian to senatorial rank, T. Petronius Taurus Volusianus, praetorian prefect, ordinary consul in 261.[4] The urban prefect of 267–8 Petronius Volusianus was probably the same person; if not, he was a close relative. Another member of the same family, L. Publius Petronius Volusianus, is recorded in an inscription from Puteoli as holding the three republican magistracies and as *sevir* and patron of Puteoli.[5] It is not certain that these Petronii belong to the same family as our Petronii nor that these Volusiani are connected with the Ceionii Volusiani, but since neither the *nomen* Petronius nor the *cognomen* Volusianus was at all common in this period, there is a strong likelihood that the families were related as suggested.

As well as being 'Anicianae domus culmen', Petronius Probus is described, this time by Ausonius, as 'stirpis novator Anniae'.[6] A similar reference is to be found in Claudian's Panegyric on Probus's sons, the consuls of 395: 'Scis genus Auchenium; nec te latuere potentes Anniadae.'[7] The name Auchenius is found in several late fourth- and fifth-century Anicii, as for example in the case of Anicius Auchenius Bassus, 'proconsul Campaniae' and urban prefect (the latter in 382).[8] Though there is no record of

[1] Claud. *In Probini et Olybrii Fratum Consulatum Panegyris.* vi. 1735 = D. 1267.
[2] vi. 1753 = D. 1267.   [3] Symm. *Ep.* I. 2. 6. v. 3344 = D. 1266.
[4] xi. 1836.   [5] x. 1706.
[6] vi. 1748.   [7] Claud., op. cit., 8 f.
[8] vi. 1679 = D. 1262.

anyone combining with the name Anicius either the *nomen* Annius or the *cognomen* from it Annianus, we do find a combination of this *cognomen* with the *nomen* Petronius, as in the case of Constantine's praetorian prefect Petronius Annianus. If we recall the connection between the Petronii and the Anicii, then we will appreciate Petronius Annianus's relationship not only with Petronius Probianus, Annius Anullinus and C. Annius Tiberianus but also with Amnius Manius Caesonius Nicomachus Anicius Paulinus, ordinary consul in 334, and with Sex. Anicius Paulinus, ordinary consul in 325 and urban prefect in 331.[1]

A poetic strain—or at least an inclination to compose verses— ran through the Petronii, so that Petronius Probus, for example, could present to Theodosius a volume of the joint poetic output of his grandfather, his father, and himself.[2] But the member of the family most given to literary pursuits was the Christian poetess Faltonia Betitia Proba, wife of Clodius Celsinus Adelphius, corrector of Campania.[3] That she was related to Petronius Probus can be seen from the name of her son Q. Clodius Hermogenianus Olybrius, who was to become a praetorian prefect under Theodosius.[4] One of Petronius Probus's sons, it will be recalled, was named Anicius Hermogenianus Olybrius. Theodosius's prefect could have got the names Hermogenianus and Olybrius only from his mother, since his father was Clodius Celsinus Adelphius.[5] But if the poetess's relationship to Probus explains her *cognomen*, what about the *nomina* Faltonia and Betitia?[6] Three Faltonii are known from the third century, two of them probably fictitious. These are Faltonius Probus, proconsul of Asia in 275,[7] and Maecius

---

[1] On the Anicii see Seeck, *Symmachus*, p. xl.

[2] Corn. Nepos, *Epigrammata*, ed. Halm, p. 101.

[3] Montfaucon, *Diarium Italicum*, p. 36 = Schenkl, CSEL xvi. p. 513. Subscriptio Vaticani Reginae 1666.

[4] vi. 1714 = D. 1271.

[5] ix. 1576 = D. 1239 Beneventum; x. 6083 Formiae. On Adelphius's correctorship see p. 55 f. He was wither identical with or related to the Clodius Celsinus recorded as consular of Numidia between 333 and 337 in an inscription from Constantina. viii. 7011 = D. 715.

[6] Proba is thought by Chastagnol to have been the daughter of Petronius Probianus and his wife Demetrias. *Fastes*, s.v. Clodius Celsinus Adelphius. See Jer. *Ep.* 130. 3; D. 8988.

[7] SHA *V. Aureliani* 40. 4.

Faltonius Nicomachus, *vir consularis*, a leading senator at the same time as Probus.[1] Both these names appear in the notoriously unreliable *Historia Augusta*, and both men appear to have taken their names from the fourth century Anicii rather than vice versa.[2] The other third-century Faltonius is a much less distinguished person than his mythical near-contemporaries, an equestrian *praeses* of Mauretania Caesariensis and *praefectus vigilum* under Gordian called Faltonius Restitutianus.[3] In view of the extreme rarity of the name he is likely to have been descended from the second-century centurion Faltonius Januarius, whose name appears in an inscription of 161 from Lambaesis.[4] It can hardly be chance that the only two Faltonii known for certain before the fourth century both came from Africa. That side of Proba's family at any rate, then, had become senatorial only a century before her time.

The name Betitius is hardly less rare than Faltonius, but has a longer aristocratic history. The family goes back to C. Betitius Pietas, who married Neratia Procilla, who is thought by Borghesi to have been a sister of L. Neratius Proculus, *legatus legionis* under Antoninus Pius.[5] The offspring of the marriage of Betitius Pietas and Neratia Procilla were Neratia Betitia Procilla[6] and C. Neratius Proculus Betitius Pius Maximillianus,[7] who in turn was the father of Betitius Pius Maximillianus:

> BETITIO PIO
> MAXIMILLIANO
> COSVLARI Cur.
> COL. CARTAGiniS
> VICE OPERVM Publicor.
> ALLECTO INTER . . .[8]

He appears to have been the first member of the family to become a senator, and probably dates from the late second century, since he

[1] SHA *V. Tac.* 5. 3.   [2] Sir R. Syme, *Ammianus and the Historia Augusta*, 156.
[3] vi. 266; Maur. Sit.; viii. 20487, 20602; *AE* 1903, 94. SHA *V. Gord.* 23. 4.
[4] D. 2452 = *Eph. Ep.* v. 1276, cf. vii., 365.
[5] ix. 1132 Aeclanum; ix. 2457 Saepinum.
[6] ix. 1163.   [7] ix. 1160–2, 1132.
[8] ix. 1121. Probably adlected 'inter praetorios'.

was the grandson of Neratia Procilla, whose brother, as we have seen, was a legate in the mid-second century. By the early third century the Betitii were an eminently respectable senatorial family, and a member of the family, C. Betitius Pius, appears as a 'v.c.' patron of Canusium among the other notables in the album of that town's benefactors of 223.[1] He may have been the same person as the C. Betitius Pius whose name appears together with that of his wife Fuscinilla on two seals[2] and in an inscription from Aeclanum.[3] The Betitii had arrived, and only the hand of a noble senator's daughter would be acceptable to them. Fuscinilla's brother, Seius Carus, whose name shares a lead pipe with hers, was a senator put to death by Elagabalus in 219 for being involved in sedition,[4] and their grandfather Seius Fuscianus was a fellow-student of Marcus Aurelius, urban prefect, and ordinary consul in 188.[5] Other members of the family were Maximilla, daughter of Betitius Calinicus, and a co-heir with her was a man called Proculus, no doubt one of the Neratii Proculi. Then there was Betitia Maximilla, wife of C. Vibius Hilarius, Betitia M . . ., Betitia C. (f. ?), (B)etitia Pia and Betitia Plotina, 'clarissima puella' from Beneventum. In the fourth century we also have two Betitii Perpetui, probably grandfather and grandson, the elder being corrector and patron of Sicily under Constantine and the younger consular and patron of Tuscia and Umbria at some time after 366.[6] The union between the Neratii of Saepinum and their neighbours the Betitii of Aeclanum was a significant one indeed. In the fourth century the Neratii were represented by two very important men and the mother of an ill-starred Caesar. The Betitii had fused with the Anicii, the poetess being 'Aniciorum mater.'[7]

But the nobility of the poetess's sons did not stem only from their mother's side of the family. Three Clodii Celsini are known from

---

[1] ix. 338 Canusium.　　　　[2] xiii. 1002246; ix. 608328.

[3] ix. 1231 Aeclanum. *Bull. Comm.* 1888, p. 397. *PIR*1 S. 242.

[4] Dio 79. 4.　　　　[5] SHA *V. Marci* 3. 8. Dio. 79. 4.

[6] Scaevola, *Dig.* 48. 10. 24. ix. 1234, 1149–50, cf. ix. 190; ix. 6083141; ix. 1570. Betitii Perpetui: x. 7204; vi. 31961 = D. 8843; vi. 1702 = D. 1251. In 366 Tuscia and Umbria were still under a corrector: *CTh.* ix. 1. 8.

[7] *Codex Palatinus*, Reifferscheid, 'Die römischen Bibliotheken', *Sitzungsberichte der kaiserl. Akademie in Wien*, phil.-hist. Kl. 1867, p. 552. See Chastagnol, *Fastes*, 132.

before the fourth century, one of them probably fictitious. He is described in the *Life* of Septimius Severus as a relative of Clodius Albinus, Severus' rival for the throne. On a milestone in Caria, probably of the third century, the name of the proconsul of Asia appears as 'Clodius Cels . . . .', and the space demands that the *cognomen* be 'Celsinus' rather than 'Celsus'.[1] We discover from a Roman epitaph that our third Clodius Celsinus had a wife called Fabia Fuscinilla.[2] We should not hesitate to link the two Clodii Celsini with our poetess's husband on the basis of the combination of the two names, and the rare *cognomen* Fuscinilla is also significant in this connection. Indeed, the only other person known to have held it was the sister of Seius Carus and wife of C. Betitius Pius, and therefore an ancestor of Faltonia Betitia Proba.[3] Adelphius, then, appears to have married a kinswoman, distant, but nevertheless related, a feature not uncommon among Roman nobles.

We can now turn our attention to the Neratii, not forgetting that through the Betitii they were linked with the Anicii. In the public baths constructed by Neratius (or Naeratius) Cerealis, a loyal servant called Cursius Satrius put up two inscriptions, one to Cerealis[4] and the other to Cerealis's son Neratius Scopius,[5] the latter being described as consular of Campania. Another inscription referring to Scopius[6] has the name of the emperor as Valerian instead of Valentinian.[7] Satrius might well be proud to serve Neratius Cerealis and his son Scopius. For, not only were Cerealis and his brother Vulcacius Rufinus among the most prominent men of their generation, and their sister Galla the mother of a Caesar, but the family could also trace its ancestry back to the Republic.

The Neratii came from Saepinum in Samnium, and we have a reference, dating probably from the late Republic, to a certain 'C. Neratius Sexti filius IIvir iure dicundo'.[8] The first known consul in the family was the distinguished governor of Galatia and

---

[1] SHA *V. Sev.* 11. 3. *V. Clod. Alb.* 4. 1; 13. 5. *BCH.* 14, 615 Iassus, Caria.
[2] vi. 31711. [3] *Bull. Comm.* 1888, p. 397. ix. 6083 [28].
[4] vi. 1745 = D. 1245. See *Hermes* 1957. [5] vi. 1746 = D. 1246.
[6] ix. 1566 Beveventum, Campania.
[7] See Mommsen's comments on ix. 1566.
[8] *Not. Scav.* 1926, 245.

9

Cappadocia under Vespasian, M. Hirrius Fronto Neratius Pansa, whose career has now been revealed to us in all its glory by Torelli's piecing together of eleven fragments of an inscription found in Saepinum. What should be noted above all else is Pansa's adlection 'inter patricios'.[1]

Next we have L. Neratius Priscus, suffect consul together with M. Annius Verus in 83 or 87 and perhaps again in 98. He was legate of Pannonia, a member of the *consilium* under Trajan and Hadrian,[2] and, if the *Historia Augusta* can be believed, was for a time generally thought to be Trajan's chosen successor.[3] The *consiliarius* had a son whose name was also probably L. Neratius Pr(iscus).[4] and who was probably the father or grandfather of Neratia Rufina Deciana.[5] L. Neratius Marcellus, a brother of the *consiliarius*, is known to have been governor of Britain in 103 and ordinary consul in 129, and also appears to have been a member of the priestly college of the Salii Palatini and to have been adlected 'inter patricios'.[6] He had estates in Ligures Baebiani and is probably to be identified with the Neratius Marcellus mentioned in a long list of noble estate-owners dated 101.[7] It should be noted that Ligures Baebiani is only a short distance away from Saepinum, the place of origin of the Neratii. Another second century member of the family was L. Neratius Proculus, whose successful senatorial career is known from a very well-preserved inscription from Saepinum.[8] Neratia Procilla,[9] wife of Betitius Pietas, is thought by Borghesi to have been his sister. She was the mother of Neratia Betitia Procilla[10] and C. Neratius Proculus Betitius Pius Maximillianus,[11] who in turn was the father of Betitius Pius Maximillianus,[12] all of them being senatorial.[13] Third-century members of the family include the consul Neratius Priscus and his daughter Neratia Marullina,[14] who married C. Fufidius Atticus, also a

[1] xiii. 1675 = D. 4537. *IGR* iii. 125. See M. Torelli: *JRS* 58 (1968) 170–5.
[2] ix. 2454. Dig. 37. 12. 5. SHA *V. Hadr.* 18. 1.
[3] SHA *V. Hadr.* 4. 8.   [4] ix. 2455.   [5] ix. 2458.
[6] *Diplomata* vol. iii. No. xxi, p. 864. ix. 2456 Saepinum.
[7] ix. 1455 col. 2, lines 16, 51, 73; col. 3, 1. 60.
[8] ix. 2457 Saepinum.   [9] ix. 1132.   [10] ix. 1163.
[11] ix. 1121.   [12] ix. 1160–2, 1132.
[13] See Barbieri, *Albo*, Nos. 968, 1489; *PIR*² B 117–19.
[14] ix. 2451–2 = D. 1131–2, ix. 2450 = D. 1130.

consul, and had three children, as we known from Saepinate inscriptions.[1]

The fourth century gives us several Neratii. (N)eratius Ju(nius), who appears in a mutilated inscription, evidently as urban prefect,[2] is probably to be identified with the Junius Flavianus who is listed in the Chronography of 354 as urban prefect in 311–12 and it is probably also to the same person, here called simply Flavianus, that a later inscription refers.[3] A Neratius Constans appears as patron of Saepinum in an inscription probably dating from some time in the fourth century.[4] Another fragmentary inscription, this time from Syracuse, reads: 'NERATIVS PALMATVS VGG/ ETIAM FRONTEM SCAENAE. O'.[5] The letters at the end of the first line have been emended to read 'v. (c). (c)', and going on to spell either 'corr(ector)' or 'cons(ularis)'. Our Palmatus may have been the same person as, or was related to, the urban prefect of 412 known to us only by his *cognomen*.[6] The only other Palmatus known to the author is a Iunius Palmatus who appears in the unreliable *Historia Augusta* as a military leader under Alexander Severus,[7] and who, whether historical or fictitious, serves to corroborate the link between Neratius Palmatus and Neratius Junius Flavianus, and also links both men with the earlier L. Neratius Junius Macer of Saepinum,[8] and with L. Junius Aurelius Neratius Gallus Fulvius Macer, who appears as a *clarissimus iuvenis* and military tribune in a Roman inscription set up to him by Fulvia Prisca c.f. evidently his mother, who was presumably responsible for introducing the name Priscus into the family of the Neratii.

The best-known members of the family in the fourth century are the mid-century praetorian prefect Vulcacius Rufinus, his sister Galla and his brother Neratius Cerealis, a leading member of the

---

[1] ix. 2451–3.
[2] vi. 37128. There has been much discussion and speculation about this inscription, Chastagnol (*Fastes*, 270–1) suggesting that Neratius be identified with Neratius Palmatus, urban prefect in 412, and the *PLRE* (s.v.) identifying him rather with Junius Flavianus, urban prefect in 311–12. This latter identification is the more likely if vi. 1718 is attributed to the PUR of 311–12 rather than to Nicomachus Flavianus. See P-W iv. 1824 (s.v. Curia); cf. *Röm. Mitt.* 1893, 281.
[3] vi. 1718 = D. 5522.   [4] ix. 2447.
[5] x. 7124 Syracusae.   [6] *CTh*. xiv. 2. 4.
[7] SHA *V. Alex*. 58. 1.   [8] ix. 2513; vi. 1433.

imperial *comitatus*, as we learn from Sozomen, who describes Cerealis together with three other senators sent by Constantius to hear the disputation of Photius and Basil of Ancyra as: οἳ ἐπιστήμῃ λόγων καὶ ἀξιώματι τότε πρωτεύειν ἐν τοῖς βασιλείοις ἐδόκουν.[1] To round off his career Cerealis was urban prefect (352–3) and ordinary consul (in 358). He is described by St. Jerome as 'clarus inter consules'.[2] Galla married Julius Constantius, brother of Constantine I, and was the mother of the Caesar Gallus.

Gallus was an old family *cognomen*, occurring as it does among the names of the young military tribune mentioned above. But, unlike his brother and sister, the great mid-century prefect is not known to have borne any of the *nomina* or *cognomina* attached to the Neratii in their long history, Vulcacius Rufinus being the only name by which he is recorded, and it is possible therefore that he was not born into the Neratii but adopted by them—unless, though a Neratius by birth, he preferred to be known by a *nomen* and *cognomen* from his mother's family which he selected from a wide array of given names. But, whether by birth or adoption, Rufinus was certainly a full member of the family, and his relationship to Galla is regarded by Ammianus as of the same degree as that of Cerealis to Galla, who is described as 'soror Rufini et Cerealis'.[3]

The family of Justus, consular of Picenum, appears to have been related to the Neratii. Justus' daughter Justina was the wife of Magnentius, and it is no doubt as a result of his support for the 'tyrant' that Justus was executed by Constantius II.[4] Justina herself, however, survived to marry the Emperor Valentinian, and was the mother of Valentinian II and of Galla, wife of Theodosius I.[5] Justus also had two sons called Constantianus and Cerealis, each of whom was at one time *tribunus stabuli*.[6] The names Cerealis and Galla in Justus' family are the pointers to their connection with Neratius Cerealis, Vulcacius Rufinus, and Galla.

Our fourth-century Neratii could look back upon an impressive array of noble ancestors and relatives. Though all the Neratii

---

[1] Soz. iv. 6. 15.
[2] Jer. *Ep.* 127. 2.
[3] Amm. xiv. 11. 27.
[4] Zos. iv. 19. 1; iv. 43. 1.
[5] Socr. iv. 3. 11; Joh. Ant. *Frag.* 187 = *FHG* iv. 609. Socr. iv. 31. 17.
[6] Amm. xxviii. 2. 10; xxx. 10. 4–5; xxx. 5. 19.

mentioned above were related one to another, they are not to be regarded as forming a single direct line of descent but rather a series of waves emerging from the ancestral home, Saepinum, into Roman public life.

It was evidently through the marriage of a daughter of C. Asinius Nicomachus Julianus to Sex. Cocceius Anicius Faustus Paulinus in the mid-third century, as we have seen,[1] that the *cognomen* Nicomachus entered the family of the Anicii. The name, which was decidedly rare, is probably a sign of the connection of the great pagan praetorian prefect of the late fourth century, Virius Nicomachus Flavianus, with these earlier Nicomachi and therefore indirectly with the Anicii. We know from innumerable letters of Symmachus that his daughter was married to Nicomachus Flavianus junior, Eugenius' urban prefect, yet nowhere does Symmachus give us his daughter's name.[2] But this marriage was not the only connection of the Symmachi with the Anicii.

The urban prefect of 418–20, Aurelius Anicius Symmachus, couples his Anicius with the *nomen* and *cognomen* of the orator's family, and it is clear therefore that there was a direct connection between the two families, perhaps as a result of the marriage of the orator's brother, Celsinus Titianus, since it was common for children to be named after an uncle.[3] Titianus himself evidently got his second name from his mother, who was probably a daughter or close relative of Fabius Titianus, praetorian prefect under Constans.[4]

With Fabius Titianus we enter a new complex of noble families, that of the Fabii-Scipiones-Gracchi-Maecii-Memmii, with whom the Symmachi, it is interesting to note, were doubly connected, because the orator's wife, Rusticiana, was the daughter of Memmius Vitrasius Orfitus, urban prefect in 353–5 and 357–9.[5]

Though Fabius Titianus himself was a staunch pagan, one of the

---

[1] See pages 109–10, above.

[2] vi. 1782–3 = D. 2947–8. Symm. *Epp.* vi. passim.

[3] Titianus was a member of one of the priestly colleges and vicar of Africa in 380. Symm. *Ep.* iii. 19; *CTh.* xiv. 3. 17. See Seeck, *Symm.*, cvi–cvii. Schuurmans, No. 733.

[4] vi. 1717 = D. 1227. See Chastagnol, *Fastes*, 107–11; Ensslin P-W 2. R. vi. 1533, s.v. Titianus 5; *PLRE*, s.v.

[5] See Stemma III.

quindecimviri sacris faciundis, the college of consulars and ex-praetors charged with the care of the Sibylline books,[1] some of his relatives belonged to Jerome's circle. The Fabii were represented in this circle particularly by Fabiola, whose first act of piety was repenting of remarrying while her first husband was still alive.[2] On her death Jerome penned a long epitaph praising her continence, her fasting, and her piety, and, in particular, her founding of a hospital for the poor.[3] The epitaph is addressed to one Oceanus, presumably Fabiola's son or, at any rate, a relative. Towards the end of the letter we read: 'Inter laudes feminae (viz. Fabiolae) subito mihi Pammachius meus exoritur. Paulina dormit, ut ipse vigilet; praecedit maritum, ut Christo famulum derelinquat. Hic heres uxoris et hereditatis alii possessores. Certabant vir et femina, quis in portu Abrahae tabernaculum figeret, et haec erat inter utrumque contentio, quis humanitate superaret.'[4] Pammachius, an old friend of Jerome's, had been active in public affairs before his conversion to Christianity. 'Antequam Christo tota mente serviret, notus erat in senatu.'[5] He had proconsular rank, but whether he had actually been a proconsul or whether his title was honorary is not known. Jerome leaves us in no doubt about Pammachius's nobility: 'et patris et coniugis nobilitate patricius';[6] 'quod patricii generis primus inter primos monachus esse coepisti'.[7] The term 'patricius' is used of his friend by Jerome in a general sense to indicate nobility rather than to refer to the new fourth century title.

Pammachius is also described as 'consulum pronepos et Furiani germinis decus'.[8] This means that Pammachius was related to Furia, another of Jerome's friends, and it is no surprise to find that Furia's mother was called Titiana.[9] Could Titiana, who was dead by 394/5, have been Fabius Titianus's daughter? If not, she was of course closely related to him. Some further pieces can now be added to the jigsaw puzzle. One is that Pammachius was related ('cognatus') to the family of his wife, Paulina, a daughter of St.

---

[1] *AE* 1893, 124 = D. 8983 Cumae.
[2] Jer. *Ep.* 77. 1–2.
[3] Jer. *Ep.* 77. 6.
[4] Jer. *Ep.* 77. 10.
[5] Jer. *Ep.* 66. 7.
[6] Jer. *Ep.* 66. 4, 13.
[7] Jer. *Ep.* 66. 13.
[8] Jer. *Ep.* 66. 6.
[9] Jer. *Ep.* 54. 1 and 6.

Paula and Julius Toxotius. Another is that Pammachius was a cousin of Jerome's favourite correspondent, Marcella,[1] and was also related to Melania and Pinianus and therefore also to the Ceionii.[2]

On the death of his wife Pammachius sold all his property, donated the proceeds to charity and became a monk.[3] It is to his charitable works in his later life that Jerome is referring in the extract quoted above. The 'femina' mentioned by Jerome with whom Pammachius vied in the doing of good works is Fabiola. That Pammachius and Fabiola were in some way related seems probable from this passage. But a surer sign of connection is the fact that Jerome wrote at least two letters addressed to Oceanus and Pammachius together. Fabius Titianus, then, was part of a very intricate and elaborate filigree of family connections.

We may rightly be sceptical about Jerome's attribution to the fourth century Fabii of descent from the line of the Cunctator of old, yet by fourth century standards the family was ancient, and through collaterals can be traced back to the first century.[4] Perhaps it is worth looking at an inscription which embraces three members of the family:

. . . .
TITIANO C.F. C. MAESI
TITIANI ET FONTEIAE
FRONTINAE CONSV
LARIVM FILIO
PATRICIO OB HONO
REM TOGAE VIRILIS
CLODIVS RVFVS EQVES ROMANVS
AMICO SVO INCOMPARABILI.[5]

It is interesting to note that the young Titianus is called 'patricius', though it is impossible to say whether his father was the first to be offered this title or whether it went back to an earlier award. His

---

[1] Jer. *Ep.* 48. 4.   [2] Pall. *Hist. Laus.* lxii.

[3] Paul Nol. *Ep.* 13. Jer. *Epp.* 66, 77, 118.

[4] Jer. *Ep.* 77. 2. *Eph. Ep.* iv., p. 154, where Mommsen gives a stemma.

[5] x. 7346 = D. 1083 Thermae, Sicilia. Notice the unusual abbreviation c(larissimo) f(ilio).

mother also came from a noble family, and must have been related to the legate of Numidia of 160 and suffect consul of 162 or 163, named, in the style of the second century, D. Fonteius Frontinianus L. Stertinius Rufinus.[1] The second part of his name, presumably from his mother's side of the family, links him with M. Stertinius Rufus, evidently the first of his line to be a senator, recorded as a member of the *consilium* of the proconsul of Sardinia under Otho in 69.[2] The link with the Aquilii is given us by another inscription:

> et Q. FABI CAESILI TITIANI
> AVO Q. AQVILIO NIGRO
> PRO COS
> SIciliAE.[3]

Q. Aquilius Niger, the proconsul of Sicily, must have been related to his namesake, consul in 117, and also to Cn. Cornelius Aquilius Niger, proconsul of Narbonensis probably at about the same time.[4]

The name Maesius Titianus, borne by the husband of Fonteia Frontina, links Fabius Titianus's family with that of another mid-fourth century noble praetorian prefect, Q. Flavius Maesius Egnatius Lollianus Mavortius. Like Titianus, Lollianus combined an eminent career in the imperial administration with service to the ancient gods of the Romans. In addition to his appointments to three urban *curatelae*, a consular governorship of Campania, a comitial post 'intra palatium', and the positions of *comes Orientis*, proconsul of Africa, urban prefect and praetorian prefect, Lollianus was 'augur publicus populi Romani Quiritium', and the dedication to him of Firmicus Maternus's astrological writings is another sign of his religious attachment to paganism.[5]

We have a record of two of Lollianus's sons. One, Placidus Severus, was later to become vicar of Rome and was married to a certain Antonia Marcianilla c.f., evidently a relative of the noble Constantinian praetorian prefect, Antonius Marcellinus.[6] The other son was called Q. Flavius Maesius Cornelius Egnatius

---

[1] viii. 2738 = D. 1082 Lambaesis. viii. 2740.
[2] x. 7852, vv. 24–5.   [3] x. 7287 Panhormus.
[4] *PIR*[2] s.v. Cn. Cornelius Aquilius Niger.
[5] x. 4752 = D. 1223 Suessa. Firm. Mat. *Math.* 8. 15.
[6] vi. 37112 = vi. 1723 = vi. 1757.

Severus Lollianus Mavortius junior.[1] By comparing the names of the sons with that of their father it is possible to work out their mother's family's names. The *nomen* Cornelius and the *cognomina* Placidus and Severus are the only ones borne by the sons which are not found among their father's range of names. Severus indeed is a name held by both brothers. Their mother's name therefore probably was Cornelia Placida Severa, a name which may link her with the Memmius-Furius-Gracchus-Scipio family complex. The names Cornelius and Placidus certainly occur in that network.

There are more certain noble ties, however, on the side of Lollianus Mavortius himself. He has a direct ancestor in L. Egnatius Victor Lollianus, a man with a very notable career in the mid-third century. Beginning as legate of Galatia under Elagabalus in 218, he became legate of Pontus and Bithynia, corrector of Achaea, and thrice proconsul of Asia. He ended his career as urban prefect in 254.[2] He was probably the son of L. Egnatius Victor, legate of Pannonia Superior in 207.[3] Both men were undoubtedly related to Egnatius Marinianus, probably legate of Arabia,[4] who in turn was related to the wife of the Emperor Valerian referred to on coins as 'diva Mariniana'.[5] That Mariniana was an Egnatia is revealed by the full name of her son the Emperor Gallienus: P. Licinius Egnatius Gallienus.

The Maesii were also an old family. Its fourth-century representatives were undoubtedly descended from C. Maesius Titianus, 'consularis', of unknown date, whom we have already encountered. The Maesii Titiani appear to have married into a family of Fabii in the late second century. Hence the names of Maesius Fabius Titianus c.p. and his sister Maesia Fabia Titiana c.f. who dedicated two inscriptions to Septimius Severus in the last years of the second century.[6] Maesius Fabius Titianus, a young boy at the end of the second century, may have been the father of C. Maesius Aquillius Fabius Titianus 'c.v. cos.', perhaps the same man as the Titianus who was ordinary consul in 245. The alliance here was of course

[1] x. 1697 = D. 1226 Puteoli.
[2] *IG* iii. 632; vii. 2510–11. vi. 1405. *PIR²* E. 36. See Chastagnol, *Fastes*, 114.
[3] iii. 11082.   [4] *IGR* iii. 1359 Gerasae.
[5] Mattingly-Sydenham, *The Roman Imperial Coinage*, v. 1. 64 f., pl. 1, 11–13.
[6] x. 7343 (197); x. 7276 (198).

with the Aquillii (or Aquilii). Q. Aquilius Niger, a descendant of his namesake, consul in 117, is known to have been proconsul of Sicily and grandfather of Q. Fabius Caesilius Titianus.[1] Another member of the family is Maesia Titiana c.f. of unknown date, whose name appears in an inscription together with that of Pomponia Fidicula c.f., to whom she was presumably related.[2]

That the senatorial rank of our fourth century Fabii goes back to the second century at least is, as we have seen, undeniable. By fourth-century standards that made them an old noble family, and in addition they were, as has been noted, patricians. It is easy to see how, though probably unconnected with the Republican Fabii of old, the fourth century family was thought of as descending from the great Cunctator, and it is not therefore very surprising to find a Fabius Maximus in the fourth century, the man in question being the first governor of Samnium as a separate province in the 350s.[3]

Fabia Aconia Paulina, wife of the great pagan praetorian prefect Vettius Agorius Praetextatus[4] and daughter of another noble praetorian prefect, Aco Catullinus Philomathius, was evidently connected with the Fabii on her mother's side.[5] Her *cognomen* recurs in the name of the late fifth-century urban prefect, Fabius Felix Pasiphilus Paulinus, a descendant of the late fourth century acting urban and praetorian prefect, Fabius Pasiphilus.[6] Paulina was also the name of one of the daughters of St. Paula and Julius Toxotius. The name Paulus, more often spelt Paullus and used as a *praenomen* rather than as a *cognomen*, was of course associated with the old Republican line of Fabii and that is no doubt the reason for its popularity among our latter-day Fabii. Can we detect a Fabian strain amid the blood-cells of the very aristocratic veins of St. Paula? Her *cognomen*, together with that of her daughter Paulina and a granddaughter also called Paula, is our only clue. So it must remain merely a possibility.

Paula's connection with the Scipiones and Gracchi and with the Maecii/Memmii is, however, far from hypothetical. She is

[1] x. 7287, Panhormus.
[2] vi. 1166–7, 1653–4, 1717.
[3] ix. 2212, 2338, 2447, 2956 = D. 5341.
[4] vi. 1779 = D. 1259.
[5] vi. 1780 = D. 1260.
[6] x. 1692 = D. 792 Puteoli. x. 1694.

described by Jerome as 'Gracchorum stirps, suboles Scipionum', and also as 'Maeciae Papiriae, matris Africani, vera et germana progenies'.[1] Notice again the Republican connotations. The Maecia which has been added to the name of the mother of the younger Africanus probably reflects fourth-century attitudes rather than accurate genealogy. The fourth-century Maecii were connected with the Scipiones and Gracchi, and it is not difficult to see how this connection was projected backwards into the Republic.

But what of the descent of the late imperial Scipiones from their republican namesakes? Can we accept this pedigree? There is a gap, it is true, of almost a century in surviving records of the family. But this gap is in the third century, when records in general are scantier than for most other periods. Moreover, when a Scipio returns to our notice at the end of the third century, in the shape of L. Cornelius Scipio Orfitus, *vir clarissimus* and an augur, we can be in little doubt that this is the same family that we last saw a century before.[2] Orfitus's position as an augur is in itself sufficient indication of his belonging to a prominent family. In addition, the name Orfitus links him with the line of Cornelii Scipiones Salvidieni Orfiti, who can be traced from the end of the second century backwards to the very early Principate, when they were adopted by the Cornelii Scipiones. Pliny the Elder has preserved for us the reaction of mingled shock and sadness which overcame the scion of another noble line when the upstart Salvidieni or Salvittones assumed the heritage of the Scipiones: '(Messala senex) cum Scipionis Pomponiani transisset atrium vidissetque adoptione testamentaria Salvittones—hoc enim fuerat cognomen—Africanorum dedecori inrepentes Scipionum nomini'.[3] Beyond this the family reaches back to the great Republican nobles who gave their names to history, back to the proud warriors whose deeds were

---

[1] Jer. *Ep.* 108. 1.

[2] vi. 505 cf. 30781 = D. 4143. vi. 402, cf. 30755, p. 3756 = D. 4396. vi. 506 cf. 30782 = D. 4144.

[3] Plin. *N.H.* Teub. xxxv (2) 8. Salvidienus was in fact not a *cognomen* but a *nomen*. Schulze, *Lateinische Eigennamen*, 104 ff. Salvidienus being a rare name, it is possible that the Salvidieni Orfiti were related to Salvidienus Rufus, executed as consul designate in 40 B.C. Dio 48, 33. 1; Vell. ii. 76. 4; Suet. *Div. Aug.* 66. 2; Appian B.C. 5. 66. 278 ff.

celebrated in rude Saturnian verse, back to the victor over the Veientines resplendent in a cuirass stripped from a king.[1]

In the late second century we encounter two members of the family among the Palatine Salian priests, a college, it should be remembered, confined to men of patrician birth. One belonged to the main line of descent from the original Salvidienus and was called Cornelius Scipio Orfitus. The name of the other, Calpurnius Scipio Orfitus, shows a link with the ordinary consuls of 172 and 175, Ser. Calpurnius Scipio Orfitus and L. Calpurnius Piso.[2] By the fourth century, however, there is no trace of the Calpurnii Pisones in the records. But in that century the Scipiones are still connected with a good number of noble lines.

Memmius Vitrasius Orfitus Honorius, whose career was as impressive as his lineage, combines in his name, as in his blood, the Scipiones with the Memmii. As well as holding all three republican magistracies and then going on to be consular of Sicily, proconsul of Africa and urban prefect (which post he held twice, 353–5 and 357–9), he was an imperial *comes*, first of the second rank —when he was placed in charge of unspecified military expeditions —and then of the first rank 'intra palatium'. In addition to his civil career, he was a priest of Vesta, of the Sun and one of the *quindecimviri sacris faciundis*, and he also set up a shrine in honour of Apollo.[3]

In view of all this it is perhaps more than slightly surprising to find Chastagnol dismissing Orfitus's nobility: 'On admettra qu'il était de naissance sénatoriale; toutefois, il n'appartenait pas à une famille de l'aristocratie: aucun membre de sa *gens* n'est attesté avant lui, et il présente tous les traits d'un *homo novus*. Il semble bien avoir été lui-même l'artisan de sa propre *nobilitas*.'[4] In fact, however, there can be no doubt that Orfitus was noble. He is described as 'nobilitate et actibus praecipuo',[5] 'genere nobili' and 'nobilitate actibusque ad exemplum praecipuo'.[6] Ammianus's description of him, which was alluded to above, accepts his nobility in contrasting his cultural attainments with his birth.[7]

[1] Liv. iv. 20. *Oxford Book of Latin Verse*, p. 3, No. 5.
[2] xiv. 3643; vi. 30865; *IGR* iv. 521.   [3] vi. 1739, 1740–2.
[4] Chastagnol, *Fastes*, 140.   [5] vi. 1739–40.
[6] vi. 1741 = D. 1243; vi. 1742.   [7] Amm. xiv. 6. 1. See above, p. 89.

His *cognomen* links Orfitus with the Scipiones. Vitrasius is a rare name, only one other holder of it being known, namely the probably late third-century *promagister* of the Salian priests, Vitrasius Praetextatus. But these were not Orfitus's only noble connections. For the Memmii were themselves a noble family and were related to other aristocratic houses.

The mid-fourth century praetorian prefect, M. Maecius Memmius Furius Baburius Caecilianus Placidus, displays in his name the multifarious noble connections of the Memmii. Our polyonymous prefect had a direct ancestor in the suffect consul and augur of unknown date, C. Memmius M. f. Quir. Caecilianus Placidus.[1] The priesthood remained in the family, as was the custom among the Romans and Placidus combines it in his career with the position of *pontifex maior* and a very noteworthy series of civil offices.[2]

The name Furius Maecius Gracchus is recorded in an inscription from Tibur as belonging to a corrector of Picenum and Flaminia.[3] Since the province went consular at some time between 350 and 352, our corrector may have been a different person from the actively anti-pagan urban prefect of 376–7 who is recorded simply as Gracchus. Another member of the same family was the early fifth-century patron of Salernum, Arrius Maecius Gracchus, who is probably to be identified with the Gracchus who received a law dated 397 as consular of Campania and may also have been the same person as the Gracchus who was urban prefect in 415.[4] From the names of our fourth-century Gracchi we can see a link between the Maecii, the Furii, and the Gracchi.

In the popular mind, as we have seen, both the Gracchi and the Maecii were connected with the Scipiones. Now the link between the Scipiones and Gracchi may be thought to be a transference from the Republic, where 'Cornelia, mater Gracchorum' was herself of course a member of the Scipionic house.[5] The truth was probably slightly more complex. The last of the Sempronii Gracchi

---

[1] xi. 5740 Sentinum. Chastagnol, *Fastes*, 128. Cf. Gatti, *Bull. Comm.* 1887 179–80.

[2] x. 1700 = D. 1231 Puteoli.

[3] xiv. 3594 = D. 5717. For his career see page 89, above.

[4] x. 520. *CTh.* xiv. 7. 1; viii. 7. 20. See R. Thomsen: *The Italic Regions*, 203–5.

[5] See Jer. *Ep.* 54. 4.

lived in the early Principate, so our sprinkling of Gracchi in the fourth century seems unlikely to have been descended from the family of the radical tribunes. Yet out latter-day Gracchi were not unrelated to their Republican namesakes. One of the ordinary consuls of A.D. 24 was called Ser. Cornelius Cethegus, a name which has associations both with the Cornelii Scipiones and with the fourth-century Gracchi. Cornelii Cethegi recur at not too wide intervals from the consul of 204 B.C. to our consul of A.D. 24. After that there is a gap of over a century, until 170, when a M. Cornelius Cethegus appears in the *Fasti* as ordinary consul. A decade later another (or the same) Cornelius Cethegus is recorded as a Salius Palatinus, so our Antonine Cethegi were far from being parvenus. But the consul of 170 and his sister, Cornelia Cethegilla, are referred to as the children of M. Gavius Squilla Gallicanus, pre-sumably by adoption. Two men, probably father and son, called M. Gavius Squilla Gallicanus were ordinary consuls in 127 and 150. It was probably the latter, also described as a proconsul, who adopted the Cornelii Cethegi. The Gavii seem to have been already related to the Cornelii Cethegi by the time the adoption took place. We know that the Cethegi were related to the Cornelii Lentuli, as we can see from a name such as Lentulus Cethegus,[1] and the Gavii in turn were related to the Cornelii Scipiones Orfiti, as is indicated by names such as that of M. Gavius Orfitus, ordinary consul in 165. Other links between the Cethegi and the Scipiones are furnished by the Salian priesthood. Retiring together with a Cethegus from the Salii Palatini was Cornelius Scipio (Orfitus), ordinary consul in 213, and in 180 the Cornelius Cethegus men-tioned above as a Salian priest retired from his priesthood.[2] The two references do not apply to the same Cethegus, since the names appearing together with each are different. That they were related can hardly be doubted, and both were undoubtedly also related to the Scipio. The connection between the Cethegi and the Scipiones is well brought out by a bronze disc bearing the name Cethegus Scipio,[3] and by a tile with the inscription 'Cethegi et Scipiones'.[4]

[1] vi. 6072.

[2] vi. 1981; vi. 1979, vv. 13–16.

[3] vi. 31964 = xv. 7147.

[4] ix. 6078[58].

Our late Empire Gracchi evidently had no direct ancestral claim to the *cognomen* Gracchus, but through their Cornelian background they were of course indirectly connected with the Republican Gracchi, which may well explain the revival of the name in a period of such strong aristocratic values as the late Empire was.

It is the *nomen* Furius which provides us with a bridge between the Scipiones-Gracchi-Maecii-Memmii and the great noble house of the Ceionii. First, the connection between the Furii and the Scipionic complex can be seen from names such as Furius Maecius Gracchus, and it should not be forgotten that our polyonymous praetorian prefect has Furius tucked away amid his collection of names. Furia, one of Jerome's devotees, was connected through her mother Titiana with the family of Fabius Titianus, which has already been discussed. Though Furia's father is not named in the sources, he is referred to by Jerome: 'Pater tuus, quem ego honoris causa nomino—non quia consularis et patricius, sed quia Christianus est—inpleat nomen suum et laetetur filiam Christo se genuisse, non saeculo.'[1] A neat pun on the name Laetus, as has been suggested by some scholars. By resorting—as on not a few other occasions—to *praetermissio*, Jerome also gives us a brief glimpse of Laetus's background. Since no Laetus appears among the ordinary consuls of the period, the description 'consularis' must refer to a suffect consulship. The word 'patricius' is probably used here in the looser sense of a noble rather than in the new fourth-century sense referring to a grant of the title by the emperor. It was probably through her father that Furia was connected with the Scipones and Gracchi. 'Cornelia vestra' is the way Jerome refers to the mother of the Gracchi brothers in a letter addressed to Furia.[2] Elsewhere in the same letter Jerome mentions Eustochium and Paula, who are described as 'stirpis vestrae flores'.[3] Now Eustochium was the daughter of Julius Toxotius and St. Paula, who is herself linked by Jerome, as we have seen, with the Scipiones-Gracchi and the Maecii.[4] A further link between this complex and the Furii is to be found in the marriage of Pammachius, 'consulum

---

[1] Jer. *Ep.* 54. 6. 3.   [2] Jer. *Ep.* 54. 4.
[3] Jer. *Ep.* 54. 2.   [4] Jer. *Ep.* 108. 1.

pronepos et Furiani germinis decus', to Paulina, another daughter
of Julius Toxotius and St. Paula.¹ After all this, it should come as
no surprise to us to learn that Laeta, another member of Jerome's
circle, is connected by Jerome with the Gracchi, or, to be more
precise, with the Gracchus who was urban prefect in 376 and who
was responsible for the destruction of a Mithraic shrine.² But Laeta
was not only related to the Scipionic network of families, for her
father, as we know again from Jerome, was the pagan priest
Albinus.³ The only senatorial Albini known to the author in the
fourth century were members of the *gens* Ceionia, and Publilius
Ceionius Caecina Albinus, consular of Numidia under Valentinian,
appears in the pages of Macrobius as a representative of the old
pagan culture and a close friend of Symmachus.⁴ It was probably
this Albinus who was Laeta's father. A further corroboration of the
link between the Furii-Scipiones and the Ceionii is the fact that
a certain Laetus is known from a letter of Ambrose to have had a
brother called Marcellus.⁵ Jerome's favourite female correspondent
—if volume is to be our criterion—was called Marcella, and we
know that her mother's name was Albina.⁶ Pammachius, who, as
we have seen, was connected with the Furii and Fabii through one
parent, was evidently descended from the Ceionii through the
other, since he was a cousin of Marcella. Pammachius' Ceionian
parent and Marcella's mother, Albina, were probably the children
of Ceionius Rufius Albinus, ordinary consul in 335 and urban
prefect between 335 and 337, who in turn was the son of the first
noble praetorian prefect known to history, C. Ceionius Rufius
Volusianus, appointed to his high post by Maxentius and called
upon to perform military as well as civil duties.⁷

The Ceionii owned land in Volaterrae in Etruria and in Africa,
and though we need not take too seriously their vaunted descent
from Volusus, the ancient Etruscan chief of the Rutuli,⁸ the family
nevertheless had a long noble lineage which can be traced back

---

¹ Jer. *Ep*. 66. 6.   ² Jer. *Ep*. 107. 2. See p. 89, above.
³ Jer. *Ep*. 107. 1.   ⁴ Macr. *Sat*. i. 2. 15.
⁵ Amb. *Ep*. 82.   ⁶ Jer. *Ep*. 45. 7; 127. 2.
⁷ Aurel Vict. *Caes*. 40. 18; Zos. ii. 14. 2. See also vi. 1708 = 31906 = D. 1222.
See p. 49, above.
⁸ Rut. Namat. i. 168.

through the Nummii to patricians of the late Republic. Gaia Nummia Ceionia Rufia Albina, 'c(larissima) p(uella), sac(erdos) pub(lica)' of Beneventum, combines the names of the Nummii and the Ceionii.[1] Among the third-century members of the family were M. Nummius Ceionius Annius Albinus v.c.,[2] urban praetor; Numnius (sic) Albinus, Prefect of Rome in 256 and 261–3;[3] M. Nummius Senecio Albinus, ordinary consul in 227; and M. Nummius Umbrius Primus Senecio Albinus, ordinary consul in 206, who in turn was undoubtedly related to three men called Umbrius Primus. The latest of these was suffect consul in 289;[4] the next was proconsul at the time of Papinian,[5] and the earliest a landowner in the time of Trajan.[6] There was also some connection between our Nummii and the Nummii Tusci, one of whom was ordinary consul in 295 and Prefect of Rome 302–3, another ordinary consul in 258, and M. Num(mius) Attidi(us) Tuscus[7] who may be the same as the Attidius (T)uscus described as a *legatus pro praetore* in a second-century inscription.[8] The connection between our Nummii and the Nummii Tusci comes out from a pottery fragment from Carthage of either the third or fourth century, reading 'Numm. Tus/ci et Albin/i cc.vv.'[9] The best known member of this branch of the Ceionian family in the fourth century was M. Nummius Albinus Triturrius, who is known to have held all three of the republican magistracies, was ordinary consul in 345 and *comes domesticus ordinis primi*, a most important appointment.[10]

A prominent fourth-century noble family probably connected with the Ceionii was the Turcii, who have already been discussed.[11]

---

[1] *AE* 1965.   [2] vi. 3146.   [3] *Chron.* 354.
[4] M. Nummius Umbrius Primus Senecio Albinus: In addition to being ordinary consul in 206 he was legate of Hispania Citerior and a member of the college of Salii Palatini and Pontifices. v. 4347, Brixia; ii. 3741, Valentia, Hisp. Tarr.; vi. 1980[14]; vi. 1982[6]. Umbrius Primus, suffect consul 289: x. 3698, 4631.
[5] *Dig.* 33, 7, 12, 40.   [6] ix. 1455, vol. 7, 78.
[7] vi. 32026.   [8] D. 8833 Ephesus.
[9] *BCTH* 1926, p. xlii; *BCTH* 1928/9, p. 284.
[10] vi. 1748. Chastagnol, *Revue Historique* 219 (1958) 234. Chastagnol, *Fastes*, 95. See also Groag, P-W xvii. 1411–12, s.v. Nummius 11. There is no need to see any incompatibility between the family's African and Etrurian connections, as does Chastagnol, *Fastes*, 52. See von Wotawa, P-W iv. 68–9 for African evidence. In addition to the land at Volaterrae, Seeck considers the name Ceionius to have an Etrurian ring. *Jahrbuch für Philologie*, 1890, 633.
[11] See above, page 55.

The link between the two families is to be found in the name of a Constantinian patron of Cillium in Africa, Ceionius Apronianus v.c.[1] The area was one where Ceionian influence was strong, as will be seen in Chapter VII. Though the Turcii did not have exclusive rights to the *cognomen* Apronianus, they are the only senatorial family in the fourth century known to have used it—and they used it repeatedly, alternating with the *cognomen* Secundus. In all, excluding our patron of Cillium, three Turcii Aproniani and three Turcii Secundi are recorded in the fourth century.

Another old senatorial line connected with the Ceionii was that of the Munatii Planci of the early Principate, as we know from a most unusual inscription found in Rome:

MVNATIO
PLANCO
PAVLINO
V.C. PRAESIDI
PANN. PER ANN. XVII
CREPEREIVS AMANTIVS
ET CAeiONIA MARINA C.F. EIVS
ABABO
SVO[2]

The Plancus mentioned in the inscription as governor of Pannonia was probably not the same person as the consul of 13 A.D. who appears in the pages of Tacitus's *Annals*, since neither in Tacitus nor in the *fasti* does the *cognomen* Paulinus appear.[3] In any event Paulinus, whose long tenure of the governorship has made Morris give him a Tiberian date, was obviously closely related to the consul of 13 and his namesake grandfather, the consul of 42 B.C. Munatia Plancina, wife of the Cn. Calpurnius Piso accused of the murder of Germanicus, was no doubt another member of the same family.[4] There is no proof that Amantius and Marina were telling the truth in claiming descent from Plancus Paulinus. And, in any case, which

[1] viii. 210, cf. p. 1179 = D. 5570.
[2] vi. 1743. See J. Morris, 'Munatius Plancus Paulinus', *Bonner Jahrbücher* 1965, 88–96.
[3] Tac. *Ann.* i. 39. 4 ff.   [4] Tac. *Ann.* ii. 43. 4.

of them was claiming this ancestry?[1] It is a very strange claim for either the Crepereii or the Ceionii, both of which were old-established noble families by fourth-century standards, for, after all, Munatius Plancus (with or without the additional Paulinus) was hardly a name to conjure with in the fourth century. A strange claim—or perhaps a true one.

Let us take a quick glance at the Crepereii, since they were connected with the Ceionii by marriage. The most distinguished member of the family was probably L. Crepereius Madalianus whose career culminated in the vicariate of Italy in 341.[2] Though the earliest known senatorial Crepereius, a certain 'L. Crepereius Rogatus qui et Secundinus c.v. pontifex Dei Solis, septemvir et insignis Lupercus', probably dates only from the third century, his three pagan priesthoods make it quite plain that he was no upstart.[3] In another inscription a 'Crepereius Ro....' appears together with well-known nobles of the late third and early fourth centuries.[4] The cognomen here should probably also read 'Rogatus'. It is possible that this Crepereius is to be identified with Secundinus and that the inscription, in which six names can now be read, originally contained a seventh as well, being a list of septemviri epulonum. The cognomen Rogatus is extremely uncommon, yet we come across it in the case of the husband of Blesilla and father of St. Paula.[5] If he was also a Crepereius, an extra strand of interconnection is added to our aristocratic network, namely that between the Crepereii and the Scipiones-Gracchi-Maecii-Memmii.

In an article on the Rufii Festi John Matthews rather tentatively suggests a possible connection between that family and the Ceionii.[6] His suggestion is based upon a letter from Libanius to a certain Postumianus, the relevant passage reading: τοῦδε μὲν οὖν σὺ κύριος, παρὰ δὲ τῶν θεῶν αἰτῶ δοῦναί μοι τὴν σὴν ἰδεῖν κεφαλὴν ἐν ἀρχομένου τάξει, καθάπερ πάλαι τὸν σὸν θεῖον ἔγνων, ᾧ παῖδα τρέφεις ὁμώνυμον ἐν τῇ πόλει τῆς θεοῦ τῆς δι' ἀγῶνος αὐτὴν λαβούσης. Postumianus was

---

[1] Dr. Morris presents us with an elaborate stemma linking Munatius Plancus Paulinus with the Ceionii. Loc. cit.

[2] xiv. 4449; viii. 5348 = D. 1228; vi. 1151 = D. 707.

[3] vi. 1397.   [4] Not. Scav. 1917, 22.

[5] Jer. Ep. 108. 3.

[6] J. Matthews, 'Continuity in a Roman Family; the Rufii Festi of Volsinii', Historia 16 (1967) 496.

evidently a Westerner, since, as we learn elsewhere in the same letter, he knew no Greek, though his uncle—whose name, which is not mentioned, was the same as Postumianus's son's—was in office in Athens. The uncle was clearly not Theodosius' praetorian prefect Postumianus, with whom Matthews identifies him, being disqualified both by name and office.[1] What we are looking for is a proconsul of Achaea who was not called Postumianus but who was related to people of that name—and we have someone who fits the bill exactly: Postumius Rufius Festus Avienius, poet, proconsul of Achaea and proconsul of Africa in the mid-fourth century.[2] The *nomen* Postumius is one pointer to the relationship between Festus and the Postumiani. Another is in the shape of a neat inscription on a bronze tablet from Rome: 'Postumiani v.c./ ex praef. praet./ et Festi v.c./ trib. et notari/ de praet. soteri/ n.n.'[3] The last two lines have caused some puzzlement, but the inscription does seem to indicate that the two men mentioned shared property and were presumably therefore related.[4] Nothing more is known of Festus, the tribune and *notarius*, but the fact that a *clarissimus*, and in this case a noble into the bargain, is found in this post is a pointer to a date late in the fourth century at the earliest. Postumianus is rather better known, being praetorian prefect of the East under Theodosius in 383.[5] Yet another clue, though dating from the following century, is the name of the consul of 448, Rufius Praetextatus Postumianus.

A passage in the notoriously unreliable *Augustan History* may serve as evidence of the relationship between the Postumiani and Ceionii. We read that Clodius Albinus, Septimius Severus' rival, 'originem a Romanis familiis traxit: Postumiorum scilicet et Albinorum et Ceioniorum',[6] and he is assigned suitably named relatives, his father's name being given as Ceionius Postumus[7] and that of a relative as Ceionius Postumianus.[8] For the light that

[1] Matthews, loc. cit. The passage quoted is from Lib. *Ep.* 1036. 8.
[2] *IG* iii. 635. Unpublished inscription from Bulla Regia kindly lent by Dr. R. Duncan-Jones. Poem: vi. 537 = D. 2944.
[3] vi. 32035 = xv. 7163.   [4] See *CIL* ad loc. and Matthews, op. cit., 495.
[5] Greg. Naz. *Ep.* 173. B*Th.* ix. 42. 10, xii. 1. 98, xvi. 7. 2, vi. 22. 7, vii. 2. 1, xii. 1. 102, xvi. 5. 11, xii, 6. 17, xii. 1. 104, xvi. 5. 12.
[6] SHA *V. Clod. Alb.* 4. 1, cf. 13. 5.
[7] Ibid. 4. 3.   [8] Ibid. 6. 1.

these statements throw on the family of Clodius Albinus, their purported subject, they might as well be ignored. But as a reflection of fourth-century family connections contemporary with the author they may not be so unreliable—and in the fourth century the *cognomen* Albinus was certainly very closely associated with the Ceionii. That the Postumiani were also connected with the Ceionii is not therefore very difficult to believe, particularly in the light of our other evidence.[1]

Going back to Libanius's letter to Postumianus we find another interesting fact: his correspondent's grandfather was consul in the year of Libanius' birth. Now the consuls of 314, the year in question, were C. Ceionius Rufius Volusianus and Petronius Annianus.[2] But which of these eminent men was Postumianus' grandfather? The name Rufius, which recurs among both the Festi and Ceionii but is otherwise rare in this period, makes Volusianus, Maxentius's praetorian prefect, the obvious choice. Some lines in Rufius Festus' *Ora Maritima*, however, point to a link with the other consul of 314. Dedicating the poem to a certain Probus, probably Valentinian's praetorian prefect Petronius Probus, Festus writes: 'his addo et illud, liberum temet loco/mihi esse(*t*) amor(*e*) sanguinisque vinculo/... quin et parent(*is*) credidi officium fore,/desideratum si tibi locupletius/profusiusque Musa promeret mea.'[3] Petronius Probus was probably a grandson, and certainly a close relative, of Petronius Annianus, one of Constantine's noble praetorian prefects.[4]

It should not be forgotten that, as has been shown above, the Petronii were related to the Ceionii as well as to the Anicii. So though Postumianus's grandfather was probably Ceionius Volusianus, his colleague in the consulship was also related to the Rufii Festi-Postumiani.

In a verse inscription found in Rome Rufius Festus claims descent from Musonius Rufus, the equestrian Stoic philosopher of the

[1] See Syme, *Ammianus and the Historia Augusta*, 154 ff.
[2] Lib. *Ep.* 1036. 8. P. Petit, *Libanius et la vie municipale d'Antioche*, 17. Matthews, op. cit., 496.
[3] Rufius Festus, *Ora Maritima*, ed. Schulten (Fontes Hispaniae Antiquae) Barcelona and Berlin, 1922.
[4] iii. 13734 = D. 8938. *AE* 1938, 85.

first century who taught Epictetus,[1] and there is no reason to disbelieve him, for the philosopher is described by Tacitus as 'Tusci generis' and we know from Suidas that he was a Volsinian like Rufius Festus himself.[2] The first senatorial members of the family appear to have been C. Rufius Festus Laelius Firmus and his sister Rufia Procula, who probably date from the second century.[3] In addition to inscriptions from Volsinii there are inscriptions from the nearby town of Viterbo celebrating members of the family,[4] and soon the family makes its appearance in Rome.[5]

The long verse inscription also gives us the names of Festus' wife and son: Placida and Placidus. The name was a rare one in this period, and where it occurs it tends to belong to a noble. We meet another (or the same?) Placida as the daughter of a certain Placidianus, 'clarissimae memoriae vir', in Symmachus' *Relationes*.[6] Placidus also occurs among the many names of Constans' praetorian prefect M. Maecius Memmius Furius Baburius Caecilianus Placidus. Finally, the son of the praetorian prefect of 354–7, Q. Fl. Maesius Egnatius Lollianus Mavortius, was called Placidus Severus.[7] One of Symmachus' *Relationes*, dated by Seeck to 384–5, deals with the legacy of a certain Postumianus, 'clarissimae memoriae vir', whose heirs were called Lolliana, Cattianilla and Severilla, the first of whom appears to have been a daughter of the dead man and the other two granddaughters. All three women are called by Symmachus 'clarissimae feminae'.[8] The names Lolliana and Severilla take us back to Mavortius and his son, the father having the name Lollianus and the son Severus as well as Placidus. Is it pure coincidence that this Placidus Severus should share his second *cognomen* (or a variant of it) with the granddaughter of a Postumianus and his other *cognomen* with the wife and son of a Rufius Festus, a close relative of Postumiani? Is it pure coincidence that a Lolliana, daughter of a Postumianus and therefore closely connected with the Ceionii, should share her name with Caecinia

---

[1] Tac. *Ann.* xiv. 59; xv. 71; *Hist.* iii. 81. 1; iv. 10. 1. Plin. *Ep.* iii. 11. 5.
[2] Tac. *Ann.* xiv. 59; Suid. s.v. Matthews, however, is sceptical. Op. cit., 491.
[3] xi. 2698 Volsinii. See Pflaum, *Carrières* i, 566 No. 215.
[4] xi. 7272 Volsinii. xi. 2997 Viterbo.
[5] xv. 7525. vi. 2153: 'Rufius Festus v.c. xv. s.f.'   [6] Symm. *Rel.* 19.
[7] vi. 1723 + vi. 1957 = D. 1225; vi. 37112 = D. 1232.   [8] Symm. *Rel.* 30.

Lolliana, wife of C. Ceionius Rufius Volusianus Lampadius, praetorian prefect under Constantius II? Quite what the ties of blood and marriage were between these various Placidi, Lolliani, Severi and Postumiani is impossible to say, but that there were ties of one kind or another seems more than likely.[1]

Sitting next to the consul of 472, Rufius Postumius Festus, in the Flavian Amphitheatre, we find a certain Rufius Valerius Messala, '(v.c.) et inl.' evidently a relative.[2] Messala was also evidently related to the Valerius Messala who was praetorian prefect in the first years of the fifth century.[3] Besides appearing as one of Symmachus' correspondents and as the recipient of a large number of imperial edicts, Messala was a man of letters and a friend of the poet Rutilius Namatianus who has some rather complimentary lines about him in his *De Reditu Suo*:

haec quoque Pieriis spiracula conparat antris carmine Messalae nobilitatus ager;
intrantemque capit discedentemque moratur postibus adfixum dulce poema sacris.
hic est qui primo seriem de consule ducit, usque ad Publicolas si redeamus avos;
hic et praefecti nutu praetoria rexit, sed menti et linguae gloria maior inest.[4]

A similar pedigree is claimed by the elder Symmachus for an earlier relative, that remarkable Constantinian official, L. Aradius Valerius Proculus Populonius:

Valerius Proculus
Cum primis, quos non oneravit gloria patrum,
Ponemus Proculum, vitae morumque decore
Haud umquam indignum magnorum Publicolarum.
Olli semper amor veri et constantia, simplex
Caelicolum cultus. Non illum spernere posses,
Et quamquam reverendus erat, non inde timeres.[5]

---

[1] Caecinia Lolliana: vi. 512 = D. 4154. viii. 25990 = 6025. See Chastagnol, 'La famille de Caecinia Lolliana', *Latomus*, 20 (1961) 744–58. On Lampadius himself see Chastagnol, 'Le sénateur Volusien et la conversion d'une famille de l'aristocratie romaine au Bas-Empire', *Revue des Etudes Anciennes* 58 (1956) 241–53. See also P. Brown, 'Aspects of the Christianization of the Roman Aristocracy', *JRS* 51 (1961) 1–11.

[2] vi. 32202.   [3] Symm. *Epp.* vii. 81–92. See Seeck, *Symm.*, clxxxvi f.
[4] Rut. Nam. *de Red. s.* 267–74.   [5] Symm. *Ep.* i. 2. 4.

The portrait is that of a republican patrician, a man upright in virtue, simple in his habits, strong and reliable in character, a worthy scion of an ancient line. But were our fourth-century Valerii really descended from the ancient Valerii Publicolae, a family with a history going back to the earliest days of the Republic ? The ancient noble house is reputed to have died with the consul of 58, M. Valerius Messalla Corvinus, and Valeria Messallina, Claudius' wife, but later in the same century we come across one Sex. Quinctilius Valerius Maximus, quaestor of Pontus and Bithynia, from whom the fourth century Valerii seem to have been descended. That the quaestor was unrelated to the old family would appear highly unlikely, in view of the fact that he was a contemporary or near-contemporary of Corvinus and Messallina. Though probably not in the direct male line, the quaestor may have been related to the Republican family through his mother, his father being a Quinctilius.

The ordinary consuls of 151 both appear to have been his grandsons, their names being Sex. Quintilius Valerius Maximus and Sex. Quintilius Condianus, two of his great-grandsons were consuls as well, Sex. Quintilius Condianus in 180 and Quintilius Maximus in 172.[1] Another member of the family was the consul of 153 and 180 L. Fulvius Bruttius Praesens Min ... Valerius Maximus Pompeius L ... Valens Cornelius Proculus ... Aquilius Veiento. In the space of a generation, therefore, there were two years, 151 and 180 in which both ordinary consuls were members of the *gens Valeria*. Late in the second century the family revived the *cognomen* Messalla, and we have L. Valerius Messalla Thrasea Priscus, ordinary consul in 196 and L. Valerius Messalla, ordinary consul in 214. The consul of 196 was probably the product of a marriage between the Valerii and the family of Thrasea Fannius Paetus and Helvidius Priscus, the aristocratic philosophers who opposed the emperors Nero and Vespasian. L. Valerius Maximus was ordinary consul in 233, and his son L. Valerius Poplico(la) Balbinus Maximus was ordinary consul in the middle of the century, perhaps to be identified with the urban prefect of 255 or the ordinary consul of 253 and 256, both referred to simply as

[1] Plin. *Ep.* viii. 24.

Valerius Maximus.[1] In the fourth century the family is represented by Valerius Maximus Basilius, whose career included appointments as urban prefect (319–23), ordinary consul (327) and praetorian prefect (327–33). This notable career, it will be seen, combines the most significant appointments with unusual length of tenure. It is very likely that Basilius was the father of Valerius Maximus, urban prefect in 361–2, and that he was also related to Valerius Hermonius Maximus, consular of Campania in 394/5.[2]

In view of this impressive array of ancestors and relatives for our Valerii, including, in the late Empire, two praetorian prefects, namely Valerius Maximus and Messalla, and an acting praetorian prefect in the shape of Aradius Valerius Proculus, the present author must reject John Matthews's view of the family, expressed in connection with Messala: 'Valerius Messala, a friend of Symmachus, was, it is true, an ostensible member of an ancient Roman *gens*, but (even if his claims were genuine) it was one which had held no important office in the late Empire till Messala himself.'[3]

The link between the Valerii and the Ceionii is not confined to our fifth-century worthies sitting side by side in the Flavian Amphitheatre. The Valerius Publicola who appears in an inscription from Beneventum as 'v.c. cons(ularis) Camp(aniae), ab atavis patronus', is very likely to have been the Publicola who was the son of Melania the elder and father of Melania the younger, who was urban praetor in about 375 and married Albina, sister of Rufius Antonius Agrypnius Volusianus, *quaestor sacri palatii*, urban prefect and praetorian prefect in the early fifth century and a member of the *gens* Ceionia.[4] In addition to their ties with the Ceionii, the Valerii were connected with the Aradii, as we have seen,[5] and also with the Brittii, as can be seen from the name of the consul of 153 and 180 mentioned above.

---

[1] Dio 77. 8. x. 408 = D. 1117; vi. 1531–2.

[2] Basilius: *CTh.* i. 5. 2 (327), For his career see Ch. III, pp. 69 and 72. Valerius Hermonius Maximus: x. 1690 = D. 589 Puteoli. For dating cf. x. 1692 = D. 792.

[3] Matthews, op. cit., 502.

[4] ix. 1591. Pall. *Hist. Laus.* 61, 54, 58. Jer. *Chron.* s.a. 377. *V. Mel* (Gr.) i. 41, 50. *V. Mel* (L.) i. 1, ii. 10, 19. Aug. *Epp.* 124–6. Jer. *Ep.* 145 = Aug. *Ep.* 202. Paul *Carm.* xxi. 281 ff.

[5] For the Aradii see p. 52 f., above.

The Brittii, can be traced back to the early second or even to the first century. There is quite a cluster of Brittii (or Bruttii) Praesentes in the third century. The consuls of 217 and 246 were both called C. Bruttius Praesens. Though Groag identifies the consul of 217 with the patron of Canusium whose name appears in the album of 223 as L. Bruttius Praesens, it is safer to regard them as close relatives.[1] Another Bruttius appears as a senatorial patron in the album of Canusium, L. Bruttius Crispinus, and it was presumably the same person who was consul in the following year. The (Pr)aesens who was co-opted into the college of Salii Palatini in 199 was probably also related.[2] The name Crispinus entered the family through the marriage of the polyonymous consul of 153 and 180 and proconsul of Africa L. Fulvius C. f. Pom . . . . . Bruttius Praesens Min . . . . Valerius Maximus Pompeius L . . . . Valens Cornelius Proculus . . . . Aquilius Veiento, with (*Val*?)eria Mar(*cia*) Hostilia Crispina Moecia Cornelia.[3] The family was very well connected, and a daughter called Crispina married the Emperor Commodus.[4] A contemporary relative was L. Bruttius Quintius Crispinus, consul in 187. The polyonymous consul of 153 and 180 was no doubt the son of C. Bruttius Praesens, ordinary consul in 139, who was in turn probably a son of Pliny's friend Praesens, whose Lucanian origin points to the likelihood of his being a Bruttius.[5] This distinguished family possessed estates in Trebula Mutuesca[6] at Amiternum, Venusia, Volcei, Grumentum and Antium.[7]

The family appears in fourth-century records as well. We have a Brittius Praesens described as 'v.c. p(ontifex) m(aior)' in an urban inscription probably dating from the 320s.[8] Another (or the same) Brittius Praesens appears as 'v.c. corrector' in Lucania at an indeterminate date in the fourth century.[9] Brittius Praetextatus Argentius, probably also a member of the same family in view of the

---

[1] ix. 338 Canusium. See *Historia* 1960. H-G. Pflaum, *Le Marbre de Thorigny*.
[2] vi. 1982–3.   [3] viii. 110.
[4] x. 408 = D. 1117 Volcei, Lucania.   [5] Plin. *Ep.* vii. 3. 1–2.
[6] ix. 4915, 4920, 4943.
[7] ix. 4232 Amiternum: ix. 425 Venusia; x. 408 = D. 1117 Volcei; x. 238 Grumentum; xv. 7796 Antium.
[8] x. 468.   [9] vi. 2153.

rarity of the *nomen*, was consular governor of Byzacena, *comes* of the first rank and a *quindecimvir*, probably at some time during the last three-quarters of the century[1] An interesting inscription from Mutina dating from the latter part of the fourth century is dedicated by a certain Fl. Vitalis to his wife Bruttia Aureliana, probably another member of our *gens* Brittia. Aureliana is described here as the daughter of Musolamius and Asteria 'c.f.' and granddaughter of Marcellinus 'ex comitibus', Marina and Gallicanus.[2] Gallicanus, who, we are told, had been ordinary consul, is probably to be identified with the consul of 330, the only man of that name in the fourth-century consular *fasti*. In view of the family background that Aureliana evidently had, judging by her Brittian connections and her grandfather's consulship, it is perhaps not going too far to suggest that her other grandfather Marcellinus, may have been one of the Antonii Marcellini. A law dated 319 in the MSS. and redated by Seeck to 313 is addressed 'ad Antonium Marcellinum, praesidem Lugdunensis Primae'.[3] The person concerned is either to be identified with the praetorian prefect of the same name or else must have been a close relative of his. The praetorian prefect is known to have been proconsul of Africa and patron of Bulla Regia from an inscription found there, in which he is also, interestingly enough, said to have come of '(*il*)lustris familiae'.[4] In addition Marcellinus is mentioned as the father (by Palladius and Jerome) or grandfather (by Paulinus of Nola) of Melania the elder.[5] Now, as was said above, Melania the elder had a son called Publicola and had evidently therefore married a Valerius, perhaps the Valerius Maximus who was urban prefect in 361–2.[6] Maximus was probably the son of Valerius Maximus Basilius, the Constantinian urban and praetorian prefect, who, as we know from Ammianus, married an unnamed sister of Neratius Cerealis, Vulcacius Rufinus, and Galla.[7] It is worth recalling at

---

[1] x. 3846.
[2] xi. 830 = D. 1280.
[3] *CTh.* xi. 3. 1.
[4] viii. 25524.
[5] Pall. *Hist. Laus.* 46; Jer. *Chron.* 2390, s.a. 377; Paul Nol. *Ep.* 29. 8.
[6] Pall. *Hist. Laus.* 61, 54, 58.
[7] Amm. xxi. 12. 24.

this point the connection, described above, between the Neratii and the Anicii. So we have come full circle in tracing the inter-relationships among our fourth-century aristocrats. For lack of a three-dimensional chart these connections have had to be divided up into three stemmata, which will be found at the end of this volume.

VI

NOBLES AS LANDOWNERS

SENATORS had always drawn their livelihood from the land and were traditionally prohibited from engaging in trade. That senators were still essentially landowners in the fourth century is a commonplace and needs no proof. Perhaps the best indication of the fact that senators were primarily landowners is to be found in the fact that the tax levied on them from the time of Constantine, the *follis*, *collatio glebalis* or *glebatio*, was, as the last two names indicate, a land-tax.[1]

The nobles were of course not the only owners of estates. All decurions and some soldiers and Christian priests, as well as new senators, were evidently in this category too.[2] Though nobles, who often inherited landed property, probably had on an average more extensive estates than their newly-arrived fellow-senators, nevertheless the general trends discernible in connection with the landholding in the late Empire are relevant to both groups of senators and also to non-senatorial estate-owners.

The whole question of landholding is bedevilled by the problem of absentee landlords, but perhaps it is best to consider the general nature of rural society in our period before indicating how the whole fabric was affected by this complication.

It was in the age of the first Flavians, more than two centuries before our period, that Pliny the elder penned his well-known stricture upon the rise of large estates: '... latifundia perdidere Italiam vero et provincias'.[3] But even in the late Empire small

[1] On the *follis* see Zosimus ii. 38. *CTh.* vi. 2 and vi. 3 passim. See also A. Bernardi, 'The economic problems of the Roman Empire at the time of its decline', *Studia et Documenta Historiae et Iuris*, 31 (1965) 154 ff. Jones, *Later Roman Empire*, i, 462–9.

[2] *CTh.* v. 2, 3 and 6.

[3] Plin.: *N.H.* xviii. 7. 35. This well-known statement has been much discussed and rejected by some as unreliable. See K. D. White, 'Latifundia', *University of London Institute of Classical Studies Bulletin* 14 (1967) 77 f.

holders were far from extinct, though their number does seem to have been on the wane. It is estimated for example that about five-sixths of the territory of Hermopolis in Egypt, and more than nine-tenths of the village of Theadelphia in the Arsinoite territory of the same province were owned by peasant proprietors.[1] This feature was probably more marked in Egypt than in the other provinces of the Empire owing to its rather unusual agrarian system which it had inherited fron the Ptolemies. In Illyricum and Thrace there was still an appreciable number of free smallholders in the sixth century, and it was from this element of the population that Justinian appears to have raised a considerable number of troops.[2] Even in the West the free peasant proprietor was not unknown. That fiery priest, Salvian of Marseilles, could hardly be guilty of manufacturing a non-existent agrarian and social system, though we may be justifiably hesitant in accepting his more vehemently passionate polemics. Through him we learn that even in Gaul the small freeholder had not entirely disappeared by the mid-fifth century when *de Gubernatione Dei* was written.[3] But the peasant who sought the protection of a great magnate would often exchange the ownership of his plot for security, and, once a smallholding was added to an estate, it would never be separated from it. The trend was for estates to grow, and there was no shortage of buyers for *latifundia*, as is shown, for example, in the sale of the extensive possessions of Melania the Younger.[4] Estates were the order of the day, but they were not all large. The land register of Magnesia, for example, shows the largest local estate in the hands of a senator, while five other people of senatorial rank are listed as the owners of six quite modest estates.[5] Landowners even of great wealth tended to have their *fundi* scattered rather than grouped together in blocks. Melania the younger owned property throughout the Western provinces, even in Britain, and we are told by Ammianus that Petronius Probus 'per orbem Romanum universum paene

[1] Jones, *JRS* 53 (1953) 59–60, 63–4.
[2] Procopius, *Bellum Gothicum*, iii. 10. 1–3. On peasant freeholders see Jones, *Later Roman Empire*, ii, 773 ff.
[3] Salvianus, *de Gubernatione Dei*, v. 38 ff.
[4] *Vita S. Melaniae Iunioris* (L) i. 15. *Analecta Bollandiana*, 8 (1889) 33.
[5] Jones, *JRS* 43 (1953), 52–3.

patrimonia sparsa possedit'.¹ Symmachus' estates were within a narrower compass, but he mentions fifteen estates in various parts of Italy as well as a considerable number of possessions in Mauretania and Sicily and three mansions in or near Rome.² Moreover, Symmachus is said by Olympiodorus to have spent 2,000 pounds of gold on his son's praetorian games—and he was considered a senator of only moderate means.³ Private estates varied greatly in size and it is not surprising to learn that some were immense. One of Melania's *saltus* is described as follows:

Erat enim possessio nimis praeclara, habens balneum infra se et natatoriam in ea, ita ut ex uno latere mare, ex alio silvarum nemora haberentur, in qua diversae bestiae et venationes haberentur. Cum igitur lavaret in natatoria, videbat et naves transeuntes et venationem in silva. Diabolus autem immitebat ei cogitationes diversas, describens pretiosa marmora et diversos ornatus vel multos reditus et censum eius omnem. Habebat enim ipsa possessio sexaginta villulas, circa se habentes quadringentenos servos agricultores.⁴

Another of Melania's estates, which she donated to the church of Tagaste, was larger than the town: 'Possessio maior erat etiam civitatis ipsius, habens balneum, artifices multos, aurifices, argentarios et aerarios; et duos episcopos, unum nostrae fidei et alium haereticorum.'⁵ Agennius Urbicus had this to say about the size of privately owned *saltus:* 'Inter res p. et privatos non facile tales in Italia controversiae moventur, sed frequenter in provinciis praecipue in Africa, ubi saltus non minores habent privati quam res p. territoria: quin immo multi saltus longe maiores sunt territoriis: habent autem in saltibus privati(s) non exiguum populum plebeium et vicos circa villam in modum municipiorum.'⁶

It is significant that both these latter examples point towards the tendency for private estates to become self-contained economic and social units. Palladius, the fourth-century writer on agriculture, assumes all along that his readers are owners of sizeable estates, and

¹ *V. Mel.* 11–12, 19–21, 37. Amm. xxvii. 11. 1.
² Symm. *Ep.* vii. 66; ix. 49. Seeck, *Symm.* p. xlvi.
³ Olympiod. Fr. 44.   ⁴ *V. Mel.* (L) i. 18.   ⁵ *V. Mel.* (L) i. 21.
⁶ Agennius Urbicus, *de Controversiis Agrorum,* Corp. Agrimensorum Rom., p. 45 (Teubner).

advises them to have craftsmen and artisans on their land so that their peasants will have no need to go to the cities: 'Ferrarii, lignarii, doliorum cuparumque factores necessario habendi sunt, ne a labore solenni rusticos causa desiderandae urbis avertat.'[1] The African mosaics corroborate this evidence, and show a multiplicity of activities going on within a single *fundus*: the tending of sheep, goats and cattle; horse-breeding; poultry-keeping, the spinning of yarn; the production of wine and oil; hunting and fishing; and of course the farming of fruit and agricultural products.[2] One of these mosaics, which depicts life on the estate of a certain Julius, also shows the villa taking on the aspect of a fortress.[3] This can also be seen in other mosaics and there is in addition no lack of archaeological evidence, even in Britain.[4] Inscriptions tell the same story: 'In his praediis M. Aureli/ Vasefanis v.p. castram se/ne cuiiusque commodum laboribus/ suis filis nepo[t]ibusque suis/ abituris perfecit. Coepta nonas/ Februarias ..... VII ...... [a]n(no) p(rovinciae) CCC.'[5] The date, the three hundredth year of the existence of the province of Mauretania, is 339. Another inscription announces: 'in his praediis/ Caeliae Maximae c.f. turres salutem saltus/ eiusdem dominae meae/ constituit/ Numidius ser(vus) ac(tor)'.[6]

An interesting example of a fortified villa is that of Zammac, brother of the rebel Moorish prince Firmus, which is described by Ammianus as constructed 'in modum urbis'.[7] The villa is also celebrated in an inscription with an acrostic down each end.[8] In his rather rambling description of the aptly named 'Burgus' of his

---

[1] Palladius, *de Re Rustica* i. 6. Cf. Varro, *de Re Rustica*, i. 17, where only farmhands properly so called are discussed.

[2] Rostovtzeff, *The Social and Economic History of the Roman Empire*, Plates lxxvii, lxxix, lxxx.

[3] A. Merlin, 'La Mosaïque du seigneur Julius à Carthage', *BCTH* 1921, 95–114.

[4] R. Paribeni, 'Le Dimore dei Potentiores nel Basso Impero.' *MDAI* (R) 55 (1940) 131–48. See also A. Schulten, *Die römischen Grundherrschaften*, Weimar 1896, espec. 21–4. A. Dauzat, *Les Noms de Lieux: Origine et evolution*, Paris, 1926, 135 ff.

[5] D. 6021 = viii. 21531 Ammi Musa, Mauretania. The words 'sene cuiiusque commodum' probably mean 'sine cuiiusque incommodo' (Dessau).

[6] D. 6020 = viii. 19328 Ain-el-Tin, Numidia.

[7] Amm. xxix. 5. 13, where Zammac is called Salmaces cf. Amm. xxix. 5. 2.

[8] D. 9351 near Saldae, Mur. Sit.

senatorial friend Pontius Leontius, Apollinaris Sidonius specifically stresses the impregnability of the walls:

> ...... non illos machina muros,
> non aries, non alta strues vel proximus agger,
> non quae stridentes torquet catapulta molares,
> sed nec testudo nec vinea nec rota currens
> iam positis scalis umquam quassare valebunt.[1]

So important was this aspect of the *fundus* that peasants tend to be
referred to by formulae such as 'coloni castelli Cellensis'.[2] Some
landowners gained imperial rescripts allowing them to collect the
taxes from their estates themselves, a custom which came to be
known as 'autopractorium' and which was outlawed in a strongly-
worded edict of 409.[3]

To this day many towns and villages in Western Europe bear
the names of the owners of such self-contained *praedia*.[4] Their
size, fortifications, and social and economic self-sufficiency made
the large estates resemble towns and their owners tended to be
placed on a par with the municipal councils. People would confuse
civitates and *possessiones* and had to be reminded of the different
titles for the administrative hierarchies in the two types of unit:
'... ordines civitatum sed procuratores possessionum'.[5] Even the
imperial government, however reluctant it may have been to do so,
had to recognize the power of the landowner within his estate.[6]

The master's power over his *coloni* was great, and a *colonus* who
left the estate to which he was attached was committing a serious
crime: 'Ipsos etiam colonos, qui fugam meditantur, in servilem
condicionem ferro ligari conveniet, ut officia, quae liberis con-
gruunt, merito servilis condemnationis conpellantur inplere'.[7]
While binding *coloni* to the estates on which they were born, this
law, issued by Constantine in 332, nevertheless makes a clear
distinction between *coloni* and slaves, and uses the threat to deprive

---

[1] Apollinaris Sidonius: *Carm.* xxii. 121–5.
[2] viii. 8777, 8701 cf. viii. 8426, 14603. See Schulten, op. cit., 44 ff.
[3] *CTh.* xi. 22. 4 (409). Though addressed to Anthemius, PPO of the East, this
practice no doubt existed in the West as well.
[4] See Dauzat, op. cit., 112 ff.   [5] Victor Vitensis: Pers. Vand. iii, 11.
[6] *CTh.* xvi. 2. 31 (398) Milan.   [7] *CTh.* v. 17. 1. 1 (332).

11

coloni of their freedom as a deterrent against the abuse which it wishes to combat. Not surprisingly, the problem of 'coloni fugitivi' was not solved by this constitution, which is only the first of a series of laws on the subject.[1] It is worth noting how the distinction between *coloni* and *servi*, which could be used as the basis of a threat in 332, had largely disappeared even by 365. Whether the distinction between *coloni* and *servi* meant anything in practical terms in 332 is not known, but by 365 even the law is well on its way to regarding *coloni* as slaves: 'Non dubium est colonis arva, quae subigunt, usque adeo alienandi ius non esse, ut, et si qua propria habeant, inconsultis atque ignorantibus patronis in alteros transferre non liceat.'[2]

A law addressed to Nebridius, proconsul of Asia in 396–7, actually uses the word 'peculium', a term traditionally associated with slaves, instead of the 'propria' of the law quoted above.[3] The subordination of the *colonus* to his master, whose title 'dominus' was also the traditional title of the slave-owner, was now complete.[4]

The whole issue of landholding is complicated by the fact that for the great majority of his estates the owner would be an absentee landlord. Does this mean that such estates were spared the development that we have been describing? No. It is not difficult to see how the term 'possessor' came to be applied to 'emphyteuticarii' or 'perpetuarii', tenants who had leases for life or in perpetuity. But probably only very few private estates had such tenants, the more usual practice being to entrust the management of such estates to short-term chief tenants known as *conductores*, or to agents termed *procuratores* or *actores*. If these were men of substance, as seems often to have been the case, they might become the effective masters of such estates. But a more important alternative, and one on which there is a considerable amount of information, was the usurpation of patrons, and it is to this subject that we now turn.[5]

On the favourite estate of a landowner all life might well revolve about him, and he might spend very little time away from it, as was the case with Sidonius' Gallic friends in the fifth century. But

[1] *CTh.* v. 17 and 18.　　[2] *CTh.* v. 19. 1 (365).　　[3] *CJ.* xi. 50. 2.
[4] For 'dominus' see *CTh.* v. 18. 1 (419), *CTh.* v. 17. 2 (386).
[5] On the management of estates see Jones, op. cit., ii, 788–92.

this was obviously not the case on all *fundi*. For the most part the estate owner was an absentee landlord, leaving the *coloni* to the mercy of *procuratores* or *conductores*.

The landowner was the natural patron of his *coloni*, but where he was an absentee landlord or a man of no great influence, the *coloni* had to look elsewhere for protection against the imperial government and particularly against tax-collectors. Our main evidence of this 'patrocinium vicorum' comes to us from the Codes and from Libanius, the Antiochene orator, who attacked the practice in a most impassioned address to the emperor.[1] All the laws are from the Eastern part of the Empire and Libanius is also concerned solely with this part of the world. But that is not to say that patronage of villages was confined to the East, and we do not entirely lack Western evidence of it, thanks to Salvian's *De Gubernatione Dei*. Though this emotive tract is far from being a systematic exposition of the workings of this form of patronage in the West, it does serve to characterize the Western brand as rather different in kind from the Eastern.

In the East the patron was very often a military man, and perhaps the best example known is Libanius' dispute with some of his own tenants, who enlisted the aid of their patron, a 'strategos', presumably the local *dux*, against him. The patron, receiving a variety of gifts from his clients, secured a favourable outcome for them.[2] We must not forget that what we have here is the testimony of the embittered loser. But even so, the influence of a patron of this kind is not difficult to believe; and the evidence of the learned rhetorician written from the point of view of an indignant landlord who has been cheated of his natural right is corroborated by the imperial constitutions written from the point of view of a government defrauded of its rightful dues.

The imperial government's concern about loss of taxes appears

---

[1] *CTh.* xi. 24. *CJ.* xi. 54. Lib. *Or.* xlvii. On patronage of villages see F. de Zulueta: *de Patrociniis Vicorum: Oxford Studies in Social and Legal History*, vol. i, ed. P. Vinogradoff, Oxford 1909. See also Harmand, *Patronat*, 449 ff. and *Discours*, 140 ff; Lecrivain, *Sénat*, 125–8. There is also a brief discussion of this, agreeing in the main with Harmand, in Gagé, *Classes Sociales*, 417 ff.

[2] Lib. *Or.* xlvii. 13–17. The text is rather corrupt here, but this would appear to be the gist of the matter. See Harmand's discussion of this episode, *Discours*, 67 ff. See also de Zulueta, op. cit., 32 ff.

explicitly in a law of 399: '... Omnes ergo sciant non modo eos memorata multa feriendos, qui clientelam susceperint rusticorum, sed eos quoque, qui fraudandorum tributorum causa ad patrocinia solita fraude confugerint, duplum definitae multae dispendium subituros.'[1] A law of 370 addressed by Constantius II to the praetorian prefect of the East and referring specifically to Egypt explains the cause for the imperial concern over the patronage of *coloni*. We learn here that patrons were men of high rank generally, *duces* being singled our for special mention.[2] A later constitution gives a more detailed array of the guilty, showing that, even in the East, holders of the illicit patronage were not necessarily military men: 'Cuiuslibet ille fuerit dignitatis, sive magistri utriusque militiae sive comitis sive ex proconsulibus vel vicariis vel Augustalibus vel tribunis sive ex ordine curiali vel cuiuslibet alterius dignitatis.'[3]

The military patron seems to have been less prevalent in the West than in the East. Though Salvian focuses his attention largely on the peasants who lose their property and become *coloni* in the service of the 'maiores', he is also not altogether silent on the subject of the patrons. Most of what he has to say about them amounts to a torrent of abuse, but a very clear portrayal emerges of the patrons as grasping estate-owners greedy for more land.[4] The province of Syria, where Libanius lived and wrote, was a particularly active one from the military point of view, and there is evidence of a close association between the people of the region and the troops.[5] Moreover, it was in the West that *latifundia* were rife, while in the East there were probably comparatively few large estates. It is not difficult to see the attractiveness as a patron of a territorial magnate with influence both locally and centrally. Such were the nobles whom we have already seen as the holders of high imperial appointments and as large landholders.

Those who came under the power of the patrons comprised not only *coloni adscripticii*, or tenants living on estates owned by others, but also freeholders,[6] some of whom may have owned more than

---

[1] *CTh.* xi. 24. 4 (399)   [2] *CTh.* xi. 24. 1 (360).
[3] *CTh.* xi. 24. 4 (399).   [4] Salvianus, *de Gub. Dei.* v. 8. 34–50.
[5] Harmand, *Patronat*, 458, quotes Mouterde-Poidebard, *Limes de Chalcis*, 239.
[6] Salvianus, loc. cit.

just a patch of land, as the terms 'possessores' and 'propria possidentes' used to refer to them may indicate.[1]

What a *colonus* sought from his patron was, above all, protection against tax-collectors and legal aid, which was the most traditional sphere of a patron's activities on behalf of his clients, dating back from the Republic if not before. And there is certainly no lack of evidence of corruption in matters of taxation and judicial proceedings. The main object of the imperial constitutions against the *patrocinium vicorum* was to prevent tax-evasion,[2] and the codes are replete with imperial attacks on the corruption and venality of officials. Patrons took advantage of these traits, and in so doing, fostered them.[3]

So much for the peasants' aims in placing themselves under a patron. Whether they obtained what they wanted is a moot point, but those of them who were freeholders tended to lose their property, as we learn from the classic statement or over-statement of their case by their champion Salvian.[4]

We are more concerned to view the whole process from the point of view of the benefits gained by the patrons. Their most obvious benefit was financial. The second constitution against patronage of this kind ends with the words: 'et non quantum patroni suscipere consuerant, sed dimidium eius fiscus adsumat'.[5] As a counter-inducement to peasants, the *fiscus* would demand only half of what they were accustomed to paying their patrons.[6] So usual did it become for patrons to receive payment that in later times in the East this due came to be known as 'patrokinion'.[7]

Patronage of villages could either benefit or harm the owner of an estate—or even do both to the same man at the same time. An absentee landlord might well find his *coloni* in the clientship of a

---

[1] *CTh.* xi. 24. 4. The heavy fines imposed upon clients (80 lbs of gold) may also be an indication of the size of their properties—or a sign of the imperial government's complete exasperation. See also *CJ.* xi. 54. 2.

[2] *CTh.* xi. 24. 4 (397) cf. *CTh.* xi. 24. 1 and 2.

[3] *CTh.* i. 16. 7., *CTh.* i. 20 (408), *CTh.* i. 16. 13.

[4] Salvianus v. 8. 38 ff.

[5] *CTh.* xi. 24. 2 (370 MSS.—368 Seeck).

[6] See the discussion as to the meaning of this clause, de Zulueta, op. cit., 20.

[7] Payment to patrons: *CJ* xi. 54. 2 (no date; Justinian ?); Lib. *Or.* iv. 4. 'Patrokinion': de Zulueta, op. cit., 21, n. 3.

neighbouring landowner, while he himself in turn might be the patron of another man's *coloni*. The tendency was for the patron to become the owner of property whose tenants were his clients, thus leading to the consolidation of neighbouring estates under a single owner and the disappearance of absentee landlords. So common indeed was it for a man to become the effective owner of an estate whose *coloni* were under his patronage that in 415 the imperial government recognized patrons who had been in this position for more than eighteen years as the legal owners of the estates concerned while forbidding the practice for the future.[1]

That the situation reflected in this law, addressed to the prefect of the East, was not confined to that part of the Empire is indicated by Salvian: 'Omnes enim hi, qui defendi videntur, defensoribus suis omnem fere substantiam suam prius quam defendantur addicunt, ac sic, ut patres habeant defensionem, perdunt filii hereditatem . . . Ecce quae sunt auxilia ac patrocinia maiorum: nihil susceptis tribuunt, sed sibi. Hoc enim pacto aliquid parentibus temporarie attribuitur, ut in futuro totum filiis auferatur.'[2] We discern, then, an unmistakable tendency for estates to become self-contained social and economic entities, and also for their owners to spend more time on them than before. That this was so can be seen from mosaics, such as that of Julius at Carthage, depicting the *dominus* hunting or dispensing justice to his *coloni*.[3]

The law of 356 fixing the quorum for meetings of the senate at fifty was probably, like so many other laws, a reaction to events rather than a positive blueprint, and in this case the cause must surely have been the decline in the number of senators present in Rome.[4] Similarly, the law dating from the second quarter of the fifth century allowing senators the right to live wherever they pleased without leave ('sine commeatu') must again be seen as a recognition rather than as an anticipation of the fact that many senators preferred not to live at Rome though legally obliged to do

---

[1] *CTh.* xi. 24. 6 (415).   [2] Salvianus, op. cit., v. 8. 39–40.
[3] A. Merlin, 'La mosaïque du seigneur Julius.
[4] *CTh.* vi. 4. 9. On the general character of the Theodosian Code as a reaction to conditions see R. MacMullen, 'Social Mobility and the Theodosian Code', *JRS* 54 (1964) 49–53; Jones, 'The social background of the struggle between paganism and Christianity', *Conflict between Paganism and Christianity* (ed. Momigliano). 34 f.

so.[1] Indeed, two laws of 354 and one of 395 had already implicitly recognized the new state of affairs in this regard, the earlier ones by their insistence that senators come to Rome to furnish games for their republican magistracies and the latter by the distinction, in connection with the payment of the *aurum oblaticium*, between 'senatores qui in sacratissima urbe consistunt, licet habeant per longinquas provincias atque diversas possessiones' and those 'qui in provinciis larem fovent'.[2] Though all those who had Roman residences also had estates elsewhere, there were evidently some who had no Roman abode at all. This is what we have on the one hand, centrifugal forces at work; but that is not to say that these nobles who lived permanently in the provinces were out of touch with Rome, which, as we can see from Symmachus' letters, was still very much the social centre of aristocratic life. There is no justification for such a dichotomy, as is made by Lambrechts, in the fourth century; and even later on when travel became more difficult and large areas were lost to the Empire, contact was not altogether broken.[3] Rutilius Namatianus, who wrote in the early fifth century, is himself a good example of such contact. His poem deals with his return from Rome to his ravaged estates in Gaul. Both he and his father held office in Italy. He himself had been *magister officiorum* and subsequently urban prefect, and his father Lachanius had been consular of Tuscia and Umbria, *comes sacrarum largitionum*, *quaestor sacri palatii* and finally prefect, though of what sort is unknown.[4] Though his career would not lead us to believe that Lachanius was a noble, his son had close contacts with the high aristocracy of Italy, apparently through office. His friend Albinus, whom he visited at Volaterrae on his way home and who was his successor as urban prefect was a member of the *gens Ceionia*, his

---

[1] *Cf.* xii. 1. 15 (undated). It has been dated by Seeck to between 426 and 442. *Regesten*, 137. For the old rule about domicile in Rome, see *Dig.* l. 1. 22. 6 (*Pauli Sententiae* 1, 1a, 8) and the discussion of it in E. Levy, *Pauli Sententiae: a palingenesis of the opening titles as a specimen of research*, Ithaca, Cornell University Press, 1945.

[2] *CTh.* vi. 4. 4 (354; MSS. 339); vi. 4. 7. (MSS. 353; Seeck, *Regesten*, 42, 354); vi. 2. 16 (395).

[3] Lambrechts ii, 108 ff.

[4] Namatianus, *Mag. Off.*, Rut. Nam. *de Red. s.* i. 561 ff.; PUR: Ibid. 156 ff. Lachanius: Ibid., 575 ff. See Chastagnol, *Fastes*, 271–3; Sundwall, *Weström. Studien*, 108; Stroheker, *Senator. Adel*, 193.

full name being Caecina Decius Aginatius Albinus. Another member of that family with whom he was friendly was Rufius Antonius Agrypnius Volusianus, whom he congratulates on his urban prefecture in 417 and whose father Albinus, no doubt Ceionius Rufius Albinus, urban prefect 389–91, Namatianus also seems to have known.[1] In addition to the Ceionii, Namatianus had some contact with the Valerii, in particular Valerius Messalla, probably the praetorian prefect of the last years of the fourth century, 'primo de consule'.[2] If these were the contacts of an outsider to the circle of the old noble families, we can gain some impression of the degree of contact within it throughout the Empire.

Even in the latter half of the fifth century, if the evidence of Apollinaris Sidonius is anything to go on, the senatorial aristocracy of Gaul had not yet lost touch with Italy. Sidonius himself was married to the daughter of Avitus, praetorian prefect of the Gauls and later emperor, who was on friendly terms with the Germanic king of Italy, Theoderic.[3] Sidonius was made prefect of Rome by the Emperor Anthemius in 468.[4]

---

[1] Aginatius Albinus, *de Red. s.* i. 466 ff. Rufius Volusianus: Ibid., 421 ff., 167 ff. Ceionius Albinus: Ibid., 167 ff.

[2] Valerius Massalla Ibid., 268 ff.

[3] Sidonius' mother was also related to Avitus. Sid. Ap. *Ep.* iii. 1. His ancestry is sketched in *Ep.* i. 3, where we learn that his 'pater, socer, avus, proavus praefecturis urbanis praetorianisque . . . micuerunt'. See Dill, *Roman Society in the Last Century of the Western Empire*, 187 ff.; Stevens, *Sidonius Apollinaris and his Age;* Stroheker, op. cit.

[4] Sid. Ap. *Carm.* ii.

VII

OFFICE, RANK, AND INFLUENCE

In the last chapter we examined the position of nobles as the owners of landed estates. In this chapter we shall look at the effect of office and rank upon their position. Our first task will be to trace the connection between office and landholding.

M. Ceionius Julianus Kamenius was patron 'a parentibus' of Bulla Regia, Valerius Publicola patron 'ab atavis' of Beneventum and Postumius Lampadius 'patronus longe a maioribus originalis' of Capua. Such terms should come as no surprise to us, since it was standard practice to grant patronage to a man and his heirs in perpetuity.[1] But what is noteworthy is that all three men also were governors of the provinces in which their client-towns were situated and that none of these men was the only member of his family to govern the province concerned.[2] In addition to Kamenius, whose proconsulate of Africa was between 326 and 333, C. Ceionius Rufius Volusianus, a close relative of his, governed the province, probably in the last years of the reign of Diocletian.[3] The governorships of Campania of Valerius Publicola and Valerius Hermonius Maximus were both probably in the last years of the fourth century.[4] Postumius Lampadius, whose Campanian governorship was also at the end of the fourth or perhaps in the first years of the fifth century, was no doubt a member of the Ceionian family and therefore related to Kamenius, our proconsul of Africa, who was

---

[1] Kamenius: viii. 25525 Bulla Regia, Publicola: ix. 1591 Beneventum Lampadius: x. 1704 Capua. On patronage of towns see Harmand, *Patronat*, 421 ff. Harmand may perhaps be guilty of attaching too much significance to such patronages (especially pp. 440 ff.) Cf. D. van Berchem, 'Note sur les diplômes honorifiques du IVe siècle à propos de la table de patronat de Timgad', *Revue de Philologie* viii (1934) 167–8.
[2] See list of patrons, p. 220, below.
[3] Aurel. Vict. *Caes.* xl. 18: Zos. ii. 14. 2.
[4] Publicola: ix. 1591. Maximus: x. 1690 = D. 792, Puteoli.

also consular of Campania in 324, as well as to Caecina Decius Albinus, who governed Campania in 397/8.[1] Is it fanciful to see in this relationship between two or more governors of a province at different times family interests in that locality ? With the possible exception of Kamenius, who may have been the son of the earlier Ceionian African proconsul, we cannot explain these inherited patronages as awards originally given to governors of the provinces concerned, though our *fasti* of African proconsuls and Campanian governors does give us some slight room for additions.[2] But, since these are among the best documented provinces in our period, it is more likely that the original holder of the patronage, at least in the cases of Publicola and Lampadius, was a local landowner; and there are also other reasons for believing this. First, Campania and Africa, it is hardly necessary to say, were two of the most favoured areas in the Empire for noble estates. Secondly, what Ammianus tells us of Petronius Probus, namely that his main aim in entering politics was to further the interests of his family and dependants, may well also be true on a smaller scale of other nobles[3] —and how better could one further one's family interests than by holding a governorship in a province containing some of the family estates ?

This view of the inherited patronage is strengthened by the description of Postumius Lampadius as 'patronus longe a maioribus originalis', by which we are surely to understand not only that the patronage of Capua had been in the family for some considerable time but also, from 'originalis', that Lampadius himself had been born there.[4] In addition, we have several noble patrons who are called just 'patroni originales', with no indication as to whether they inherited the patronage or were themselves awarded it in the first place. They are Anicius Paulinus, consular of Campania and urban prefect in 380, Petronius Probus and Nicomachus Flavianus junior, another consular of Campania.[5] Paulinus and Probus were

---

[1] Albinus: *AE* 1909, 223 and *AE* 1933, 159; viii. 7034 = D. 5789. Symm. *Epp.* vi. 23, vii. 38; vii. 40, vii. 45–9. Seeck: *Symm.* p. clxxxii. See also Chastagnol: *Fastes*, 259.

[2] *Fasti, PLRE.*   [3] Amm. xxvii. 11. 1.   [4] x. 1704.

[5] Paulinus and Petronius Probus: Unpublished inscriptions from Capua communicated to the Fifth Epigraphical Conference, Cambridge, 1967. Flavianus: D. 8985, Naples.

patroni originales of Capua, Flavianus of Naples. If a noble was born in any place other than Rome, and especially if it was in an area so well known for noble estates as was Campania, it is not very daring to conjecture that our three *patroni originales* were born on estates near Capua or Naples, as the case may be, and that the families concerned still had those estates when our three nobles were patrons. For, families such as the Anicii, Petronii or Nicomachi—all incidentally interrelated[1]—would not tend to sell up their estates. Again, therefore, governorships appear to be connected with local landholding.

Nor is this the only evidence of the connection between land and office. The Aradii, for example, had a long-standing link with Africa, going back as it did at least to the suffect consul, probably of the early third century, Q. Aradius Rufinus Optatus Aelianus and his wife Calpurnia Fidiana Aemiliana, who were patrons of Bulla Regia.[2] An Aradia Roscia was patroness of Bulla Regia probably at some time in the third century, and it was at Thuburbo that Q. Aradius Rufinus, also of the third century, set up his inscriptions to the sun and moon.[3] In the fourth century not only were both Q. and L. Aradii Proculi governors of Byzacena, but the latter also went on to become proconsul and vicar of Africa and there were two other Proculi who were African proconsuls, one in 319 and the other in 340, both no doubt members of the *gens* Aradia.[4] Another example of local family ties is the Ceionian connection with Numidia, four of whose twenty-four consulars known in the fourth century being Ceionii: Ceionius Italicus (before 343), Publilius Ceionius Caecina Albinus (364/7), Alfenius Ceionius Julianus Kamenius (before 381), and Caecina Decius Albinus

---

[1] See Chapter V and Stemma II for the interrelationship.

[2] Unpublished inscription from Bulla Regia kindly communicated to the author by Dr. R. Duncan-Jones.

[3] Aradia Roscia: viii. 14470. Aradius Rufinus: viii. 14688 = D. 3937; viii. 10602 = 14689 = D. 3938.

[4] Proculus procos. Afr. 319: *CJ*. viii. 52. 2; *CTh*. xv. 3. 1; vi. 35. 2; iv. 16. 1. For the dating see Seeck, *Regesten*, 55, 57. Chastagnol, *Fastes*, 96, sees him as possibly a brother of Q. and L. Aradii Proculi. Proculus, procos. Afr. 340: *CTh*. xi. 30. 21. Chastagnol, op. cit., 102, regards him as the elder son of L. Aradius Proculus, the younger one being the Aradius Rufinus who was urban prefect in 376. There is no warrant for such a precise relationship, nor for the view of the proconsul of 319 as a brother of our two *praesides* of Byzacena.

(c. 390).[1] Similarly, over a fifth (thirteen) of the sixty-four pro-
consuls of Africa known in the fourth century were Anicii, Ceionii
or collaterals,[2] as were five of the ten noble vicars of Africa: C.
Annius Tiberianus (325–7), Petronius (340), Virius Nicomachus
Flavianus (377), Faltonius Probus Alypius (378), and Alfenius
Ceionius Julianus Kamenius (381).[3]

It is hardly accidental that those provinces which tended to be
governed by nobles in the fourth century were also the provinces
noted for aristocratic landed possessions. The Italian, African, and
Spanish provinces in particular fall into this category, though Gaul,
another favourite area for noble estates in the late Empire as a
reader of Rutilius Namatianus or Apollinaris Sidonius need not be
reminded, was not often governed by nobles at the provincial
level and never at the diocesan level, so far as our records go. It was
also, as we have seen, in Italy, Africa, and Spain that the first consular governorships were created by Constantine, a designation
which may well have been introduced to pander to aristocratic
pride, which might be offended by the title 'praeses', latterly
confined to equestrians and imbued perhaps with too plebeian a
character. An appointment to an area such as Campania or Numidia would enable the appointee to safeguard any property he
might have there and also to add to it. Petronius Probus, according
to Ammianus, was actually compelled ('cogebatur') to seek appointment as praetorian prefect 'iurgiis familiarum ingentium',[4] and
the number of appointments, favours, and recommendations of
which a praetorian prefect could dispose is impossible to calculate,
but it must have been immense. Even the influence of lesser officials
could be quite considerable.[5] This of course applies whether the

---

[1] Ceionius Italicus: viii. 7012–3, Constantina, Numidia. Albinus: viii. 20156 =
D. 5536; viii. 7975 = 19852 = D. 5910; viii. 4767 = 18701 = D. 5571; viii.
2388 = D. 5554. Kamenius: D. 1264; vi. 1675 and p. 155, vi. 31902; vi. 31940;
AE 1953,238. Caecina Decius Albinus: See p. 156, n. 1.

[2] The figures for the proconsulate of Africa are based on the *fasti* of the *PLRE*,
anonymi not being counted in the total.

[3] Tiberianus: *CTh.* xii. 5. 1; xii. 1. 15; *CJi* vi. 1. 6: *CTh.* iii. 5. 6.; Jer. *Chron.*
s.a. 336.; *ILT.* 814 Tubernuc. Petronius: *CTh.* ii. 6. 5; *CTh.* x. 15. 3. Flavianus:
vi. 1782–3 = D. 2947–8. Alypius: vi. 1657; vi. 1185 = D. 783; vi. 31975[199].
Amm. xxviii. 4. 1–2. Kamenius: See n. 1 above.

[4] Amm. xxvii. 11. 3. The reading is here in doubt.

[5] See e.g. *CTh.* i. 16, where examples are given of the venality of officials

officials concerned were noble or not. But with their wealth and their close web of family alliances nobles could probably benefit more from their official positions than could non-noble officials in general.

There was a general bar on purchases while in office of land, houses, or slaves, and this was applicable to all office-holders irrespective of rank. This prohibition first appears in the *Theodosian Code* in an extract from a case of 334 presided over by Constantine, who formulates the law as follows: 'Sed iure continetur, ne quis in administratione constitutus aliquid compararet, unde quidem nihil interest, an in suo pago an in alieno comparavit, cum constet contra ius eundem comparasse. Et adiecit: ignoratis fiscale effici totum, quidquid administrantes comparaverint?'[1] The same rule is reiterated in laws of 364, 365, and 397, a sign that the imperial government was experiencing some difficulty in eliminating this offence.[2] The reason for the prohibition of what might appear to be an innocuous practice is not difficult to fathom. The influence wielded by men in official positions was no doubt sufficient to adjust the price that they were required to pay for a purchase to suit themselves. A reduction in price or an appropriate gift might also serve to bring its own reward in the shape of office or a reciprocal favour on the part of the administrator, and of course, the higher up in the imperial hierarchy one was the more influence one would tend to have. Petronius Probus, as Ammianus tells us, possessed estates in almost every part of the Empire—'iuste an secus, non iudicioli est nostri': a polite and non-committal way of raising doubts about Probus's methods of accumulating property.[3] His power also enabled Probus to protect his dependants: 'Namque fatendum est numquam ille, magnanimitate coalitus, clienti vel servo agere quicquam iussit illicitum, sed si eorum quemquam crimen ullum compererat admisisse, vel ipsa repugnante Iustitia, non explorato negotio, sine respectu boni honestique defendebat.'[4] A grateful client might even record his gratitude for posterity, as did T. Aelius Poemenius, who erected an inscription to his patron,

Justice was an expensive luxury if one had to pay one's way through a series of bureaucratic barriers to appear in court. (*CTh.* i. 16. 7).
[1] *CTh.* viii. 15. 1. [2] *CTh.* viii. 15. 3, 4, 8.
[3] Amm. xxvii. 11. 1. [4] Amm. xxvii. 11. 4.

T. Fl. Postumius Titianus, through whose 'suffragium' he had been appointed *procurator aquarum*.[1]

In the year 451 Valentinian III, Emperor of the West, issued a law revoking the ban on purchases by office-holders. Though this novel purports to be merely a reiteration of a law issued by Honorius, no trace of the earlier law survives, and in any case Valentinian does not claim that his predecessor's law was decisive on the score of administrators' purchases, but rather that it could be interpreted as freeing office-holders from their former restrictions in this regard:

Quae plerique in legibus constituta dissimulant, necesse est recenti iussione sanciri, ut omni ambiguitate submota instauratione solidiora reddantur. In administratione enim et in militia positis emendi licentiam denegatam superflua nonnullorum dicitur esse persuasio, cum lex divi Honorii ad Palladium ppo missa, in Theodosianum redacta corpus, hanc copiam talibus legatur dedisse personis.[2]

It would seem unlikely that this was the intention of Honorius' law, since we know that he endorsed his brother Arcadius' law issued by 397 repeating the standard injunction against purchases by or gifts to office-holders.[3]

Valentinian III's novel is phrased in such a way as to imply that it had never been illegal for office-holders to make purchases while in office, and this is probably to be seen as a tactical face-saving device. The Emperor's admission that he had changed the law would only serve to mark him out as the submissive tool of his own officials. It is hardly irrelevant to note that the reign of Valentinian III (423–55) saw a succession of praetorian prefects of Italy whose names were representative of the noblest houses of the late Empire: Flavius Anicius Auchenius Bassus, Rufius Antonius Agrypnius Volusianus, Caecina Decius Aginatius Albinus, Anicius Acilius Glabrio Faustus, Nicomachus Flavianus, Petronius Maximus.[4] In these circumstances it is difficult not to see the revocation of the ban on purchases as a result of noble pressure.

Another example of the influence resulting from office is

---

[1] vi. 1418 = D. 2941.
[2] *N. Val.* 32. 1.
[3] *CTh.* viii. 15. 8.
[4] See Sundwall, *Weström. Studien*, s.vv.

furnished by a constitution of 380 dealing with betrothal gifts made
by provincial governors:

Si quis in potestate publica positus atque honore administrandarum
provinciarum, qui parentibus aut tutoribus aut curatoribus aut ipsis,
quae matrimonium contracturae sunt, potest esse terribilis, sponsalia
dederit, iubemus, ut deinceps, sive parentes sive eaedem mutaverint
voluntatem, non modo iuris laqueis liberentur poenaeque expertes sint,
quae quadruplum statuit, sed extrinsecus data pignera lucrativa habeant,
si ea non putent esse reddenda.[1]

We have here a very clear picture of the sort of pressure that a
governor could exert on people. The key word is 'terribilis'. The
law contrives to protect a family forced into an alliance with a high
official against their will. Not only are they entitled to break off the
betrothal with impunity but they can also retain the official's
betrothal gift.

A creditor wishing to hasten payment of a debt would sometimes
transfer the debt owing to him to a powerful man. The fact that the
potens now appeared as the creditor was evidently sufficient to have
the desired effect, and this practice was also outlawed, the penalty
being the loss of the debt.[2] Indeed, so successful was this sort of
ploy that the name of a powerful man might be used in litigation
even when in fact he had not given his consent: 'Animadvertimus
plurimos iniustarum desperatione causarum potentium titulos et
clarissimae privilegia dignitatis his, a quibus in ius vocantur,
opponere.'[3] It says much for the efficacy of the influence of the
powerful that people were even prepared to perpetrate a fraud in
order to lay claim to it.

Another sphere in which influence could prove efficacious was in
evading taxation. The difficulty of collecting taxes from senators in
general is well demonstrated by the imperial contortions in a vain
effort to find an effective way of extracting money from these errant
subjects. Decurions were no doubt cowed or bribed by the great
magnates, and the duty of collecting taxes from senators was
transferred from them at an unknown date to members of the
governors' *officia*. But in 397 the task reverted to the decurions.
We do not have to read between the lines, easy enough though it

---

[1] *CTh*. iii. 6. 1.   [2] *CTh*. ii. 13. 1 (422).   [3] *CTh*. ii. 14. 1 (400).

would be to do so; we are told in a 397 law that in some provinces only half of the senatorial taxes had been paid.[1]

In 399 the praetorian prefect of Gaul received a constitution abolishing all grants of favours to landowners: 'Omni amoto privilegio beneficiorum possessores sublimitas tua praecipiet universos muneribus adstringi . . .'[2] Though we are not told what form these 'beneficia' took, we can only infer from the law that they were some form of tax-exemption or reduction extended by the emperor to certain landowners, presumably those who had contacts at court to influence the emperor in their favour. This law probably refers to *ad hominem* awards by the emperor, for seven years later we have a hint that *illustres* were in a privileged position as regards taxes. In a constitution addressed to the praetorian prefect Anthemius, it is decreed that the daughters of the Emperor (Arcadius) 'tantum inlustribus privilegiis ac debitis potiantur' in the amount of tax that they should be required to pay on their land.[3]

A powerful man could use his influence to ease not only his own tax burden but also that of others. Such a man would evidently sometimes take a tradesman under his wing and, no doubt in return for a share of his profits, help him to evade payment of the *collatio lustralis*, a tax imposed upon all those engaging in trade.[4] Though there is no evidence as to how the protector set about shielding his protégé from the *fiscus*, we can assume that, as in other matters, personal influence was the decisive factor here. It was of course the loss of imperial revenue that prompted Theodosius to issue a law against this practice.[5]

The influence of the powerful can also be seen in the imperial decrees of Valentinian and Valens instituting *defensores civitatum* or *defensores plebis*. The new officials, who were to protect the plebeians 'contra potentium iniurias'[6] were to be drawn from among former governors, barristers, *agentes in rebus*, *palatini*, and *principes* of the *officia* of prefects or vicars, while other officials and decurions

---

[1] *CTh.* vi. 3. 4.   [2] *CTh.* xi. 1. 26.
[3] *CTh.* x. 25. 1 (406).   [4] *CTh.* xiii. 1. 1–2.
[5] *CTh.* xiii. 1. 15 (386).
[6] *CTh.* 1. 29. 1 (364). For precursors of this post in Egypt see A. Hoepffner, 'Un aspect de la lutte de Valentinien Ier contre le sénat: la création du "defensor plebis"', *Revue Historique*, 182 (1938) 226; E. Stein, *Geschichte* i, 278.

were explicitly debarred.[1] It is not difficult to account for the Emperors' choice of *defensores*. All of these were either high-ranking officials or, as in the case of the *palatini*, came to the localities concerned from the imperial court, and were therefore much more influential than ordinary officials attached to governors' *officia*. The choice of the *agentes in rebus* may have been prompted by their 'secret service' activities,[2] and the exclusion of decurions is attributable to the fact that they themselves were among those needing protection.[3] In all, then, and not surprisingly, the choice of Valentinian for his new post fell upon those office-holders who he thought would be most efficacious in protecting the *plebeii*.

But who were the *potentes* against whom the *defensores* were to defend them? To Hoepffner the term 'potentes' is not suitable as a description of officials as such and so he identifies them with 'l'aristocratie sénatoriale'.[4] Though he admits that later emperors did regard the function of the *defensores* as protecting the humble against imperial officials, he sees this as a change in the purpose of the institution.[5] Yet from a letter of 365 sent by Valentinian to a

---

[1] *CTh.* I. 29. 1 and 3.

[2] On the 'secret service' work of the *agentes in rebus* see Aur. Vict. *Caes.* xxxix. 44, *CTh.* vi. 29. 4, and the discussion of the question in Jones, *Later Roman Empire*, ii, 581–2.

[3] *CTh.* i. 29. 7 (392) describes the duty of *defensores* as follows: 'Plebem tantum vel decuriones ab omni improborum insolentia et temeritate tueantur.'

[4] Hoepffner, art. cit., 226 ff. But cf. Harmand, *Patronat*, 464 f.

[5] Hoepffner, ibid. and 233. Having come to this conclusion for no very apparent reason, Hoepffner proceeds to date the institution of the new office to 368. But, though *CTh.* i. 29. 1 is redated by Seeck from 364 (the MS. date) to 368 (*Regesten*, 91–2), *CTh.* i. 29. 2, which is addressed to a *defensor*, is undoubtedly correctly dated in the MSS. to 365, as Seeck points out (*Regesten*, 32), since another part of the same constitution (*CTh.* viii. 15. 4) refers to a law of 364 (*CTh.* viii. 15. 3) as recently ('proxime') issued. *CTh.* i. 29. 1, which in any case refers only to Illyricum, would not appear therefore to be the earliest law about the new office, which must have been instituted before 27 June 365, the date of *CTh.* i. 29. 2. Hoepffner, however, argues that the *defensores* cannot date before 368, since Valentinian was on good terms with the Senate until then (p. 228). Though, as Hoepffner points out, Valentinian issued a law in 364 confirming Constantius' institution of *defensores senatus* (*CTh.* i. 28. 1–2), yet the appointment to the urban prefecture of one Viventius, a Pannonian (Amm. xxvii. 3. 11) and almost certainly a non-noble—a step hardly calculated to win the favour of the aristocracy—took place in 365 or 366. (See Seeck, *Regesten*, 117. The *PLRE* dates Viventius's entry into office as PUR to 365, but gives no explanation.) *CTh.* xiv. 3. 7. Another act hostile to pagan nobles was the promulgation of the law against sacrifices, dated September 364. (*CTh.* ix. 16. 7), and in January 365 a law was issued revoking Julian's immunity to senators from arrest. (Julian: *CTh.* ix. 2. 1 (362).

certain Seneca, evidently a *defensor*, it is clear that at least one of his
functions was to act as a judge of first instance, deciding minor
cases and sending more serious ones on to the governor.[1] This does
not conflict with later laws on the subject, and one of them shows
how important it must have been for the humbler and poorer
elements of society to have cheap or free access to the courts, since
justice tended otherwise to be a very expensive luxury.[2] In this
regard the *defensores* cannot be regarded as aimed specifically
against the aristocracy, though a noble governor might well be as
venal as a non-noble one. A similar view of the post is shown by a
law of 392 in which Theodosius calls upon the *defensores* to remove
'patrocinia quae favorem reis et auxilium scelerosis inpertiendo
maturari scelera fecerunt'.[3] If the patrons whose activities were
censured here were men whose influence stemmed from office or
wealth or both, it is more than likely that some nobles were included in their number.

A very real advantage that noble-office-holders had over non-
noble office-holders was the elaborate interlocking skein of relationships and family connections that are represented in our
stemmata at the end of this volume. From this all the major aristocratic families appear to have been connected one with another.
Marriages tended to be within the same aristocratic circle. This
would tend to have knitted together the various noble families into
a more united social stratum which it was not easy for an outsider
to enter, though Symmachus himself was only the second or third
generation of his family to be born noble. This inter-related
family structure must also have served as a network of communica-
tion and influence for the aristocracy. Even if a particular noble
was not himself in office, he would be likely to have relatives in
high office at any given time upon whom he could count to further
his interests at a higher level of government.

The fact that nobles were concerned, as we have seen, to link
themselves with the distant past by claiming descent from the

---

Valentinian: *CTh.* ix. 2. 2 (365)). A similar view of Hoepffner's on the phases of
Valentinian's policy towards the senate is expressed by Schuurmans, *Samenstelling*, 565 ff., *Ant.Class.* 18 (1949) 25–38. Cf. Alföldi, *Conflict of Ideas*, 39 ff.
  [1] *CTh.* i. 29. 2 (365).   [2] See p. 158, n. 5.   [3] *CTh.* i. 29. 8.

aristocratic figures of the Republic is in itself an indication that the late Empire was a period of aristocratic values. Lineage and birth were accorded great respect—another advantage that aristocratic office-holders had over their non-noble colleagues. St. Jerome's obvious esteem of noble birth is no doubt a reflection of a common popular attitude rather than of an idiosyncratic preference on his part.[1]

As urban prefect and also in his earlier posts Symmachus had considerable experience in judicial procedure. In this period the judicial side of a governor's duties would often be the most important, and the urban prefect was primarily a judge. It is instructive therefore to discover what the orator's view of justice was: 'Ratio quidem semper habenda iustitiae est, sed circa nobiles probabilesque personas plus debet esse moderaminis, ut perspiciatur in discretione iudicium.'[2] Though the category of 'nobiles probabilesque personae' was probably much wider than just the aristocracy and no doubt included men of substance and 'respectability' in general, it is interesting to find such blatant bias as a principle of justice on the part of a man who can be taken without much hesitation as a representative spokesman for the aristocratic office-bearers.

This aristocratic view of justice did not square with the view held, for example, by Constantine, who, not surprisingly, regarded with no great favour the overmighty subject who attempted to pervert the ends of justice. A law of 328 instructs provincial governors to report any such person whom they were unable to punish or who disrupted the proceedings of a case either to the praetorian prefect or to the emperor himself.[3] Whether any such 'insolentiores potiores' were nobles is not known, but if their methods were, as they appear to have been,[4] bribery and largess rather than armed force, it is not at all unlikely that they included some nobles. Julian, on the other hand, issued a law in 362 in which he said that it was necessary to protect the rights of senators and the authority

---

[1] See, for example, *Epp.*54. 2; 107. 1; 108. 1.
[2] Symm. *Ep.* ix. 40.   [3] *CTh.* i. 16. 4.
[4] *CTh.* i. 16. 6 (331) for example, insists that cases be judged in public and crowded court-rooms to prevent the bribery that could and no doubt did take place in judges' private chambers.

of the senatorial order, 'in quo nos quoque ipsos esse numeramus'.[1] The law goes on to give accused senators immunity from arrest until convicted. Three years later, however, Valentinian decreed that judges should refer to the Emperor 'vel causae meritum vel personae qualitatem' but that in the meantime anyone suspected of a crime should be arrested, 'cuiuscumque honoris esse dicatur'. This is hardly surprising in an emperor who was a sincere and dedicated champion of the 'laesi minores'.[2]

In an age in which bribery and corruption was as rife as the Theodosian Code shows it to have been wealth was obviously a factor of great importance in exerting influence. So venal do governors appear to have been in their capacity as judges that they were forbidden to receive visitors from their own province in the afternoon.[3] It is hardly surprising that in so deferential a society as the late Empire the clarissimate should carry with it certain privileges. In addition to negative privileges such as immunity from curial duties, senatorial rank accorded its holders some positive influence and is specifically mentioned, for example, in the law of 400 quoted above dealing with the illicit use of the 'tituli potentium' in court cases.[4]

Another example of such influences is to be found in a novel of Theodosius II: 'Sed et quod motibus se iudicum reverentia subtrahunt dignitatis, publicis commoditatibus noxium esse perspicitis. Cessat enim debitorum conpulsio, si debitori deferat executor.'[5] The law then goes on to forbid entry to the Senate on the part of decurions—a prohibition first enacted a century previously.[6] The evidence is clear that even the clarissimate was invested with sufficient aura to swing the result of a court action.

---

[1] *CTh.* ix. 2. 1 (362).
[2] Valentinian's decree of 365: *CTh.* ix. 2. 2. On Valentinian's hostility to nobles see *Amm.* xxx. 8. 10. For his predilection for Pannonians see Alföldi, *Conflict*, 13–27. For his policy as regards appointments to office see Chapter IV, above. The term 'laesi minores' occurs in a Constantinian law, *CTh.* i. 16. 4.
[3] *CTh.* i. 16. 13 (377).
[4] Immunity from curial duties: see *CTh.* xii. 1, *passim*. See discussion of this in Jones, *Later Roman Empire*, ii, 741 ff. Law of 400: *CTh.* ii. 14. 1, quoted above, p. 161, n. 3. See Jones, op. cit., ii, 535 ff.   [5] *Nov. Theod.* xv. 1. 2 (439).
[6] *CTh.* xii. 1. 18 (326; the date is in question, MSS. giving 329 and other laws which appear to be parts of the same constitution being dated 354. See Seeck, *Regesten*, 43, where the date 326 is preferred); xii. 1. 25 (338).

Senatorial rank connected a man with a glorious past, a history going back to the establishment of the Republic. The ethos had survived though the senate as an assembly was no longer of any real significance and few members seem to have attended meetings.[1] The senatorial traditions, however, were far from dead. New members of the 'club' were gradually absorbed and partook of the ethos which had its origins in the mists of history. Even in the latter part of the fifth century, in the writings of Apollinaris Sidonius, we find strong echoes of the ancient fellowship. On being asked to recommend a bishop for the see of Bituriges (previously Avaricum, now Bourges), Apollinaris discussed the relative merits of actual and hypothetical candidates. Rank was also taken into account and Sidonius admits that two candidates, namely Eucherius and Pannychius, were 'rightly' thought superior to the man of his own choice, Simplicius, because they were *illustres*. Simplicius' election could be secured only by pointing out that his rivals were canonically ineligible since both were remarried.[2]

Membership of the Senate still counted for something in the late Empire. But to place beside evidence of the clarissimate's influence we have evidence of senators suffering at the hands of people below them in the social scale: 'Senatoriae func[tion]is curiaeque sit nulla coniunctio et ne laeden[di cu]rialibus praebeatur occasio per apparitores rect]orum provinciae de senatorum fundis fis[calia] postulentur habeatque hanc dispondendi cu[ram, c]ui defendendi senatus sollicitudo mandata [erit].' From this it would appear that not all senators were men of influence, though extortionate practices on the part of decurions collecting taxes might be difficult even for an influential senator to check, given the scattered nature of landed possessions. It is worth noting that all the laws in the Theodosian Code dealing with *defensores senatus* are Eastern laws, no doubt a reflection of the fact that such protection was needed more by the senators of that half of the Empire than by their Western counterparts.[3] As can be seen from the statistical

---

[1] See *CTh.* vi. 4. 9 (356) and the discussion of it above.

[2] Ap. Sid. *Ep.* vii. 9. 18, quoted on p. 106, above.

[3] Extract quoted: *CTh.* vi. 3. 2 (396). Laws on *defensores: CTh.* i. 28. 1–4; vi. 3. 2–3. *CTh.* i. 28. 1 (361—Constantius II) is addressed 'ad senatum' and no provenance is given, but vi. 4. 12–13, which seem to be part of the same law, are

tables at the end of the volume, the number of nobles appointed to Eastern offices in our period was very small by comparison with noble appointments in the West, and most of those appointed to Eastern positions were Westerners, men such as Q. Clodius Hermogenianus Olybrius, Postumianus, Vettius Agorius Praetextatus, Maecius Memmius Caecilianus Placidus or Vulcacius Rufinus, the first two of whom were praetorian prefects of the East, the third being proconsul of Achaea and the last two *Comites Orientis*.[1] It was in the West that the large estates of the senatorial aristocracy were concentrated, and Eastern senators are more likely to have been poorer than their Western brethren. Also the Eastern Senate seems to have been made up of self-made men with no elaborate family connections or long established local position.[2]

The advantages attaching to senatorial rank and the much greater benefits accruing to the holders of high office were of course far from being the monopoly of the aristocracy. But nobles had the added advantage of wealth and intricate family networks which could serve to conduct the influence of nobles in office to those living in retirement on their estates. For of all the sources of influence office was undoubtedly the most important, and the emperor's ear was clearly the most valuable commodity in the Empire, as can be seen, for example, in the successful appeals of Praetextatus to Valentinian.[3] The addition of office to the previous amalgam of birth and wealth gave the senatorial aristocracy a more potent compound that was possessed by any other element of the civil population.

marked as given at Gyfyra (Gephyra) (See Seeck, *Regesten*, 208, s.a. 361). The Senate to which the law is addressed could of course be either that of Rome or Constantinople.

[1] Olybrius: vi. 1714 = D. 1271. Postumianus: *CTh.* ix. 42. 10; xii. 1. 98; xvi. 7. 2; vi. 22. 7; vii. 2. 1; xii. 1. 102; xvi. 5. 11; xii. 6. 17; xii. 1. 104; xvi. 5. 12. Praetextatus: vi. 1779 = D. 1259; vi. 1777 = D. 1258 and vi. 1778. *Hell.* iv., p. 24, Thespiae. Placidus: x. 1700 = D. 1231, Puteoli. Rufinus: vi. 32051 = D. 1237.

[2] See Jones, *Later Roman Empire*, i, 133–4; ii, 551 ff. For the origins of the Eastern assembly see Soz. ii. 3; Zos. iii. 11; Euseb. *V. Const.* iv. 67; Amm. xxii. 24. The history of this Senate is related by Lecrivain, *Sénat*, 217 ff.

[3] Zos. iv. 3; Amm. xxviii. 1. 11.

CONCLUSION

T HE usual view of the power-structure of the Later Roman Empire is summed up in the terms used to describe it. It is labelled 'the Dominate' or 'Oriental Despotism' in the belief that it was a period of absolute monarchy. The results of my research have led me, however, to a very different conclusion.

Conscious that imperial power and senatorial power were at opposite ends of a political see-saw, emperor after emperor encroached upon the power of the Senate from the early Principate onwards until it was left with only ceremonial functions. But though the Senate as an institution was of no account, the men who comprised it continued to have a monopoly of most of the high state posts, notably provincial governorships. At first emperors worked through the Senate, subverting the position of the older families by introducing their own nominees into the Senate and then appointing them to governorships, and thus keeping within the traditional constitutional framework. But the third century saw a change. Particularly in the latter half of the century emperors tended to by-pass the Senate, advancing non-senators directly to high office without bothering to make them senators first. This tendency was systematized by Diocletian, in whose reign senators were debarred from all but a few high state offices and the senatorial career became a *cul-de-sac*. A low-born military man who cultivated an aloof manner and kept an ostentatious court, Diocletian had achieved the aim of more than one of his predecessors. He was indeed an autocrat.

In the conventional view, which still holds the consensus, the reign of Diocletian marks the beginning of 'the Dominate'. For me, however, the reign of Diocletian was not a beginning but an end. Constitutionally the position of Constantine was not inferior to that of Diocletian. But Constantine reversed the anti-senatorial trend in government, which can be traced back to the military dynasts of the Republic. Now, after a generation's gap, Constantine appointed members of old senatorial aristocratic families to high civil posts in the West once again. Nor was this only a momentary interlude, for his successors continued this policy for as long as there was an emperor in the West—and beyond. The change in policy became clear to me from a close study of the careers and family origins of imperial appointees in the period.

But how is the change to be explained ? To explain it in terms of an idiosyncratic predilection on Constantine's part for aristocrats is inadequate—unless we are to suppose that this predilection was hereditarily transmitted not only to successors of his own blood but also to others not related to him at all, such as the emperors of the Theodosian house. It is important to note that, while nobles were now regularly appointed to high office in the West, the East continued for the most part to be governed by non-nobles. The Greek-speaking East was much more urbanized and also more Christian than the Western half of the Empire, which was still largely rural and pagan. The appointment of members of the aristocracy to imperial posts by Constantine may best be understood as an attempt to placate and win over this ardently pagan class, whose considerable landed wealth and local influence were concentrated in the West. Even an emperor like Valentinian I (364–75), who made no secret of his dislike of the aristocracy and who had genuine sympathy for the man at the bottom of the social and economic pyramid, conformed to the Constantinian pattern, giving a free hand in the West to a noble—and corrupt—praetorian prefect.

The emperor had given the aristocracy a share in the ruling of the Empire—a share which was to increase at the emperor's expense. Office-holders could use their position as a lever to enhance their wealth and local influence, and noble office-holders in general had two main advantages over most of their non-noble colleagues. First, they tended to be better endowed with wealth and land, and circumstances favoured the large landowner. The barbarian incursions in the latter half of the fourth century forced many a free peasant smallholder to barter his land in return for the protection of a neighbouring estate-owner. In this way large estates could be consolidated and on each of them, with its walls and self-sufficient economy, the estate-owner was an autocrat.

Secondly, being a close-knit intricate network of inter-related families, the aristocracy had ready-made channels for the conduction and distribution of favours and influence within their exclusive group. For, though now part of the imperial administrative machine, nobles utilized their position for the benefit of their families in the localities. The aristocracy was essentially a centrifugal force, which helped to undermine the position of the imperial administration from within while war and invasion threatened it from outside.

How does our new view of the role of the aristocracy affect our interpretation of the period in general? The consensus of scholars and laymen alike still labels the period as one of 'decline and fall' in the West, and the Germanic invaders are still seen as the culprits, though there is a variety of explanations for their victory. But what was it that the invasions caused to collapse? The central imperial administration. Yet, in eliminating the emperor the invasions only strengthened the underlying amalgam of economic, social, and political forces in society, centrifugal in tendency and aristocratic in tone, which had been prominent since the reign of Constantine and which were to continue to dominate Western Europe for close on a thousand years.

APPENDIX: SELECTED PROSOPOGRAPHY

The names appearing here are those of office-holders who could not be discussed in the main body of the text but whose careers or backgrounds are nevertheless interesting or problematical.

1. *Acilius Clarus*

MOENIA QVISQ. DOLET NOVA CONDERE SVCCESSORI
INCVLTO MANEAT LIVIDVS HOSPITIO
ACILIVS CLARVS V. COS. P.P.N.
SIBI SVCCESSORIB. FECIT.[1]

This rather unusual inscription comes from Lambaesis in Numidia, and of course the letters 'P.P.N.' in the third line stand for 'praeses provinciae Numidiae', and Acilius Clarus himself was a 'v(ir) co(n)s(ularis)'.

As is remarked by its editor in the *Corpus*, the inscription probably refers to the change of the provincial capital from Lambaesis to Cirta, which was then renamed Constantina to fit it to its new role. This took place under Constantine, but we do not know when in his reign. It cannot, however, be later than 320, when the province is first recorded as governed by a consular, Domitius Zenophilus. Since Constantine gained control of Africa in 312, Acilius Clarus must have been *praeses* at some time between 312 and 320. The designation 'vir consularis, praeses' may be seen as at only one remove from the title 'consularis', and since it is likely that the title of the governor was changed at the same time as the seat of government, this would place Clarus nearer 320 than 312.

In addition, however, we have an inscription dated 286 from Aquileia, in which we are told that one Acilius Clarus was corrector of Italy.[2] Identified with this corrector, our *praeses* has naturally been assigned a date before 286, since a praesidial governorship is junior to a correctorship.[3] But there is no need to identify the namesake governors, though they must have been related. As we have seen, the most probable date for the governorship of Numidia was some thirty years later than the correctorship of Italy. The *praeses* could therefore have been the son, or even the grandson of the corrector. Both men must have been members of the noble family of the Acilii.

---

[1] viii. 2729 Lambaesis, Numidia.
[2] v. 8205 Aquileia.
[3] This identification is made by Groag *PIR*² A 55, the *PLRE* (s.v.) and E. Birley, 'The Governors of Numidia A.D. 193–268', *JRS* 40 (1950) 66.

2. *Domitius Zenophilus*

After a correctorship of Sicily[1] he became 'cons(ularis) sexfascalis'of Numidia, in which post he is recorded in 320.[2] Zenophulis was therefore the first known consular of that, or indeed of any, province.[3] At some time between 326 (the execution of Crispus) and 333, when Zenophilus became ordinary consul, he was proconsul of Africa.[4] The career adheres to the fourth-century standard senatorial *cursus*. Though Zenophilus' family cannot be traced, his clarissimate already as corrector indicates senatorial birth, since one was unlikely to be elevated to senatorial rank to become a corrector, a position which could be held by *perfectissimi* as well as *clarissimi*.

The *nomen* Domitius was one of the commonest in the Empire, but it is just possible that Zenophilus was related to Domitius Latronianus, who, like Zenophilus, was corrector of Sicily and proconsul of Africa, holding this latter post while Zenophilus was consular of Numidia.

Zenophilus' career as we know it was successful, but only moderately so. If he was the first consular to be appointed, that must be accounted a great honour. But an even greater honour, and one which is very difficult to explain in view of Zenophilus's apparently rather modest attainments, was his ordinary consulship—an honour normally accorded by Constantine to members of the Imperial family and men who had reached high positions in the service of the Empire. What were Zenophilus's qualifications? If he was the proconsul of Africa who, among other things, was also proconsul of Asia and Achaea, but whose name is missing from an inscription charting his impressive course through life, we can easily understand why he became consul afterwards.[5] Of course Zenophilus

---

[1] x. 7234 Lilybaeum, Sicilia.

[2] *AE* 1915, 30 Lambaesis, Numidia.

[3] Opt. *App.* 1. Aug. *c. litt. pet.* iii. 57. 69. Aug. *ep. ad cath.* 18. 46. Aug. *c. Cresc.* iii. 28. 32, 29. 32. iv. 56. 66. *Epp.* 43. 17, 53. 4.

[4] viii. 1408 = D. 5359 Thignica. For a history of the administration of Numidia see Chastagnol, 'Les Consulaires de Numidie', *Mélanges Jérôme Carcopino*, 215–28.

[5]   . . . eximiae potestatis et moderationis
et bonitatis ac praedicabili, c.v. post
correcturas et consularem dignitatem,
Acaiae, Asiae iterum et Africae IV procos.
sacro iudicio Constantini Maximi victoris
ac triumfatoris semper Au[g] et beatissimorum
Caes[*arum*] . . .
I.L. Afr. 456 Bulla Regia, Afr. Procos.

There is nothing here which conflicts with Zenophilus' career as we know it. He was a corrector and a consular as well as proconsul of Africa at some time after 324, as this inscription requires, the epithet 'victor' giving us that date. If this is Zenophilus, we must add to his career a correctorship of an unspecified province, and proconsulships of Achaea and Asia.

is not the only candidate for this inscription, but he is a strong one.[1] Yet, irrespective of it, an ordinary consulship is in itself a strong pointer to noble birth in the absence of the other qualities which marked men out for this ancient magistracy.

3. C. Caelius Censorinus

His career begins with a praetorship and, significantly, a suffect consulship. Then, after a series of traditionally senatorial *curatelae*, Censorinus becomes *comes* of Constantine—the only indication of date in the inscription. As 'exactor auri et argenti' Censorinus was probably responsible for the collection of the *aurum oblaticium*, a tax imposed on senators on the accession of an emperor and on each fifth anniversary after that. This curious appointment is followed by consular governor-ships of Sicily and Campania, and it was while in the latter post that the people of Atella recorded their gratitude to him for his benefactions.[2]

It is significant that Censorinus was a genuine *consularis*, in the sense of an ex-consul, when appointed to his consular governorships, and, though we know nothing of his ancestry, Caelius being so common a *nomen*, his suffect consulship is sufficient indication of wealth and nobility.[3] His namesake recorded as *consularis sexfascalis* of Numidia in 376/78, was probably his grandson.[4]

4. Agricola

All we have to guide us here is a fragmentary inscription from Chusira in Byzacena, in which (A)gricola is described as 'v.c. presid(e)', presumably of Byzacena.[5] This is clear enough in itself, but what we lack is a date. There were no *praesides* in Byzacena before the provinces were, in Lactantius's phrase, 'in frusta concisae' by Diocletian.[6] In particular, proconsular Africa was now only a meagre remnant of the former imposing senatorial province, the rest of the old proconsulate being divided

---

[1] It could also be a description of the career of M. Caeionius Julianus Kamenius, Maecilius Hilarianus, or Tertullus, all of whom were, like Zenophilus, proconsuls of Africa. The only one of these in addition to Zenophilus to become ordinary consul was Maecilius Hilarianus, but Zenophilus is more likely to be the anonymous triple proconsul than Hilarianus because of his Greek *cognomen*. Both the additional proconsulates were in the Greek-speaking half of the Empire, and it is not too fanciful to associate Zenophilus with a Greek-speaking background because of his *cognomen*—and besides, he had already been corrector of Sicily, which was evidently still largely Greek-speaking. The identification must, however, remain hypothetical. See Chastagnol, *Fastes* 89/90 n. 105, who seems to favour Kamenius. Groag, *Reichsbeamten von Achaia*, 24–5, expresses no preference.

[2] x. 3732 = D. 1216.   [3] See article 'Adlectio', P-W i. 366–8.
[4] viii. 2216.   [5] *AE* 1946, 45.
[6] Lactantius: vii. 4. No attempt is made in the *PLRE* to date Agricola more precisely than to the early fourth century.

up into two provinces, Tripolitana and Byzacena. The latest date for a *praeses* of Byzacena is 338, since the province was first placed under consulars at some time between 321 and 338, as is explained in the discussion on Cezeus Largus Maternianus, probably the earliest known consular of Byzacena. So Agricola could have been *praeses* of Byzacena at any time within the period between 284 and 338. Most important, we cannot tell whether he was governor under Diocletian or Constantine. One point is worth considering, however; Diocletian divided the old proconsulate of Africa into three provinces, the new proconsulate and two praesidial provinces. In view of his general policy of excluding senators from state posts, it seems unlikely that he would appoint a senator to one of the praesidial provinces which he had just created, bringing two-thirds of the old province back under senatorial control. Moreover, we know of three senatorial *praesides* of Byzecana under Constantine. It is therefore much easier to believe that Agricola was a Constantinian rather than a Diocletianic *praeses*.

5. *Cezeus Largus Maternianus*

An inscription dating from between 326 and 333 found near Vaga in Proconsular Africa describes his as legate to the proconsul and patron of the town.[1] From another African inscription we learn more about him:

CEZEO LARGO CV
PATRONO COLONIAE
MAGNIFICO ATQ PRAES.
TANTI ET SENATORIAE DIG
NITAtis ORNAMENTO
PRAEtORIO VIRO EX CON
SVLARi bYZACENAE PRo
VINCIAE TERTIO PROCON
SVLI PRoVInclAE AFRICAE[2]

All the appointments were in Africa. That Maternianus had close ties with Africa is inescapable, as we can see from his patronage of both the towns where the inscriptions were set up. As legate of Africa Maternianus was under Ceionius Julianus, a member of another family with close African ties. Perhaps proconsul and legate were related, which was not infrequently the case. As legate Maternianus already appears as 'v.c.' But how did he get this title? Was it the result of senatorial birth, or did he gain it later on? He could not have been adlected, since the only adlections known in the fourth century were 'inter consulares', but Maternianus was only 'vir praetorius' even as proconsul of Africa. Nor could he have held any office automatically conferring the clarissimate before becoming legate, since all such posts, proconsulships and vicariates

---

[1] viii. 14436 = D. 5518 nr. Vaga, Afr. Procos.   [2] *ILAlg* 4012 = *AE* 1922, 17.

for example, were higher than a humble legation. To consolidate our view of Maternianus as a man of senatorial origin we have the words in the second inscription 'magnificus atq. praestans et senatoriae dignita(tis) ornamentum'.

6. *Aginatius*

Recorded as consular of Byzacena in 363,[1] he is better known as vicar of Rome—which post he held from 368 to 370—because of his clash with Maximinus, his successor and architect of his death. The story is recounted in full detail and with more than a dash of melodrama by Ammianus, and there is no need fo repeat it here.[2] For our purpose it is significant to notice that, though Maximinus was a favourite of Valentinian's, it took him some time to act against Aginatius, displaying unwonted caution in his attack. He was even afraid to have a known accomplice of his put Aginatius to death, and it appears to have been four years after the end of his own vicariate before Maximinus felt able to pounce on his foe, through the agency of a Gaul called Doryphorianus, for whom Maximinus, now a praetorian prefect, arranged an appointment to the vicariate of Rome to accomplish his bloody purpose. Ammianus's explanation of Maximinus's great caution in action against Aginatius is instructive: a death warrant from the Emperor was easy enough to obtain, but it was because Aginatius was 'homo patriciae stirpis' that Maximinus was afraid to act too rashly against him.[3]

We also know of Aginatius's noble birth from other passages in Ammianus where he is referred to as 'senator perspicui generis'[4] and 'iam inde a priscis maioribus nobilis'.[5] That Aginatius was of noble birth is therefore clear, though Ammianus adds to this last description: '. . . ut locuta est pertinacior fama; nec enim super hoc ulla documentorum rata est fides'.[6] This is to be taken as scepticism not about Aginatius's nobility—which, as we see fron the other references, Ammianus fully accepts—but of the antiquity of his lineage. In any case, the name Aginatius, of which there is no record before our vicar, recurs later in the ranks of both the Anicii and the Ceionii, the Ceionian link being represented by the name of the urban prefect of 414 and 426, Caecina Decius Aginatius Albinus, and the Anician link by the consul of 483, Anicius Acilius Aginatius Faustus.

7. *Caelestinus*

The address 'Caelestino consulari Baeticae' in a law of 357 is the only reference to this governor.[7] In addition to a very fragmentary inscription

---

[1] *CTh.* xi. 20. 1.   [2] Amm. xxviii, 1. 30–5, 50–6.
[3] Amm. xxviii. 1. 52.   [4] Amm. xxviii. 1. 54.
[5] Amm. xxviii. 1. 30.   [6] Ibid.
[7] *CTh.* ix. 42. 3.

which seems to read 'Caelestinae c.f.'[1] and a reference to a Caelestinus in the life of Valerian in the *Augustan History*,[2] the only other Caelestini known are members of the family of the Granii Caelestini, namely Q. Granius Caelestinus, described as 'c.v., quaestor . . . senator splendidissimus', probably of the early third century,[3] and Q. Attius Granius Caelestinus, 'v.c. cu(r) alv. Tib. et cloac. s.u.' in the time of Constantine.[4] In view of the extreme rarity of the name Caelestinus and the near-contemporaneity of the urban curator and the Spanish governor, it is not a very daring step to assume a link between them, perhaps as father and son. The African senator would then in turn be the grand-father or great-grandfather of the curator.

8. *Aemilius Maximus*

PACIS ET QVIETIS
AVCTORI LIBERTATIS
RESTITVTORI ET VICTORI
HOSTIVM D.N. FLAVIO
CONSTANTINO MAXIMO
PIO FELICI INVICTO AVG.
AEMILIVS MAXIMVS VC
. . . . MIDIVC/I
. . . .[5]

It is unfortunate that the text fails us just at the point where it would have given us Maximus' position. The letters visible in the eighth line are incomprehensible. What we do know is that Maximus was a *clarissimus* and that he set up an inscription to Constantine in Gallaecia. The occasion must have been Constantine's defeat either of Maxentius or of Licinius. The title 'invictus' was assumed after the victory over Maxentius in 312 and was often replaced by 'victor' after the 324 victory against Licinius. Though 'victor' appears in this inscription, it is used informally and does not appear among the official titles of the Emperor. The date is probably, therefore, between 312 and 324. The public nature of the dedication makes it certain that Maximus was a state official. He was probably *praeses* of the province, Gallaecia, though it is just conceivable that he might have been vicar or *comes provinciarum*. If, as is most likely, he was *praeses*, we may safely assume that his clarissi-mate came to him by birth, though nothing is known of his family.

9. *Numerius Albanus*

The only reference that we have to him is a short inscription on the walls of baths in Lisbon.[6] The date is 336 and Albanus is 'v(ir) c(larissi-

1 xi. 7283 Volsinii.
2 SHA *V. Valeriani* 8. 1.
3 *IRT* 532 Lepcis Magna.
4 vi. 1143.
5 *Eph. Ep.* viii. p. 403, 1117, Bracara, Gallaecia.
6 ii. 191 = D. 5699 Olisipo.

mus) p(raeses) p(rovinciae) L(usitaniae)'. The name Numerius was a rare one, but it is difficult to connect our man with anyone in particular. There was another Numerius Albanus, a *tribunus cohortis* and *praefectus classis* in the first half of the second century, who may have been an ancestor of our *praeses* as Dessau rather tentatively suggests.[1] Of course the title *clarissimus* in itself tells us nothing about a man's birth, but only that he was of senatorial rank at the time. But in the case of a *praeses* the clarissimate may be taken as sufficient sign of senatorial birth. For it is hardly conceivable that a man should be adlected into the Senate or granted the *latus clavus* only to be appointed to an ordinary provincial governorship which was usually held by an equestrian. The same argument also applies to T. Septimius Januarius, Constantinian *praeses* of Sardinia.

10. *Pompeius Appius Faustinus*

He was 'v.c. pr(aetor) ur(banus)'[2] then 'v.c. corr. Campaniae' under Constantius I[3] and finally urban prefect 300–1. His career is clearly that of a man of senatorial birth, and he was related to Pompeius Faustinus Severianus, a suffect consul of the first half of the third century recorded in an African inscription.[4]

11. *Virius Gallus*

'V.c. corr. Campaniae', and ordinary consul together with Anicius Faustus in 298, he was clearly of senatorial birth. He may have been related to Virius Lupus, consular of Campania in the mid-fourth century and the line of the Virii Lupi.[5]

12. *Julius Festus Hymetius*

His career is recorded in an inscription reading:

HYMETII
... IVLIO FESTO HYMETIO C.V.
CORRECTORI TVSCIAE ET VMBRIAE PRAETORI VRBANO
CONSVLARI CAMPANIAE CVM SAMNIO
VICARIO VRBIS ROMAE AETERNAE PROCONSVLI
PROVINCIAE AFRICAE ...[6]

The date of the inscription is 376. Hymetius may still have been proconsul of Africa at the time, or else he had recently retired. In either case

---

[1] Numerius Albanus: vi. 221 = D. 2160; *PIR*[1] N. 160. Septimius Januarius: x. 7950, x. 7974. *Epp. Ep.* viii. 783 = *AE* 1889, 35.
[2] vi. 314 d.   [3] x. 4785 Campania.   [4] viii. 1438.
[5] x. 3867 = D. 6310 Capua, Campania. Cf. Domitius Zenophilus, App. 2. See Virius Lupus, App. 13.
[6] vi. 1736 = D. 1256.

he had a long tenure of the position, since we have a law addressed to him as proconsul of Africa dated 368 by Seeck and 367 in the MSS.[1] We have a reference in 362 to Hymetius as Vicar of Rome,[2] and his consular governorship of Campania and Samnium must have been held no later than in the 350s, in which decade Samnium became a separate province.[3] The position of the praetorship after a correctorship of Hymetius's career may be thought to indicate that he was not of senatorial birth. It is possible that the order as we have it is the error of a stonemason, who, omitting the praetorship, added it in later. But in the absence of any proof of such a slip we must accept the order in the inscription as historical. Even so, however, it is conceivable that a man of senatorial birth postponed holding the praetorship because of the considerable expense attached to it. Such speculations would be quite futile if it were not for the fact that we have positive proof of Hymetius's nobility. He is described by Ammianus as 'praeclarae indolis vir',[4] and St. Jerome tells us that a man whom he calls simply Hymetius had a wife called Praetextata and was 'patruus Eustochiae virginis'.[5] In another passage we learn: '(Paula) tali igitur stirpe generata iunctaque viro Toxotio, qui Aeneae et Iuliorum altissimum sanguinem trahit. Unde etiam Christi virgo, filia eius, Eustochium Iulia nuncupatur et ipse Iulius, a magno demissum nomen Iulo.'[6] Since the father of Eustochium (or Eustochia) was called Julius Toxotius and since Hymetius was Eustochium's 'patruus', he was therefore Toxotius's brother and presumably therefore also had the *nomen* Julius. This is sufficient to identify Jerome's Hymetius with the vicar Julius Festus Hymetius. Jerome endows the family with a very imposing lineage but to take this literally and connect Hymetius with the family of Julius Caesar would of course be folly. We can quickly acquit Jerome of any partiality towards this pagan stalwart.[7] In holding that Hymetius and his brother Toxotius were members of an ancient noble family Jerome must have been expressing a current belief.

We do have some senatorial Julii Festi of the third century. First there was Tib. Jul(ius) Festus, legate of Moesia under Severus Alexander.[8] Then we have Julius Festus, v.c. *praetor urbanus* under the tetrarchy, who put up a dedication to Hercules.[9] Finally there is a Julius Festus whose name appears in a list of donors, and who may be the same person as the praetor.[10] The family was connected by marriage with some of the noblest houses in the Empire. Toxotius married Paula, who is

[1] *CTh.* ix. 19. 3. [2] *CTh.* xi. 30. 29.
[3] See Thomsen, *The Italic Regions*, 210–17.
[4] Amm. xxviii. 1. 17. [5] Jer. *Ep.* 107. 5.
[6] Jer. *Ep.* 108. 4. [7] See Jer. *Ep.* 107. 5.
[8] Pick, *Münzen Nordgriechenlands* 1, 283–8 n. 995–1022. A. Stein, *Die Legaten von Moesien, Dissertationes Pannonicae*, i. 11. 1940, 96, n. 3.
[9] vi. 314 c. [10] vi. 37118, 12.

described as 'Graccorum stirps, suboles Scipionum'[1] on her mother's side.[2] This is a genuinely old family, and can be traced back, through an adoption, to the Cornelii Scipiones of the Republic, as is shown in the discussion of it in Chapter V.

The name of Hymetius's wife, Praetextata, is far from common and may well indicate some connection with the praetorian prefect Vettius Agorius Praetextatus. Hymetius and Praetextata were pagans, and Jerome attributes their deaths to their attempts to dissuade Eustochium from devoting her life to the church by clothing her elegantly and by having her hair modishly waved.[3] This paganism was also not calculated to win the favour of the Emperor Valentinian, and, on a suspicion of embezzlement, which seems to have been ill-founded, Hymetius was fined.[4] Then, to add to his difficulties, he was implicated with a soothsayer named Amantius and was eventually (371/72) tried before Ampelius, Prefect of Rome, and Maximinus, Vicar of the City. In expectation of the death penalty, Hymetius appealed to the Emperor, who delegated jurisdiction to the Senate. The Senate banished Hymetius to Boae in Dalmatia, to Valentinian's indignation, as Ammianus would have us believe. It is difficult to see why Valentinian handed the case over to the Senate if he really wanted Hymetius to be executed. It looks very much as though the Emperor was deliberately shielding an important noble from his ardent pagan-baiting officials. It is in the context of Hymetius's trial and banishment that we must see the dedication and the two gilt statues put up in his honour by the African provincials in the year after Valentinian's death.[5]

13. Virius Lupus

We know from Symmachus that a certain Lupus was consular of Campania under Julian, between 361 and 363,[6] and the name Virius has been reconstructed from the letters 'rius' in a fragmentary inscription.[7] If this is correct, Lupus must have been related to the Virius Lupus who was proconsul of Africa, under Constantius and to the Virii Lupi of the principate, three of whom are known, one being legate of Britain under Septimius Severus and another called L. Virius Lupus Julianus being legate of the proconsul of Asia in Lycia and Pamphylia. The one with the most interesting career was also the latest in time, living as he did in the late third century.

.. viriO LVPO C.M.V.
cos. ord. PRAEF. VRBI PONTIF. D.S.

[1] Jer. *Ep.* 108. 1.
[2] Jer. *Ep.* 108. 3.
[3] Jer. *Ep.* 107. 5.
[4] Amm. xxviii. 1. 17 ff.
[5] Ibid.; vi. 1736 = D. 1256.
[6] Symm. *Rel.* 40. 3, 5.
[7] x. 3858 Capua.

iudici sACRARVM coGNITION.
per asiam ET PER ORIeNTEM PRAES.
syriae COLES ET ARABIAE

. . . . .¹

Lupus was urban prefect 278–80 and is no doubt to be identified with the Lupus who was ordinary consul in 278. He apparently combined the governorships of Syria and Arabia simultaneously with the appellate jurisdiction of the East as a whole, a position similar to that later to be held by L. Aelius Helvius Dionysius. Both these men were forerunners of the *Comites Orientis* who made their first appearance under this title in the latter part of Constantine's reign.

If our Campanian consular's *nomen* was Virius, as seems most likely in view of the *cognomen*, he had an impressive array of ancestors.

14. *Avianius Valentinus*

Known only as 'v.c. cons. Camp.' under Valentinian, he may have been related to Symmachus the orator, with whom he shares his *nomen*. Symmachus is known to have had three brothers, Celsinus Titianus and two unnamed ones who died before 380, one of whom Seeck has identified with Avianius Valentinus, and Chastagnol sees the other in a later consular of Campania, Avianius Vindicianus.²

15. *Anicius Paulinus*

In a series of tributes to great men of the age set up by Oecumenius Dositheus Asclepiodotus, consular of Crete, is one in honour of Anicius Paulinus, described as: ὁ λαμπρότατος ἀπὸ ἀνθυπάτων καὶ ἀπὸ ἐπάρχων τῆς βασιλευούσης Ῥώμης.³ Paulinus' urban prefecture was in 380, as we know from the Theodosian Code,⁴ and an unpublished inscription from Capua indicates that he was proconsul of Campania.⁵ Paulinus' relative and presumably his successor as governor of Campania, Anicius Auchenius Bassus, was also a proconsul, and Caecina Decius Albinus, governor of Campania at the end of the century, is called 'spectabilis vir', the title for vicars and proconsuls. The upgrading must have been an *ad hominem* grant in each case, since the province appears to have had a consular again between Bassus and Albinus, namely Valerius Hermonius Maximus and once again returns to consulars after Albinus' governorship.

---

¹ Proconsul of Africa: viii. 994 and p. 928 Carpi. Legate of Britain: Ulpian *Dig.* 28, 6, 2, 4. Legate of Asia: vi. 31774. Inscription quoted: vi. 31775 = D. 1210.
² x. 1656 = D. 764 Puteoli, Campania. Seeck P-W 2R iv. 1158 (20). J. A. MacGeachy, *Quintus Aurelius Symmachus*, p. 7 n. 1. Symm. *Ep.* iii. 6. 2. Chastagnol, *Fastes*, 160.
³ *AE.* 1933, 193 Creta.   ⁴ *CTh.* xv. 7. 4–5.
⁵ Unpublished inscription communicated to the Fifth International Epigraphical Conference, Cambridge, 1967.

The only explanation for the unusual designation is a desire on the part of the emperor to gratify these representatives of the two most prominent noble families of the day with a suitably flattering title. Paulinus' inherited patronage of some regions in Campania is an example of the combination of state post with local influence.

16. Anicius Auchenius Bassus

AVCHENII
ANICIO AVCHENIO BASSO V.C. QVAESTORI CANDIDATO
VNO EODEMQVE TEMPORE PRAETORI TVTELARI
PROCONSVLI
CAMPANIAE PRAEFECTO VRBI TRINI MAGISTRATVS
INSIGNIA FACVNDIAE ET NATALIVM SPECIOSA LVCE
VIRTVTIS
ORNANTI QVI CLARITATEM GENERIS PATERNIS
AVITISQVE FASTORVM
PAGINIS CELEBRATAM INIMITABILIVM IN
REMPVBLICAM MERITOR.
PRAE PROPRIA LAVDIS INDVSTRIA REDDIDIT
AVCTIOREM
PROSAPIAE LVMINI AEQVE DISERTO AC NOBILI
PROVISIONE
EFFICACIA VIGORe ELOQVENTIA EGREGIA
MODERATIONE
PRAESTANTI IN IPSO FLORE IVVENILIS AETATIS
FRVGEM
MATVRAE AVCTORITATIS . . .[1]

It was apparently regarded as an achievement to hold the quaestorship and praetorship simultaneously, otherwise it would not have received so much emphasis as the words 'uno eodemque tempore' give it.

As was said above, Bassus is the only known proconsul of Campania other than Anicius Paulinus. Since Paulinus is specifically described in an inscription as the first proconsul of the province, Bassus' proconsulship must be dated no earlier than 380, and since his proconsulship is recorded only in the reign of Gratian, it was probably not later than 383.[2]

In three inscriptions he is described as 'vice sacra iudicans' or by some other term to represent appellate jurisdiction.[3] The only explanation for the unusual title is that Bassus had more duties than an ordinary

---

[1] vi. 1679 = D. 1262.
[2] xiv. 2917 = D. 1263 Praeneste, xiv. 1875 = D. 1292 Ostia, x. 3843 Capua, AE 1892, 143 = D. 8984 Naples, ix. 1568–9 Beneventum, x. 6656 = D. 5702 Antium (379/83). CIG 2597 = Inscr. Cret. iv. 314 Gortyn, Crete.
[3] ix. 1568–9, x. 6656 = D. 5702.

consular, and was given a suitably flattering title. Bassus' last post was his urban prefecture in 382, during which he was later suspected of embezzlement.[1] The ordinary consul of 408 called Anicius Auchenius Bassus was probably our prefect's son.[2]

Not surprisingly, Bassus was patron of three Campanian towns, Naples, Beneventum, and Fabrateria Vetus.[3] Of Naples he was 'patronus originalis' and of Beneventum 'ab origine patronus', both terms indicating that he had inherited the patronage of these towns from his ancestors. In addition Bassus was patron of the 'regio Esquilina' in Rome, probably the area where the family town-house was.[4]

Bassus is described as 'restitutor generis Aniciorum',[5] but it is not certain to what this refers, for the family was not lacking in male heirs, since Petronius Probus, himself described as 'Anicianae domus culmen'[6] was also 'consulum pater', the consuls of 395, Olybrius and Probinus, both being his sons.[7] But, since Probus was not himself a member of the Anicii, or at least not through the male line.[8] Bassus' epithet could well refer to the fact that he alone of the direct male line of the family had an heir to succeed him.

His wife was Turrenia Honorata, probably related to L. Turranius Gratianus,[9] and the Anicius Auchenius Bassus who was consul in 408 was probably their son. Tyrrania Anicia Juliana, wife of the urban prefect of 368–70, Q. Clodius Hermogenianus Olybrius, is thought by Chastagnol to have been the daughter of Bassus and Honorata. The names make this a plausible suggestion but the dates do not, and all we can say with certainty is that they were related.[10]

The Anicii were among the first noble families to convert to Christianity: 'Non Paulinorum non Bassorum dubitavit prompta fides dare se Christo, stirpemque superbam gentis patriciae venturo attollere saeclo.'[11] Bassus himself is probably to be identified with the Christian Bassus who acquitted bishop Ephesios of heresy.[12]

---

[1] Symm *Rel.* 23. 4–7; 26. 2, 34. 7.

[2] *CTh.* i. 6. 8. (Nov. 382).

[3] ix. 1568 Beneventum, D. 8984 = *AE* 1892, 143 Neapolis, x. 5651 Fabrateria Vetus.

[4] ix. 1569.

[5] xiv. 2917 = D. 1263; see also x. 5651 and ix. 1568. Cf. Chastagnol: *Fastes*, 212.

[6] D. 1267.   [7] D. 1267–8.

[8] Claudian refers to 'vetus Probinus', i.e. Petronius Probinus, PUR 345–6, as practically a member of the *gens Anicia* (Claud. *de cons. Olybrii et Probini* v. 29), which has led Seeck to believe that he married an Anicia, thus making his son, Petronius Probus, a member of the *gens.* If this is correct, Probus married a relative.

[9] PUR 290–1—Chron. 354.

[10] vi. 1714 = D. 1271.

[11] Prudentius *contra Symm.* i. 558–60.

[12] Coll. Avell. 2. 54–5.

17. *Meropius Pontius Paulinus*

> Paulino Ausonius. metrum sic suasit, ut esses
> tu prior et nomen praegrederere meum
> quamquam et fastorum titulo prior et tua Romae
> praecessit nostrum sella curulis ebur.[1]

So writes Ausonius to his friend and pupil Meropius Pontius Paulinus, better known to history as Paulinus of Nola. There are two other references in his works to his friend's consulship:

> hic trabeam, Pauline, tuam Latiamque curulem
> constituis, patriosque istic sepelibis honores ?[2]

and

> Paulinum Ausoniumque, viros, quos sacra Quirini
> purpura et auratus trabeae velavit amictus.[3]

The phrase 'fastorum titulo prior' should refer only to ordinary consuls, who alone were entered in the *fasti* and gave their names to the year. But Paulinus was not an ordinary consul, since no ordinary consul in the second half of the fourth century is recorded with that *cognomen*. Ausonius' consulship in 379, on the other hand, was ordinary; indeed he was *consul prior* in that year. His use of the term 'fasti' to refer also to his friend's suffect consulship is an easily understandable combination of poetic licence and flattery.

Paulinus's nobility is brought out very clearly by St. Ambrose in describing the reaction to his entering the Church: 'Haec ubi audierint proceres viri, quae loquentur: ex illa familia, illa prosapia, illa indole, tanta praeditum eloquentia migrasse a senatu, interceptam familiae nobilis successionem: ferri hoc non posse.'[4] 'Paulinum splendore generis in partibus Aquitaniae nulli secundum'.[5] It is clear from this that Paulinus was of noble origins and we can undoubtedly link him with C. Pontius Paulinus, a consul probably of the late second or early third century,[6] and with Pontius Paulinus, a senator under Septimius Severus.[7]

The family possessed property at Fundi in Campania as well as at Ebromagus in Spain,[8] and it is not therefore surprising to find Paulinus as consular of Campania, a post which he occupied in 381.[9] It is interesting to note that he got married in Spain, presumably on a visit to the family estates there,[10] and remained there for some time, since his son

---

[1] Aus. *Ep.* 24. 1–4.   [2] Aus. *Ep.* 29. 60–1.
[3] Aus. *Ep.* 27. 64–5.   [4] Amb. *Ep.* 58. 3.
[5] Amb. *Ep.* 58. 1.   [6] ix. 3079.
[7] Ulpian *Dig.* 24. 1. 3. 1.
[8] Paulinus *Ep.* 32. 17; 11. 14; Aus. *Ep.* 27. 126–7.
[9] Paul. *Carm.* xxi. 374–76, 395–6; xiii. 7–9.
[10] Paul. *Carm.* xxi. 397–401. Amb. *Ep.* 58. 2; Amb. *Epp.* 27–9.

was born there[1] and he was ordained a priest in Barcelona in 394.[2] It is not without significance that Nola, the town where he was first a priest and later bishop, was in Campania.[3] Paulinus's family was from Bordeaux, his father also being called Paulinus.[4] There can be no doubt that the later consular of Campania (probably in 409) Pontius Proserius Paulinus, called 'junior' presumably to distinguish him from the bishop, was a relative.[5] Proserius is 'ab origine patronus' of Puteoli, again an example of state posts and local influence going hand in hand.[6]

18. *Virius Audentius Aemilianus*

We know him as consular of Campania, and proconsul of Africa with appellate jurisdiction under Gratian as senior Augustus, that is between 379 and 383.[7] All his inscriptions describe him as 'v.c.' except for an African inscription dating from his proconsulship, which calls him 'clarissimus et eminent(issimus)',[8] from which it has been concluded that he was 'Stellvertreter des Proconsuls von Afrika zwischen 379 and 383'.[9] There is absolutely no warrant for such an explanation, for proconsuls' legates were normally just simple *clarissimi*, nor should we expect so lowly a senatorial post to carry any other title—and certainly not the title traditionally reserved for praetorian prefects. Indeed, if it were not for the reference to the legate of Numidia in the inscription, no one would have hesitated for a moment to regard Aemilianus as a praetorian prefect, which may yet be the correct interpretation. If not, the 'eminentissimus' added to the clarissimate must be seen as an indication that its bearer was in some way superior to a mere *clarissimus*, whether in position or in birth—and the latter is more likely than the former, since the title 'spectabilis' was already coming in to differentiate proconsuls from their lesser senatorial brethren.[10] In either case, it is by no means impossible that a man who was consular of Campania and proconsul of Africa, both posts normally occupied by men of senatorial birth, was related to Virius Nicomachus Flavianus or Virius Lupus, or both.

---

[1] Paul. *Carm.* xxxi, 601–10, 619–20.   [2] Paul. *Ep.* i. 10, 2–4.   [3] Paul. *Ep.* 5.
[4] Uranii presb. *Ep. ad Pacatum* 2; Amb. *Ep.* 58. cf. Paul *Carm.* xxi. 397–8. Father's Name: Aus. *Ep.* 25. 105.
[5] x. 1128 Abellinum. x. 1702–3. Puteoli. *AE* 1961, 136 Beneventum.
[6] x. 1702.
[7] Campania: x. 3714 = D. 5478 Liternum: Capua: x. 3842, x. 3866. Africa Proconsularis: viii. 14728 Ghardimau near Thuburnica; Carthago: viii. 24588 = D. 9356, viii. 24589.
[8] viii. 14728.
[9] P-W i. 542 n. 12 (Virius Audentius Aemilianus).
[10] The earliest examples occur in the reign of Constantius II. D. 733 (see also D. 1296 and D. 9043).

19. *Pontius Paulinus*

A mutilated inscription from Formiae describes a man of this name as 'cons.', presumably 'cons(ularis Campaniae)'.[1] He is probably to be identified with either Meropius Pontius Paulinus or Pontius Proserius Paulinus.

20. *Pontius Salutus*

In view of his *nomen* and his position as consular of Campania, it is likely that he was related to Pontius Proserius Paulinus and his more famous relative Meropius Pontius Paulinus of Nola.[2]

21. *Olybrius*

After a series of at least three correctors of non-senatorial origin, Tuscia and Umbria was placed under consular governors of whom Olybrius was the first. He can be exactly dated, being the recipient of a law of May 370.[3] Though all we have is his *agnomen* Olybrius, this name occurs in the fourth century, so far as is known, only among the Anicii, where it recurs several times, notably in the cases of the urban prefect of 370–2 and consul of 379, consular of Campania and proconsul of Africa, and of the consul of 395. That our consular of Tuscia and Umbria was also an Anicius, therefore, seems more than likely.

22. *Julius Agrius Tarrutenius Marcianus*

IVLIO AGRIO TARRVTENIO MARCIANO V.C. ET INL.
NOBILITATE IVSTITIA ELOQVENTIA ET AVCTORITATe
CONSPICVO ET A PRIMO AETATIS FLORE
PROBATO QVAEST. KANDIDATO PR. kand.
CONSVL. SICILIAE PROCONS. ORIENTis
LEGATO AMPLISSIMI ORDINIS TERTIum praef.
VRBI IVDICI SACRARVM COGNITIonum
ITERVM[4]

As the inscription tells us, Marcianus held his quaestorship and praetorship at an early age. The title 'Proconsul Orientis', otherwise unknown, may be a mistake for 'Comes Orientis' or may be a title specially created for Marcianus. For the *comes Orientis* was in fact a vicar and may have had the same rank as one, namely a lower rank than a proconsul. Moreover, while vicars and presumably *comites Orientis* were subordinate to the praetorian prefects, proconsuls were theoretically independent of their jurisdiction.

The career is Western with the exception of the proconsulate of

---

[1] x. 6088 Formiae.   [2] *AE* 1927, 137 Capua.
[3] *CTh.* xii. 1. 72.   [4] vi. 1735.

Oriens, which must presumably therefore be dated to the reign of Theodosius I, the latest date when we can expect to find a Westerner in an Eastern post. Such a date would also not be incompatible with an urban prefecture under Attalus in 409–10, when we know that the urban prefect was called Marcianus.[1]

Neither the name Agrius nor the name Tarrutenius was at all common. There was an Agrius Celsinianus, 'co(n)s(ularis) vir', and curator of Bulla Regia in Africa,[2] who was probably the same person as Celsinianus, 'consularis vir' and curator of Thuburbo, whose mother Aelia Celsinilla was already a 'consularis femina'.[3] The family probably became senatorial during the third century, and Q. Agrius Rusticianus, thrice procurator under Caracalla, may have been the author of his family's elevation.[4]

Only two people are known to have borne the name Tarrutenius before our man. The name Tarrutenia Paulina appears in an inscription from Rome, but nothing is known about its bearer.[5] A corrupt inscription, perhaps from the third or early fourth century, and quoted in Appendix 35, gives us the name (No)nius Tineius Tarrut(enius) Atticus, who, described as 'c(larissimae) m(emoriae) v(ir) pr(aetor) tut(elaris), XV v(ir) s(acris) f(aciundis)', was clearly of senatorial birth.[6] Other signs of Marcianus's nobility are the words 'nobilitate . . . conspicuo' in the inscription quoted above and the fact that he held both the quaestorship and the praetorship—and both of them at an early age.

A later member of the family was Tarrutenius Maximilianus, who was consular of Picenum 'anno aetatis nonodecimo', presumably at some time after 398, when Picenum was separated from Flaminia.[7] He was then vicar of Rome, and finally, following in the footsteps of his kinsman Marcianus, he was a member of two senatorial delegations, probably to the emperor, as we know from an inscription put up to Maximilianus by his son-in-law Anicius Acilius Glabrio Faustus in or after 438, the year of Faustus' consulship.[8]

There are pointers to the identification of Tarrutenius Maximilianus with both the Maximilianus and the Maximianus mentioned by Zosimus in connection with the senatorial embassy to Honorius in 409. Two

[1] Attalus's urban prefect: Zos. vi. 7. 2. Chastagnol (*Fastes*, 268) identifies Attalus's urban prefect with the vicar Marcianus who received a law dated 384 (*CTh.*i x. 38. 7) and with the Marcianus recorded as proconsul of Africa under Eugenius in 394, (*Carmen adv. Flavianum*, v. 78, ed. Riese: *Anthologia Latina* i, 13, No. 19), but probably neither identification is justified, because the inscription quoted gives us a detailed *cursus*, even mentioning the republican magistracies and senatorial embassies, which are frequently omitted. It is hardly likely that so detailed an inscription would omit a vicariate or proconsulate.
[2] viii. 25523 Bulla Regia.   [3] Cagnat—Merlin, *ILAfr.* 414.
[4] viii. 11163 Afr.   [5] *Bull. Comm.* 1892, 355.
[6] xiv. 3517, Tibur.   [7] vi. 1767 = D. 1282.
[8] Ibid.

references in Zosimus, one to Maximianus, and the other to Maximilianus, son of Marinianus, clearly deal with the same person. Maximianus, we are told, was one of the senatorial envoys sent to Honorius; Maximilianus is the name used when the envoy is held to ransom by Alaric and freed on payment of 30,000 gold pieces by his father.[1]

His nobility and the fact that, as we know from his inscription, Tarrutenius Maximilianus was twice a senatorial envoy lead us to see in him Zosimus' Maximianus/Maximilianus. To go so far as to suggest that his father Marinianus was really Julius Agrius Tarrutenius Marcianus may be somewhat rash, but, in view of the rarity of the *nomen* Tarrutenius and the fact that both Marcianus and Maximilianus were clearly nobles, we can hardly doubt that the two men were related. Maximilianus is probably also to be identified with Symmachus' correspondent of that name who was consular of Sicily at some time before 396 and subsequently held an undefined, but apparently high, court post.[2]

23. *Pontius Atticus*

He was corrector of Lucania and Bruttium in 374,[3] and his name also appears in a list of three names, dated 376. Though Atticus himself is referred to in this list simply as 'v.c.', his name appears between that of Turcius Secundus Asterius, described as 'v.c. XVvir s.f.' and Sextilius Aedesius, 'v.c. p.p. hierof. Hecatar.'[4] What this short list represents is difficult to say. Atticus himself was presumably not a priest, so the three men may have been donors to some fund. It has been suggested that Atticus may have been descended from Fl. Atticus v.c., whose name appears in a list of pagan priests and philosophers probably in the 320s, but the *cognomen* is too common to make this hypothesis anything more than conjecture.

24. *L. Nonius Verus*

L. NONIVS VERVS V. CONS. BIS CORRECT. APVLIAE ET
CALAB.

---

[1] Maximianus: Zos. V. 44. 1. Maximilianus (or Maximillianus), son of Marinianus: Zos. V. 45. 4.

[2] Governor of Sicily: Symm. *Ep.* ix. 52. Court post: Symm. *Ep.* viii. 48. With more than his usual degree of perversity, Chastagnol identifies Attalus's urban prefect (called Marcianus by Zosimus—vi. 7. 2) not with Julius Agrius Tarrutenius Marcianus but with Maximilianus's father Marinianus. Indeed, Chastagnol banishes Julius Agrius Tarrutenius Marcianus from the fourth century and makes him, without giving any reason at all, a mid-fifth century urban prefect instead. (Chastagnol, *Fastes*, 268–9 and *Historia* 4 (1955) 178–9).

[3] *AE* 1913, 227 Rhegium, Bruttium.

[4] vi. 31118. Cf. *PLRE* s.v., which considers Atticus was a priest and a descendant of Fl. Atticus.

VENETIARVM ET ISTRIAE COMES PATRONVS
MVTINENSIVM AQVILEIEN.
BRIXIANORVM ET VNIVERSARVM VRBIVM APVLIAE
CALABRIAEQVE
VINICIAE MARCIANE C. F. FIL. CAECILIANI P.V. BIS
RATION.
VRBIS ROMAE ET AFRICAE PRAES. LVSITANIAE CORR.
APVL. ET CALAB. VIC. PRAEF. PER ITAL.[1]

Verus is not recorded as ordinary consul, so his title 'vir cons(ularis)' must refer to a suffect consulship which he had held. This, together with the absence of equestrian posts from his career, is a clear pointer to his being of senatorial birth, though his father-in-law was a non-senatorial vicar. It is interesting to note that both Caecilianus and Verus were correctors of Apulia and Calabria, a post which Verus may have gained through the influence of his father-in-law, since he himself appears to have come from the North, with his patronage of Mutina and Brixia. His other patronages evidently came to him through his official positions, for Aquileia was in Venetia and, in addition, he was patron of all the towns of Apulia and Calabria.

25. *Attius (Insteius T)ertullus Populonius*

The only record of this man's career that we have is a mutilated inscription which exists only in MS.: 'Populonii. Attio (*Insteio T*)ertullo v.c., quaes(*tori cand.*), praetori can(*d. consuli, correctori*) Apu(*liae et Calabriae*)...e..............'.[2] Though no trace of the word 'consuli' could be seen by the recorder, it is required by the spacing.

The name Insteius has been restored on the analogy of the name of the urban prefect of 307–8, Attius Insteius Tertullus, but our man is not to be identified with the urban prefect, who was corrector of Venetia and Histria but not of Apulia and Calabria.[3] The urban prefect was presumably our corrector's father, grandfather or uncle.

The *signum* Populonius is shared with Tertullus by the brothers Aradii who were governors under Constantine, and may indicate some relationship, or a common origin from Populonia in Etruria.

The family of the Insteii Tertulli can be traced back to the early third century. In addition to the urban prefect of 307–8, who was suffect consul before Diocletian,[4] we have a short tombstone inscription from Africa, possibly of the fourth century, dedicated by Insteius Tertullus to Insteia Diogenia, 'feminae merenti'.[5] Another inscription possibly dating from the fourth century is dedicated to 'Attius . . . (*T*)ertul(*l*)us

[1] xi. 831 = D. 1218 Mutina.   [2] vi. 1697.
[3] vi. 1696, v. 2818 Padua. On the question of identification see Chastagnol, *Fastes*, 48–50, who shares the view expressed in the text.
[4] vi. 1696, v. 2818.   [5] viii. 876.

qui et Populonius', described as v.c., quaes(*tori*), praetori can(*d*)...
Apu.'[1] Next we have a very worn inscription on which the letters
RTVLLI.......VC can be made out. The name is probably 'Tertullus', but it is not certain whether he was an Insteius or not.[2] Whether
these four inscriptions refer to four different men or whether two or more
of them refer to the same person is difficult to say. We also have seals,
probably of a later date than the inscriptions, with simply the names
Insteius Tertullus and Stefanilla Aemiliana, presumably husband and
wife.[3] We have another Insteius Tertullus in the third century listed as
magister sodalium Augustalium Claudialium in the year 214.[4]

He is the only one of these Insteii whose *praenomen* is recorded, and
it is Lucius, which, together with the fact that Insteius was far from
being a common name, might point to a link between the Insteii Tertulli and L. Insteius Flaccianus, L.f., who was a *decemvir stlitibus
iudicandis, sevir turmarum, quaestor, tribune* and *praetor candidatus*,
probably in the early third century. Flaccianus appears in an inscription
together with Claudia Papia Netonia Insteia Praenestina, presumably
his daughter.[5] The connection with Praeneste is repeated in the case of
one Q. Insteius, whose *cognomen* is missing, a tribune, a praetor, suffect
consul and legate of an unknown province, honoured by the people of
Praeneste.[6] The only difficulty here is that, while Flaccianus was a
Lucius, son of a Lucius and a member of the Horatian tribe, Q. Insteius
was the son of a Titus and belonged to the Pupinian tribe.

26. *Volusianus*

The existence of a vicar of this name in 365 or 366 depends upon the
dates, addresses, and content of two laws. One, dated 6 August 365, is
addressed 'ad Volusianum v.c. vic.',[7] and the other, addressed 'ad
Volusianum p.u.', bears the subscription: 'Prolata litteris sub die XII
kal. Mart. Rom. acc. IIII kal. April. Venabri (sic) conss. Valentiniani
et Valentis AA. (sic).'[8] On the basis of the grammar, Seeck adds a
'post' after 'Venabri', thus making the next word 'consulatum' and the
year 366. He attributes both constitutions to Volusianus, vicar of Rome,
the Venafrum law because the urban prefect had no jurisdiction in
Samnium, and the other law because he sees the contents as indicating
'dass der Empfänger über die Provinz Tuscia und die Stadt Tarracina
zu gebieten hatte, was sehr gut zu der Kompetenz des Vicarius Urbis
passt'. The *PLRE* follows Seeck on the Venafrum law, but, though no
reason is given, it is undecided whether the other law should be assigned
to the vicar or to the urban prefect of 365, who was also called Volusianus,
or, to give him his full name, C. Ceionius Rufius Volusianus Lampadius

---

[1] vi. 1697.   [2] vi. 32208.   [3] vi. 37126 = Diehl *ILCV* 136.
[4] vi. 1987.   [5] vi. 1429 = 31652.   [6] xiv. 2924 Praeneste.
[7] *CTh.* xiv. 6. 3.   [8] *CTh.* viii. 5. 22.

(praetorian prefect in 355). At the other end of the spectrum Chastagnol assigns both laws to the urban prefect, though he fails to explain why.

Seeck's attribution of the Venafrum law to a vicar of Rome called Volusianus must be endorsed, whether the year is taken as 366 or kept as 365. Indeed, if we retain 18 February 365 as the date, there is no question of attributing the law to the urban prefect, since the urban prefect then was still the elder Symmachus.

The other law, however, poses a more complex problem. On 6 August 365, the MS. date, which is not in question, the urban prefect was Volusianus Lampadius, but the law deals with the supply of lime for the upkeep of public buildings in Rome, a matter which falls into the province of the urban prefect rather than that of the vicar. Yet the second clause of the law relieves the decurions of Tuscany of the duty of providing 900 loads of lime and the last sentence seems to be addressed to someone other than the urban prefect.

The attribution of this law must remain in doubt, but the existence of a Volusianus as vicar of Rome in 365 or 366 rests on the basis of the Venafrum law. Perhaps the two addresses were accidentally swopped, not an uncommon occurrence in the compilation of the Theodosian Code.[1]

Volusianus was nothing if not noble, for his *cognomen* was uniquely associated in the fourth century with the Ceionii, and he must therefore have been related to his contemporary, C. Ceionius Rufius Volusianus Lampadius.

27. Valerius Severus

The first we hear of him is as the recipient of a law dated March 382 concerning municipal delegations to the Emperor. Though Severus is addressed as urban prefect, and we know that he was urban prefect on 1 April of that year, the law does not seem appropriate to an urban prefect, and it is marked as posted up at Carthage. It is possible, therefore, that Severus was proconsul of Africa before becoming urban prefect.[2] Severus' first laws as urban prefect would then be those of 1 April, but on each of the next two days he received a law addressed to him as praetorian prefect, and then we find two more laws with him addressed as urban prefect, one from June and the other from August.[3]

---

[1] Seeck, *Regesten*, 118–19. *PLRE* s.v. Chastagnol, *Fastes*, 168. C. Ceionius Rufius Volusianus Lampadius: p. 82. Symmachus the elder: His last two laws as urban prefect were *CTh.* x. 1. 9 (9 March 365) and *CTh.* i. 6. 4 (10 March 365).

[2] *CTh.* xii. 12. 8. That this law could be a sign of a proconsulate of Africa is the view of A. H. M. Jones, 'Collegiate Prefectures', *JRS* 54 (1964) 84. *PLRE* s.v. Seeck sees it as an indication of a praetorian prefecture, an untenable view unless one revives the now dead theory of collegiate prefectures (Seeck, *Regesten*, 115).

[3] First laws addressed 'ad Severum pu.': *CTh.* vi. 6. 1, xiv. 6. 4 (both 1 April 382). Addressed 'ad Severum ppo.': *CTh.* vii. 18. 6 (2 April 382), *CTh.* viii. 2. 13

Is the designation 'praetorian prefect' mistaken, or was Severus perhaps acting praetorian prefect between the two Syagrii, at the same time as being urban prefect?[1] We know from Palladius's *Lausiac History* that Pinianus, husband of Melania the Younger, was the son of Severus, an ex-prefect.[2] Now Pinianus's full name was Valerius Pinianus, as we discover from the poems of Paulinus, so there can be little doubt that his father was our Valerius Severus.[3] Another Pinianus was urban prefect from 385 to 387, no doubt a member of the same family, perhaps a brother of Valerius Severus, and in addition we know that Pinianus junior had a brother called Severus.[4] The family cannot be traced back further with any degree of certainty, Valerius being so common a name, but in view of the two urban prefectures and Pinianus's marriage with Melania the Younger, daughter of two nobles, Valerius Publicola and Albina, a member of the *gens Ceionia*, we can be well assured that Valerius Severus was also of noble birth.[5]

28. *Petronius*

Nothing is known of him other than that he received two laws both dated 340, as vicar of Africa. Though we have only his *nomen*, the fact that he had an African office could mean that he was a member of the noble house of the Petronii, who were closely connected with Africa. Of the fourth-century proconsuls of Africa, seven were Petronii/Anicii: Amnius Anicius Julianus (*c.* 300), Petronius Probianus (315–16), Sex. Anicius Paulinus (before 325), Sex. Claudius Petronius Probus (358), Q. Clodius Hermogenianus Olybrius (361), Petronius Claudius (368–70), and Claudius Hermogenianus Caesarius (before 374).[6]

(3 April 382). Later laws addressed 'ad Severum pu.'; *CTh.* xiv. 18. 1 (20 June 382), *CTh.* viii. 9. 2 (1 August 382).

[1] This latter view is that of A. H. M. Jones, loc. cit., while Chastagnol (*Fastes*, 209, n. 70) sees the Severus who was praetorian prefect as a different person from the Severus who was urban prefect. Palanque even goes so far as to repudiate Severus as the addressee of the laws where he is called PPO, and replaces his name with that of Syagrius. (*Essai*, 66–7).

[2] Pall. *Hist. Laus.* 61. 12.

[3] Paul. *Carm.* xxi. 216–24, 294–5.

[4] Pinianus, PUR 385–7: Coll. Avell. 4. *CTh.* vi. 35. 13, xiii. 3. 13, vi. 28. 4. For further sources see *PLRE* s.v. and Chastagnol, *Fastes*, 229–30. Severus, brother of Pinianus junior: V. Mel. Gr. 10. 12. V. Mel. Lat. i. 10. 12.

[5] Chastagnol's linking of Severus with Valerius Proculus, though far from implausible, is gratuitous, since there is no evidence (Chastagnol, op. cit., 210–11). Seeck (*Symm.* cxci–cxcii) followed by Chastagnol (*Fastes*, 210) identifies the recipient of a letter from Symmachus (viii. 6) called Severus with Valerius Severus.

[6] Petronius's two laws: *CTh.* ii. 6. 5, *CTh.* x. 15. 3. Proconsuls of Africa: The dates given are those of the *fasti* of the *PLRE*.

29. *Julius Eubulides*

IVLIO EVBVLIDAE
C.V. CORR. TVSCIAE
XVIRO PRAEFECTO AERARIIS SATVRNI (sic)
OB INLVSTRIA IPSIVS
MERITA ET AMOREM IVX
TA CIVES ORDO INTE
RAMNATIVM PATRONO.[1]

The earliest well-attested corrector of Tuscia and Umbria was C.
Vettius Cossinius Rufinus under Maxentius, but in view of the rarity of
the name Eubulides, which is not found anywhere else, it is likely that
our corrector is to be identified with the Eubulides who received a law
dated 344 as vicar of Africa.[2] More interesting than his two governorships, however, are his two other positions as *decemvir* and *praefectus
Aerarii S(acri) Saturni*. The latter post goes back to the earliest days of
the principate, and from the time of Nero it was in the hands of *praetorii*
nominated by the emperor. It was therefore an old senatorial position,
though by the fourth century merely titular.[3] The decemvirate is slightly
more puzzling, since nothing is said about its sphere of activities, but
the only attested decemvirate is that concerned with 'stlitibus iudicandis',
which, though last recorded in 242, must be the one held by our vicar.[4]
Eubulides' senatorial birth is therefore beyond doubt, though nothing
is known of his family.

30. *Septimius Acindynus*

He first appears as vicar of the Spains in an inscription dating from
between 317 and 326.[5] More than a decade pater, between 338 and 340,

---

[1] xi. 4181 = D. 1233. Interamna Nahars (Terni), Tuscia et Umbria. In the
third line either the wrong case has been used in the word 'Aerarium' or the s.
= 'sacri', the latter view being that of Hirschfeld, *Verw.* 23, n. 1.

[2] *CTh.* viii. 102.

[3] Tac. *Ann.* xii. 29. See also Cassius Dio, liii. 16 and 22. The office is last
recorded in the late second or early third century: D. 1167 Egnatius Proculus.

[4] Bormann (ad xi. 4181) thought that it was *Decemvir urbis Romae*, a title not
otherwise known but thought to be the same as *duodecimvir urbis Romae*, a
priesthood which is last recorded in 377, and which was held by Consius Quartus
Junior. D. 1233; D. 1249 (Quaestor) D. 4148 (377). There is no need to reduce the
size of this ancient college so arbitrarily just in order to accommodate Julius
Eubulides. The last recorded *decemviri stlitibus iudicandis*: D. 1199 C. Passienius
Cossonius Scipio Orfitus, D. 1197 M. Rubrenus Virius Priscus Pompeianus
Magianus Proculus, D. 1192 M. Aelius Aurelius Theo. D. 1188 . . . Annianus
(242).

[5] II. 4107 Tarraco. He is described as 'agens per Hispanias v.c.p.t. vice sacra
cognoscens'. Though 'v.c.p.t.' is not a recognized abbreviation for anything,
the sense is clear enough. Acindynus could hardly have been anything other
than a vicar, as the words 'agens per Hispanias' indicate. We would expect the

we encounter him again, this time as praetorian prefect in the East and consul in the latter year.[1] The prefect of Rome from 293 to 295 was also called Septimius Acindynus and was no doubt a relative of our prefect, probably his father or uncle.[2] Our vicar and prefect was, therefore, almost certainly of senatorial birth, though nothing is known of the origins of Septimius Acindynus senior.

Symmachus became the owner of an estate at Bauli near Misenum which had previously belonged to his father-in-law Memmius Vitrasius Orfitus, urban prefect 353–6, and before him to Septimius Acindynus the younger, of whom Symmachus writes in a poem about the house: 'hic consul clarum produxit Acindynus aevum'. Of course Acindynus could have sold the estate to Orfitus—or was there some relationship, a marriage alliance perhaps, between the two families ?[3]

31. *Albinus*

He was vicar of the Spains in 341.[4]

There were several Albini in the late Empire, all of whom were members of the *gens Ceionia*, the only doubtful case being that of a man whose name appears in a forged letter implying treasonable intentions on the part of Silvanus. The letter purported to be from Silvanus to his friends 'inter quos et Tuscus erat Albinus'.[5] If his name was Tuscus Albinus, then he too must have been a Ceionia, since the name Tuscus was connected with the Ceionii as well as was the name Albinus.[6] In view of the solidity of the phalanx of late Empire Albini—not a rare name in the High Empire—in the *gens Ceionia*, we must conclude that our vicar was also a Ceionius.

32. *Volusius Venustus*

Together with Clodius Octavianus, Aradius Rufinus and Turcius Apronianus, Venustus was a member of the senatorial delegation that went to see the Emperor Julian in 362.[7] He had begun his career as

---

full title to read 'agens per Hispanias vic(es) p(raefectorum) p(raetorio)', as is suggested by the editor in the *Corpus*, and it is likely that this is what the stone-mason was instructed to write. The Caesar whose name was obliterated in the second line was probably Crispus who was created Caesar in 317 and executed in 326.

[1] *CTh.* ii. 6. 4. (Dec. 338), *CTh.* viii. 5. 3 (MSS. 326, Seeck 339), *CTh.* ix. 3. 3 (340). *BGU.* i. 21. Consul: *Fasti.* That Acindynus was prefect in the East is shown by the fact that the law of December 338 is marked 'p(ro)p(osita) . . . . . Antioch.' See also Palanque, op. cit., 19; *PLRE*, s.v.

[2] *Chron.* 354. See Chastagnol, *Fastes*, 21; Barbieri, *Albo Senatorio*, 334, No. 1920.

[3] Symm. *Ep.* i. 1. See Seeck, *Symm. L.*

[4] *CTh.* xi. 36. 5 (vic. Hisp.) *CJ* vii. 62. 20 (341).   [5] Amm. xv. 5. 4.

[6] See p. 131.   [7] Amm. xxiii. 1. 4.

corrector of Apulia and Calabria under Constantine,[1] later became consular of Sicily,[2] and was rewarded by Julian with the vicariate of Spain.[3] In 370 he again appears in Ammianus in a senatorial embassy, this time to Valentinian, to appeal against the harsh sentences and torture being inflicted upon nobles in Maximinus's onslaught against them in the law-courts.[4]

Macrobius gives the name of Flavianus's father as Venustus.[5] This Venustus was probably the same person as our Volusius Venustus whose *nomen* may be a sign of connection with the Ceionii, among whom the *cognomen* Volusianus is frequently found.[6]

The family may also have been connected with the Anicii, among whom the *cognomen* Nicomachus makes an early appearance. The name entered the *gens Anicia* in the mid-third century through the marriage of Sex. Cocceius Anicius Faustus Paulinus with the daughter of C. Asinius Nicomachus Julianus. Both sides were notable even at this point in the third century, the father-in-law being the proconsul of Asia and the son-in-law proconsul of Africa.[7] Two members of the family, thought by Seeck to have been the products of this marriage, have names which point strongly towards a link between the Anicii and the Nicomachi Flaviani. They are: Junius Caesonius Nicomachus Anicius Faustus Paulinus, *consul ordinarius* in 298 and prefect of Rome in the following year; and M. Cocceius Anicius Faustus Flavianus, described in an inscription as 'patricio, consulari'. Finally there is Amnius Manius Caesonius Nicomachus Anicius Paulinus Honorius, proconsul of Asia, and urban prefect and ordinary consul both in 334. Nichomachus is not a common name, and the occurrence not only of this name but also of Flavianus among the Anicii of the third or early fourth centuries may well indicate some connection with that noble house on the part of Nicomachus Flavianus, probably on his mother's side.[8]

33. *Volusianus*

We have an isolated reference to a certain Volusianus as recipient of a law 'de medicis et professoribus' dated 'Crispo et Constantino CC. conss.', without specifying which of their consulships it was. The year could therefore be either 321 or 324. Volusianus' office is not mentioned.

---

[1] ix. 329 = D. 5557ª Canusium, Apulia.
[2] Symm. *Ep*. iii. 71 ad Eusignium. See Seeck, *Symm.*, cxiii ff.
[3] Amm. loc. cit.   [4] Amm. xxviii. 1. 24–25.
[5] Macrob. *Sat*. i. 5. 13.   [6] ix. 329 Canusium.
[7] Cocceius Paulinus: viii. 1437. Asinius Nicomachus Julianus: *CIG* 5498. See *PIR*², s.vv.
[8] Seeck: Symm., xc–xciii. Anicius Paulinus: vi. 315. Cocceius Flavianus: viii. 7040. Amnius Nicomachus Paulinus: vi. 1682, 1652, 1141. For the history of the Anicii see p. 109 ff.

14

but the other similar laws in the same section of the *Theodosian Code* are mostly addressed either to praetorian prefects or to prefects of Rome.[1] Could this law had been addressed to C. Caeionius Rufius Volusianus, praetorian prefect under Maxentius in 310 and urban prefect 310–11 and 313–15? It could certainly not have been addressed to him in any of those capacities unless we are prepared to tamper with the date. Then, was this great man again praetorian prefect in the 320s? He would have been in his seventies by then, and, in any case, it would have been unusual for a man to return to the praetorian prefecture after being urban prefect and consul. So the praetorian prefect of 321 or 324 was probably not Maxentius's old prefect but another member of his family. The name Volusianus was far from common, and indeed the only bearers of it in the late Empire known to the author all belonged to the same family, namely the Ceionii. The Ceionian pedigree is treated in Chapter V.[2]

34. *Sextus Claudius Petronius Probus*

His career began with the quaestorship and urban praetorship, followed by the proconsulship of Africa.[3] An unpublished inscription, recently discovered in Capua, has added two new pieces of information to what was already known about Probus.[4] First, it has given him the additional *nomen* Claudius, a name found among several fourth and fifth century Anicii but usually written in the 'plebeian' manner as 'Clodius', Probus is now the earliest known bearer of this name in the family, the next being Q. Clodius Hermogenianus Olybrius, Gratian's praetorian prefect. This links the Petronian branch of the Anician family as well as the main line with Clodius Celsinus Adelphius.

The other new fact we learn is that Probus was praetorian prefect and proconsul of Africa simultaneously, which harks back to Aradius Proculus. But, though Proculus was only acting prefect, Probus had the full office. The date of Probus' first praetorian prefecture is unknown, but it must have been before 364, when he is recorded as praetorian prefect of Illyricum.[5]

Probus was prefect of Gaul in 366,[6] after which comes his seven-year

---

[1] *CTh.* xiii. 3. 1.

[2] Chastagnol (*Fastes*, 57–8) assigns this praetorian prefecture to C. Ceionius Rufius Volusianus, Maxentius's praetorian prefect, while the *PLRE* rejects prefecture altogether (*Fasti*). See p. 97 f.

[3] Quaestorship and praetorship: *AE* 1934, 160 Forum Traiani, Roma. Proconsulship: *CTh.* xi. 36. 13 (June 358); vi. 1751–3. For further sources see *PLRE*, s.v.

[4] Unpublished inscription from Capua communicated to the Fifth Epigraphical Conference, Cambridge, 1967.

[5] *CTh.* i. 29. 1.

[6] *CTh.* xi. 1. 15 dat. Remis.

tenure of the prefecture of Italy and Africa, and Illyricum.[1] It is not without significance that Probus survived Valentinian in office,[2] and for the rest of Gratian's reign he appears to have been out of office. But in 383 he reappears as praetorian prefect of Italy, Africa and Illyricum, being left in sole control of the West since Gratian was busy fighting the Alamanni and Valentinian II was only a young boy at the time.[3] Probus was still alive in 387, when Magnus Maximus invaded Italy, and he left for Thessalonica together with the young Valentinian.[4] Sozomen's statement that Probus was praetorian prefect in Italy at the time has been regarded as false, yet there is no reason to reject it.[5] Though Eusignius is known to have been praetorian prefect between January 386 and May 387, it is not known whether his prefecture embraced Italy or not, the only reference to the region he controlled being in a law of July 386 referring to Macedonia, Dacia Mediterranea, Moesia, and Dardania.[6] He could, therefore, have been prefect of Illyricum alone, while Probus governed Italy. Though only Sozomen specifies that Probus accompanied the imperial family into exile, Socrates tells us of Probus' shift of abode to Thessalonica, for fear of the usurper, and in the next chapter we find Theodosius visiting Valentinian II in Thessalonica,[7] a fact mentioned also by Sozomen. The very fact that Probus and the Emperor both went to Thessalonica strengthens the possibility that Probus was praetorian prefect at the time.[8] Moreover, Valentinian did not leave Milan before September 387, so even if Eusignius' prefecture included Italy, he appears to have relinquished his post several months before the retreat.

It was during his long prefecture under Valentinian that Probus was ordinary consul. The year was 371, and Probus' fellow-consul was the young Gratian.

35. *Flavius Nonius Atticus Maximus*

He was praetorian prefect of Italy in 384 and received one law in this capacity.[9] In 397 he was ordinary consul together with Flavius Caesarius, and he is said by Symmachus to have owned land at Tibur.[10] This must have been the family seat, since it is near Tibur that the tombstone was

[1] Amm. xxvii. 11. 1, Amm. xxviii. 1. 31, Amm. xxx. 3. 1, *CTh.* iv. 17. 1 (374).
[2] Rufinus *HE.* ii. 12.
[3] *CTh.* xi. 13. 1. Soc. v. 11. 3. Soc. vii. 13. cf. Symm. *Ep.* i. 58.
[4] Soz. vii. 13 cf. Soc. v. 11. 11–12.
[5] The *PLRE*, s.v., regards Sozomen's statement as incorrect, though gives no reason.
[6] Eusignius: *CTh.* xvi. 1. 4 (Jan. 386) *CTh.* i. 32. 5 (July 386 Illyricum), *CTh.* xi. 30. 48 (May 387).
[7] Soc. v. 11 and 12, Zos. iv. 43. 5; Philostorg. x. 8.
[8] Clinton, *Fasti Romani*, s.a. 387.
[9] *CTh.* xiii. 1. 12.   [10] Symm. *Ep.* vii. 31.

found of what must be our prefect's father or grandfather: '(*No*)nio Tineio Tarrut/(*enio*) Attico c.m.v./ (*q.k. pr*)aetori tutelario/ (*XViro*)/s.f. qui vixit an. XXVIII/ . . . . . a Maxima c.f. a solo/ . . . . oriam fecit coiugi/ . . . . issimo cum quo/ (*vixi*)t ann. VIII m. vii d. xi.'[1] It was then from his mother or grandmother that Maximus received his last *cognomen*, the rest being from the noble pagan priest whose early death had deprived him of a civil career. The rare name Tarrutenius must link Maximus with the other Tarrutenii who were his contemporaries, Tarrutenius Marcianus and his son Maximilianus.[2]

[1] xiv. 3517 Castelmadama, Latium, nr. Tibur.
[2] See Julius Agrius Tarrutenius Marcianus, App. 22.

FASTI AND STATISTICAL TABLES

INTRODUCTION

THE aristocracy of the fourth century is portrayed particularly in the pages of Symmachus and Ammianus as intent upon 'otium senatorium', but the love of leisure and the pursuit of power are not mutually exclusive, as a glance at the late Republic will reveal, and Symmachus himself, the personification of *otium senatorium*, was not averse to political manipulation, as his numerous letters of recommendation bear witness.

A man would evidently not normally hold a particular post for more than a few years, as is indicated by offices such as the urban prefecture, the proconsulate of Africa and the prefecture of Egypt, of which we have detailed *fasti*, but this fact in no way vitiates the importance of office-holding as a gauge of political significance. Though the average office-holding noble might spend only a fraction of his life in office, a number of noble office-holders in one particular post or a collection of nobles in various high state posts at the same time can hardly be disregarded.

It is impossible to know what percentage of nobles held state posts, but even if we had certain evidence that those nobles who entered public life formed only a small minority of the senatorial aristocracy, we would not be justified in waving them aside, both for the reasons mentioned above and because the aristocracy, more than any other element of society, formed an intricate and unified network of family connections which served as a conductor of influence. The example of Petronius Probus was probably repeated on a smaller scale in many other noble office-holders. In all, what we have is a circular process. For example, Petronius Probus' main and indeed sole qualification for office was the fact that he was the head of the wealthiest and most influential noble family of the day. Office then in turn gave him the opportunity to enhance his wealth and influence. And, as was shown in Chapter VII, there was a link between governorships and landholding.

The *fasti* of *praesides*, consulars, vicars and praetorian prefects are essentially those of the *PLRE*, with the addition of social origins. Where necessary, sources have also been added, usually just one or two of the main sources for the person concerned or, where available, sources which throw light on his social origins. If a man is discussed in the main body of the work, the appropriate page reference is given. Similarly, those who are discussed in Appendices or whose names appear in the Stemmata are marked accordingly. For further biographical details of the people concerned the reader should refer to the *PLRE*. The lists of noble patrons, *comites*, pagans, and republican magistrates include only those nobles (and known relatives) in each category who also were provincial governors, vicars, or praetorian prefects, the aim being to show the link between office, birth, religion, and land. The list of suffect consuls, however, is complete. The statistical tables have been compiled on the basis of the *PLRE*, no *anonymi* being counted however.

The statistics pose a problem. First, we have no way of knowing what proportion of nobles in our period is represented in our sources. Moreover, we obviously lack all trace of a good number of office-holders, and even of those whose names are preserved there are many—the majority in most cases—whose social origins cannot be worked out. Are we more likely to know the origin of a noble than of a non-noble? In the fourth century, as we have seen, the equestrian titles went out of use and the holders of most high posts became *clarissimi*, thus making the title meaningless as an index of social origin, except for the holders of certain offices such as praesidial governorships. The main criteria used to determine nobility are nomenclature and explicit or indirect indications in the sources. To establish non-senatorial birth it is necessary to rely on direct or indirect statements in the sources, and in an age which laid much store by high birth it is hardly to be expected that the number of known non-noble office-holders should represent as high a proportion of the actual number of non-noble office-holders as the number of known noble office-holders represents of the actual total of noble office-holders. In other words, if we take: X to represent the total number of known office holders who were noble, whether we know their origin or not; x to represent the number of office-holders known to us to have been nobles; Y to represent the total number of known office-holders who were non-noble, whether we know their origin or not; y to represent the number of office-holders known to us to have been non-noble; then the fraction x/X is likely to be greater than the fraction y/Y, and the ratio $x:y$ is therefore unlikely to be the same as $X:Y$. The degree of noble office-holding is rather to be found by considering the number of noble office-holders in any one post as a fraction of the total number of holders of that post in a specified period or as a fraction of the total number of the holders of specified posts at a given time.

The statistical noble bias inherent in the sources, it must be noted, is not such as to fluctuate from year to year or reign to reign, and the difference between the amount of noble office-holding under the tetrarchy and under Constantine and his successors cannot but be seen as statistically extremely significant. Another striking contrast is that between the number of nobles in Western posts and those in Eastern ones.

In the case of the most important office of all, the praetorian prefecture, we are probably not very far short of a complete list of office-holders. If we include all Constantine I's praetorian prefects (who do not appear to have been regional)[1] and all praetorian prefects in the West from 337 to 395, we find that nineteen out of sixty-two, or almost a third, are known to have been noble. The significance of this figure is indisputable, especially if we consider that until Maxentius' appointment of Ceionius Rufius Volusianus not a single noble had held the praetorian prefecture.

[1] Instead, one seems to have been attached to each of the Augusti and Caesars. A list of the Constantinian prefects dated in accordance with this principle appears among the *fasti* of the *PLRE* and is explained in an as yet unpublished article by Mr. J. R. Martindale, who was kind enough to let me consult it.

The total of sixty-two, it should be noted, includes none of the PPOs of Maxentius, Galerius, Maximinus Daia or Licinius, but all the PPOs of Constantine and his sons from 315 (when the first of Constantine's PPOs whose names are known is recorded) to 337.

FASTI

An arabic numeral attached to a name refers to an appendix.

GOVERNORS OF NUMIDIA

Praesides

NS	Tenagino Probus	v.p.	*SEG* ix. 9, *AE* 1936, 58	268–9
NS	Severinius Apronianus	v.p.	D. 5788	?276/82
NS	M. Aur. Decimus	v.p.	D. 2291	283/4
NS	Fl. Aelius Victorinus	v.p.	*AE* 1908, 240	LIII/EIV
NS	Fl. Flavianus	v.p.	viii. 2480–1, 17970, 4325	286/93
NS	Aur. Diogenes	v.p.	viii. 2573–5	286/93
NS	Aur. Maximianus	v.p.	D. 5786	290/3
NS	Aur. Pi. . . . . nus	v.p.	*AE* 1918, 30	293/305
NS	Val. Concordius	v.p.	xiii. 3672 *Cf* ix. 9. 27	295
NS	Val. Florus	v.p.	*PLRE*	303
NS	Aur. Quintianus	v.p.	*PLRE*	303
NS	C. Val. Antoninus	v.p.	*PLRE*	305–6
NS	Val. Paulus	v.p.	viii. 18905	313/4
NS	Julius Antiochus	v.p.	*PLRE*	314/7
NS	Aur. Almacius	v.p.	*PLRE*	293/305 or 314/20
SB	Acilius Clarus 1	v.cos.viii. 2729; ST. II		312/20

Consulares

SB	Domitius Zenofilus 2	v.c.	*AE* 1915, 30	320
OU	M. Aur. Val. Valentinus	v.c.	xi. 5391 Assisi *CTh.* xvi. 2. 7	330
SB	Clodius Celsinus	v.c.	p. 112 ff; ST. II	333/7
SB	Vulcacius Rufinus	v.c.	pp. 76, 117 f. before 342	
SB	Ceionius Italicus	v.c.	viii. 7012–3; ST. I.	343
OU	Maximus	?	*BCTH* 1887, p. 83, n. 184	337/61
OU	Ilicus		*CTh.* i. 15. 3	351 or 357
OU	Ulpius Mariscianus	v.c.	viii. 17896, viii. 4771 = 18684	361/3
SB	Publilius Ceionius Caecina Albinus	v.c.	viii. 20156 = D. 5536; viii. 7975 = 19852 = D. 5910	364/7
OU	Ulpius Egnatius Faventinus	v.c.	*PLRE*	366/7
ns	Fl. Simplicius	v.c.	Vic. Rom. adviser of Maximinus D. 5535, Amm. xxviii 1. 44–5	367/74
OU	Annius . . . . . mianus	v.c.	viii. 7015 and p. 1847 = D. 5555 Constantina	367/75
SB	Caelius Censorinus 3		viii. 2216	375/8
OU	Felix Juniorius Polemius	v.c.	viii. 10702 el-Ghussa, Num. before 378	

OU	L. Aemilius Metopius		
	Flavianus	v.c. viii. 18328 = D. 5520	379/83
SB	Alfenius Ceionius		
	Julianus Kamenius	v.c. D. 1264, p. 50	before 381
SB	Caecina Decius Albinus	v.c. AE 1909, 223; SE 1933,	
		159; viii. 7034 = D. 5789;	
		p. 100	388/92
OU	Fl. Herodes	procos. Afr., CSL AE 1954, 155	
		before 394	

Praesides Mauretaniae Caesariensis

NS	M. Aur. Victor	v.e. D. 548	263
NS	Aelius Aelianus	v.p. PLRE	M/L III
NS	Fl. Pecuarius	v.p. PLRE	288
NS	T. Aurelius Litua	v.p. PLRE	290/3
NS	Ulpius Apollonius	v.e. PLRE	293/305
NS	.... ianus	v.p. PLRE	? 297
OU	? Claudius ?	Anal. Boll. ix (1890) 116–23	c. 303
NS	M. Valerius Victor	v.p. PLRE	306
NS	Valerius Faustus	v.p. PLRE	311/12
NS	Fl. Terentianus	v.p. PLRE	324/37
OU	Fl. Hyginus	v.c. ii 2210 = D. 6116 Corduba	
		Chr.	? MIV 361/3
OU	Athenius	Opt. ii. 18	361/3

Praesides Mauretaniae Sitifensis

NS	Titus Atilius		PLRE	LIII (after 293/IV)
NS	Septimius Flavianus	v.p.	PLRE	315
NS	Fl. Terentianus	v.p.	PLRE	318(?) and 324/37
NS	Jucundius Peregrinus	v.p.	D. 5964	340/50
NS	Fl. Augustianus	v.p.	viii. 84754 p. 972 (?)	351/4
NS	Claudius Helpidius	v.p.	viii. 20592	351/61
NS	Fl. Felix Gentilis	v.p.	viii. 20266	379/83
OU	Fl. Maecius Constans		D. 5596	388/92
OU	(Ae)desi(us)	v.c.	viii. 8397	IV/VE

GOVERNORS OF BYZACENA

Praesides

NS	.... cius Flavianus	v.p. PLRE	293/305
OU	Vibius Flavianus	AE 1953, 45	? LIII/EIV
SB	Aco Catullinus	pp. 78–9, ST. III	313/4
SB	Q. Aradius Rufinus		
	Valerius Proculus	v.c. pp. 52–3; ST. I	321
SB	L. Aradius Valerius		
	Proculus	v.c. pp. 52–3, 65; ST. I	before 324
sb	Agricola 4	v.c. AE 1946, 45	E IV
OU	.... tianus	v.c. viii. 701	E IV

Consulares

SB	Cezeus Largus Maternianus 5	v.c.	viii. 14436 = D. 5518; *AE* 1922, 17	E/MIV
SB	Brittius Praetextatus	v.c.	x. 3846, pp. 140–1; ST. I	c. 330/95
OU	Victorinus	v.c.	viii. 11184 and p. 2337	IV
OU	Constantius		viii. 11333	IV
SB	C. Ceionius Rufius Volusianus Lampadius	v.c.	p. 50; ST. I	before 354
SB	Aginatius 6		*CTh.* xi. 20. 1; Amm. xxviii. 1. 30–5, 50–6	363
OU	Honoratus		*CJ* i. 331	368
OU	Fl. Synesius Filomatius	v.c.	*AE* 1912, 178	383/408
OU	M. Ael . . . . Candidianus	v.c.	*AE* 1954, 69	IV/V
OU	Q. Avidius Felicius		viii. 11932	IV/V
OU	Superius	v.c.	Aug. de cura ger. pro mort. 13	LIV/EV

GOVERNORS OF BAETICA

Praesides

NS	Aur. Julius	v.p.	a(gens) v(icem) p(raesidis) ii. 1115 = D. 593 (Florianus) ii. 1116 (Probus)	276
OU	?Diogenianus?		*AASS* Jul. 4 pp. 583–6	LIII/EIV
OU	Octavius Rufus		ii. 2204	? 312/24
NS	Egnatius Faustinus	v.p.	*PLRE*	337
OU	Decimius Germanianus	v.c.	Amm. xxvi. 5. 5	MIV

Consulares

OU	Decimius Germanianus	v.c.	ii. 2206 PPO	337/71
sb	(Q. Attius Granius) Caelestinus 7	v.c.	*CTh.* ix. 42. 3	357
?ns	Tanaucius Isfalangius		Amm. xxviii. 1. 26 = PUR ?	368/71

Praesides Gallaeciae

sb	Aemilius Maximus 8	v.c.	*Eph. Ep.* viii, p. 403, No. 117 ? Praeses Gallaeciae ?	312/24
SB	Aco Catullinus	v.c.	pp. 78–9	before 338

GOVERNORS OF LUSITANIA

Praesides

NS	Aur. Ursinus	v.p.	*PLRE*	? 293/305
NS	C. Sulpicius . . . . s	v.p.	*PLRE*	315/319
NS	Caecilianus	v.p.	D. 1218	EIV
sb	Numerius Albanus 9	v.c.	ii. 191 = D. 5699	336
NS	Julius Saturninus	v.p.	*AE* 1927, 165	337/40

Consulares

SB	Vettius Agorius Praetextatus	v.c.	pp. 61, 101	before 362
OU	Volventius		proconsul (Lusitania) *PLRE*	382/3

Correctors in Italy

SB	Pomponius Bassus	corr. totius Italiae vi. 3836 =	
		31747 = *IGR* i. 137 cos. 259,	
		procos, PUR 270/1	c. 268/9
SB	C. Pius Esuvius Tetricus	corr. Lucaniae Noble fam: Vict.	
		Caes. 33. 14. Eutr. ix. 10. 4	273/5
OU	M. Aur. Julianus	corr. (N. Ital.) Vict. *Caes.* 39. 10,	
		Zos. i. 73. 1	283/4
SB	C. Ceionius Rufius	v.c. corr. Ital. per ann. octo/vi.	
	Volusianus	1707, cf. p. 3173 = D. 1213;	
		ST. I.	289/91
OU	Paetus Honoratus	corr. Ital. D. 614 = v. 2817	
		Patavium	284/305
SB	Acilius Clarus 1	v.c. corr. Ital. v. 8205; ST. II	286
SB	T. Aelius Marcianus	v.cos., corr. Ital. xi. 1594	
		Florentia	287
ns	L. Aelius Helvius		
	Dionysius	v.c., corr. utriusque Ital.	? 288/96
OU	Numidius	corr. Ital. *CJ.* vii. 35. 3 fare	
		name: only one other in D and	
		PIR (1)	290
SB	T. Flavius Postumius	v.c., corr. Ital. regionis Trans-	
	Titianus	padanae vi. 1418 = D. 2941;	
		ST. I.	? 291/2

GOVERNORS OF CAMPANIA

Correctors

SB	T. Fl. Postumius Titianus	v.c.	vi. 1418 = D. 2941; ST. I.	? 292/3
SB	Pompeius Appius			
	Faustinus 10	v.c.	x. 4785	293/300
SB	Virius Gallus 11	v.c.	x. 3867 = D. 6310	after 298
OU	? Maximus ?		Praeses (in Campania)	
			AASS Jun 3	270–3
				c. 304
SB	Vettius Cossinius Rufinus	v.c.	p. 60	307/12
SB	P. Helvius Aelius Dionysius	v.c.	p. 41	before 324
SB	Clodius Celsinus Adelphius	v.c.	pp. 55 f., 112 ff., ST. II	
				before 324

Consulares

SB	M. Ceionius Julianus			
	Kamenius	v.c.	p. 57; ST. I.	324
SB	Caelius Censorinus	v.c.	x. 3732 = D. 1216	314/37
OU	Junius Valentinus	v.c.	x. 1482 Naples	324/37
SB	Q. Fl. Maesius Egnatius			
	Lollianus	v.c.	pp. 80 f., 122 ff; ST. III	328/34
OU	Barbarus Pompeianus	v.c.	D. 1219 Praeneste	333
NS	C. Julius Rufinianus	v.c.	x. 1125 = D. 2942, pp. 11,	
	Ablabius Tatianus		86 f.	after 337
OU	Julius Aurelianus	v.c.	unpub. inscr. Chastagnol,	
			sub Magnentio aut	
			Eugenio	? 352/4
				or 393/4

SB	Julius Festus Hymetius 12	v.c.	cons. Camp. cum Samnio pp. 91, 107, 129; ST. III c.	355/62
SB	Naeratius Scopius	v.c.	p. 115, ST. II in or after 358	
SB	Q. Clodius Hermogenianus Olybrius	v.c.	p. 101, ST. II before 361	
OU	Virius Turbo	v.c.	x. 3868	? 361/3
SB	Virius Lupus 13	v.c.	Symm. *Rel.* 40. 3. 5; x. 3858	361/3
OU	Buleforus		*CTh.* ix. 30. 2; xv. 15. 1; viii. 5. 24	364/5
SB	Avianius Valentinus 14	v.c.	x. 16561 = D. 764; ST. II	364/75
OU	Amphilochius		*CTh.* xii. 1. 71	370
SB	Anicius Paulinus 15	v.c.	procos. *AE* 1933, 193; unpublished inscr. 5th International Epigraphical Conference, Cambridge, 1967; ST. II	378/9
SB	Anicius Auchenius Bassus 16	v.c.	procos. Camp. vi. 1679 = D. 1262; ST. II	379/82
SB	Meropius Pontius Paulinus 17		Paul. Carm. xxi. 374–6, 395–6; xiii. 7–9	381
SB	Nicomachus Flavianus	v.c.	D. 8985; p. 119; ST. II before 382	
SB	Virius Audentius Aemilianus 18	v.c.	x. 3714 = D. 5478 before 383	
SB	Valerius Hermonius Maximus	v.c.	p. 139; x. 1690 = D. 589; ST. I.	? 394/5
SB	Caecina Decius Albinus		p. 100; *AE* 1909, 223; *AE* 1933, 159	397/8
OU	Tanonius Marcellinus	v.c.	ix. 1589 = D. 6506	IV
OU	Hortensius		x. 1247 Nola	IV/V
OU	Septimius Rusticus	v.c.	x. 1707 = D. 5692	IV/V
OU	Domitius Severianus	v.c.	D. 5693	IV/V
OU	Claudius Julius Pacatus	v.c.	D. 6505 Beneventum	IV/V
OU	Virius Vibius		x. 3869	IV/V
SB	Pontius Paulinus 19		x. 6088	IV/V
SB	Pontius Salutus 20	v.c.	*AE* 1927, 137	IV/V
OU	Fl. Lupus		*PLRE*	? LIV
SB	Valerius Publicola	v.c.	ix. 1591; p. 139; ST. I.	? LIV
SB	Avianius Vindicianus 14	v.c.	x. 1683, x. 6312–3; ST. II ? LIV	
SB	Acilius Glabrio Sibidius	v.c.	vi. 1678 = D. 1281; ST. II LIV	

GOVERNORS OF SAMNIUM

SB	Fabius Maximus	v.c.	rector provinciae (in Samnium) p. 90 f; ST. III	352/7
NS	Fl. Uranius	v.c.	rector provinciae (in Samnium) *PLRE*	352/75
OU	Antonius Justinianus		praes. prov. Samnitium D. 5588 Aesernia x. 4858	
NS	Maecius Felix		Venafrum (Campania)	MIV
		v.p.	rector Samnii *PLRE*	M/LIV

NS	Fl. Julius Innocentius	v.p.	praes. Samnii *PLRE*	M/LIV
OU	Quintilianus		governor of Samnium,	
			x. 4865 Venafrum	? M/LIV

GOVERNORS OF TUSCIA AND UMBRIA

Correctores

SB	C. Vettius Cossinus			
	Rufinus	v.c.	p. 60	307/12
NS	C. Julius Rufinianus			
	Ablabius Tatianus	v.c.	pp. 11f., 86 f.	c. 337
SB	L. Turcius Apronianus			
	Asterius	v.c.	D. 1229; ST. I.	342
SB	Julius Eubulides	v.c.	corr. Tusciae D. 1233	
			Interamna	before 344
SB	P. Publilius Ceionius			
	Julianus	v.c.	vi. 1159, xi. 4118	353/70
SB	Julius Festus Hymetius	v.c.	pp. 91, 107, 129; ST. III	
				before c. 355
?ns	Dynamius		corr. Tusc. 'Actuarius	
			sarcinalium principis	
			iumentorum Amm.	
			xv. 5. 3–14	after 355
SB	Vettius Agorius	v.c.	vi. 1779 = D. 1259; pp. 61,	
	Praetextatus		101	before 362
OU	Auxonius		corr. Tusc. *CTh.* viii. 1. 6.	
			vic. As., PPO	362
NS	Terentius		corr. Tusc. 'humili genere in	
			urbe natus et pistor'	
			Amm. xxvii 3. 2. *CTh.*	
			xii. 1. 61	364–5
NS	Maximinus		corr. Tusc. Amm. xxviii.	
			1. 6. *CTh.* ix. 1. 8	366

Consulares

NS	Lucilius Constantius	v.c.	praes. 'Mauretaniae et	
			Tingitanae, v.c.' D. 1252	
			Luna, Etruria	p. 366
SB	Betitius Perpetuus			
	Arzygius	v.c.	vi. 1702 = D. 1251; ST. II	p. 366
sb	Olybrius 21		cons. Tusc. *CTh.* xii. 1. 72	370
OU	Claudius		cons. Tusc. *CTh.* ii. 4. 5	389
OU	Lachanius		governor of Etruria—father	
			of Rutilius Namat. *de*	
			red. s. 579–80, 595–6,	
			CSL, QSP, PUR	LIV

GOVERNORS OF FLAMINIA AND PICENUM

Correctors

NS	Claudius Uranius	v.p.	*PLRE*	325
OU	M. Aur. Val. Valentinus		xi. 5381 Assisi	a. 330
SB	L. Crepereius Madalianus	v.c.	xiv. 4449; viii. 5348 =	
			D. 1228; pp. 58f., 133;	
			ST. I.	c. 335

SB	Fabius Titianus	v.c.	pp. 82, 119 ff; ST. II–III a.	337
SB	L. Turcius Secundus			
	Asterius	v.c.	p. 54; ST. I.	340/50
SB	M. Aur. Consius Quartus	v.c.	p. 84 f.	a. 350
SB	Furius Maecius Gracchus	v.c.	p. 89	a.c. 350

Consulares

OU	.... meius	v.c.	*PLRE*	350/2
OU	Fl. Ro(ma)nus	v.c.	*AE* 1951, 17 (sub Magnetio)	350/2
OU	Gnaeus Aquilius Romanus			
	Eusebius	v.c.	*PLRE*	p. 350
SB	Justus		governor of Picenum p. 83; ST. II	MIV
OU	Paturinus		consularis (in Picenum) Amm. xv. 7. 5	p. 355
OU	Valentinianus		cons. Pic. *CTh.* ix. 30. 4	365
OU	Sophronius		cons. Pic. *CTh.* xii. 1. 71	370
SB	Tarrutenius Maximilianus 22	v.c.	consularis Piceni vi. 1767 = D. 1282	LIV

Correctores Lucaniae et Bruttii

SB	Pius Esuvius Tetricus		'corrector Lucaniae'	273/5
SB	Q. Sattius Fl. Vettius			
	Gratus	v.c.	pp. 34–5	LIII/IV
OU	Rufinus Octavianus		*CTh.* i. 16. 1	313
OU	Claudius Plotianus		*CTh.* xi. 30. 1 (D. 6349)	313
OU	Maecilius Hilarianus		procos. Afr. cos. 332, PUR, ?PPO *CTh.* xii. 1. 3.	316
SB	L. Turcius Apronianus		? governor of L. and B. ? ST. I. p. 54	323
OU	Alpinius Magnus	v.c.	*PLRE*	324/6
SB	Brittius Praesens	v.c.	p. 140; ST. I.	? EIV
OU	Marius Artemius		*CTh.* viii. 3. 1.	364
SB	Q. Aur. Symmachus			
	Eusebius	v.c.	p. 119; ST. II	365
SB	Pontius Atticus 23	v.c.	*AE* 1913, 227; vi. 31118	374
OU	Rullus Festus	v.c.	x. 212	IV/V
OU	Annius Victorinus	v.c.	x. 519	IV/V

Correctores Apuliae et Calabriae

NS	Ulpius Alenus	v.c.	ix. 687	305/7
SB	L. Nonius Verus 24	v. cons.	xi. 831 = D. 1218	317/24
SB	Volusius Venustus	v.c.	p. 92; ix. 329 = D. 5557ª; ST. II	317/33
SB*	Clodius Celsinus	v.c.	corr. (Camp.) pp. 55 f., 112 ff; ST. II	a. 333
NS	Caecilianus	v.p.	D. 1218	EIV
SB	Attius Insteius Tertullus 25	v.c.	vi. 1697	? E/MIV
NS	Annius Antiochus	v.p.	D. 724, 749	355/61

* I do not accept Celsinus as governor of Apulia and Calabria, but the *PLRE* does. See p. 55 f.

OU	Furius Claudius Togius		
	Quintillus	v.c. ix. 1127, D. 5700 ix. 282	IV
OU	Flavianus	ix. 282	? IV
OU	Flavius Cornelius	v.c. ix. 1579 Beneventum	
	Marcellinus	Native of Benev.	? IV
NS	Fl. Sexio	v.p. Symm. Ep. ii. 43, D. 780	379/94
NS	Aelius Restitutianus	v.p. ix. 430	IV/V

Praesides Sardiniae

NS	L. Septimius Lenticus	v.e. procurator Sard. Eph. Ep.	
		viii. 745	268/70
NS	P.... tius	v.p.	270/5
NS	Septimius Nigrinus	v.e. proc. (Augusti in Sard.)	270/5
NS	Julius..... nus	v.e. PLRE	282
NS	M. Aelius Vitalis		282/3
NS	Valerius Fl... nus	v.p. PLRE	286/305
NS	Aur. Marcus	v.p. PLRE	293/305
NS	Valerius Domitianus	v.p. also v.e., proc.	305
OU	Maximinus	Eph. Ep. viii. 780	? 305/6
OU	Cornelius Fortunatianus	D. 672	306/9
NS	L. Papius Pacatianus	v.p. i. 372 sub Domitio	
		Alexandro	308/9
sb	T. Septimius Januarius 9	v.c. Eph. Ep. viii. 783, x. 7950,	
		x. 7974	312/24
OU	Festus	CTh. ix. 40. 3.	319
NS	Florianus	v.p. AE. 1889, 34	312, 323 or
			330
NS	Helennus	v.p. proc. (in Sard.)	335/7
NS	Fl. Octavianus	v.p. PLRE	335/7
NS	Munatius Gentianus	v.p. PLRE	337/40

VICARS OF ROME FROM THE ACCESSION OF CONSTANTINE TO THE
DEATH OF THEODOSIUS

OU Januarinus, 'agens vicariam praefecturam', CTh. ix. 34. 3, ix. 21. 2—320.
OU Silvius Paulus, 'mag. It.', CTh. i. 15. 1—325.
OU Philippus, 'civ. urb.', CTh. x. 4. 1 (MSS. 313)—326.
NS C. Caelius Saturninus, 'vicarius praeff. praet. in urbo Roma', vi. 1704 =
      D. 1214—a. 334.
OU Junius Tertullus, 'vicarius', Chron. 354—340.
OU Eustathius, 'PPO', CTh. ii. 1. 1, xi. 7. 6—349.
(OU Junius Bassus, 'recens promotus urbi praefectus', died 359. Amm.
      xvii. 11. 5. No indication that his previous post was vic. Rom., which
      PLRE regards him as having been.)
OU Artemius, 'curans vicariam potestatem', Amm. xvii. 11. 5—359.
OU Julianus, 'ex vicario', Amm. xxii. 11. 1, CTh. xiv. 1. 1—360.
OU Fl. Sallustius, 'v.c. vic. urb. Rom.', D. 1254—a. 361.
SB Julius Festus Hymetius pp. 91, 107, 129; ST. III—362.
SB Clodius Octavianus, p. 85—a. 363.
OU Hypatius, 'vic. urb. Rom.', CTh. iii. 5. 8.—363, Feb. 21.
SB L. Aurelius Avianius Symmachus, 'v.c. pro-praeff. praet. in urbe
      Roma finitimisque provinciis', vi. 1698 = D. 1257, p. 83 f. ST. II—
      a. 364.
SB Placidus Severus p. 122; ST. III—364-5.

15

SB 26   Volusianus, *CTh*. xiv. 6. 3, viii. 5. 22; ST. I—365–6.
OU   Magnus, 'vic. urb. Rom.', *CTh*. vii. 13. 3–4—367.
SB 6   Aginatius, 'vic. Rom.', Amm. xxviii. 1. 30–5, 50–6—368–70.
NS   Maximinus, 'regens vicariam praefecturam', Amm. xxviii. 1. 5, 12 ff;
      p. 94—370–71.
OU   Ursicinus, Amm. xxviii. 1. 44–5—371.
ns   Fl. Simplicius, Amm. xxviii. 1. 45—grammaticus; p. 87—374–5.
NS   Doryphorianus, Amm. xxviii. 1. 53–7—375/6.
OU   Aquilinus, *Epist. Imper.* 13—378/9.
OU   Potitus, 'vic. urb.', *CTh*. vi. 28. 1, iv. 22. 2—379–80.
OU   Val. Anthidius, 'a.v. praeff. praet.' D. 5906—381.
OU   Hellenius, 'vic. urb.', *CTh*. xii. 11. 2—386.
OU   Orientius, 'vic. urb. Rom.', *CTh*. ix. 7. 6—390.
OU   Leporius, Symm. *Ep*. ix. 10—394.
SB   Fabius Pasiphilus, 'v.c. agens vicem praefectorum praetorio et urbi',
      x. 1692 = D. 792, x. 1694; ST. III—394–5.

VICARS OF ITALY FROM THE TETRARCHY TO THE DEATH OF THEODOSIUS

NS   Caecilianus, 'v.p., vic. praef. per It.', D. 1218—EIV.
OU   Julius Severus, 'vic. It.', *CTh*. xi. 30. 9—318.
OU   Helpidius 'a.v. p.p.' *CJ*. 8. 10. 6—321.
SB   L. Crepereius Madalianus, 'v.c. vic. It.', pp. 58/9, 133; ST. I—341.
OU   Faventius, 'vic. It.', *CTh*. xi. 1. 12—365.
OU   Italicus, 'vic. It.' *CtTh*. xiii. 1. 10—374.
OU   Catafronius, 'vic. It.', *CTh*. viii. 5. 31, xvi. 2. 24—376–7.
SB 27   Valerius Severus, ST. I—382.

VICARS OF AFRICA FROM THE TETRARCHY TO THE DEATH OF THEODOSIUS

NS   Val. Alexander, 'v.p. a.v. praeff. praet.' *AE* 1942/3, 81—303–6.
NS   L. Domitius Alexander, 'agrestibus ac Pannonicis parentibus', *Vict.
      Caes.* 40. 17—308.
OU   Patricius, vic. praeff. praet. Eus. *H.E.* x. 6. 4—c. 313.
OU   Aelafius, Opt. *App.* iii—313/4.
OU   Aelius Paulinus, 'a.v. pp.' ('vir spectabilis' prob. interpol.) Opt. *App.*—
      314.
NS   Verus, 'v.p. vic. praef per Afr.', Aug. *c. Cresc.* III. 70, 81; *Ep*. 88. 4—315.
OU   Domitius Celsus, 'vic. Afr.', *CTh*. ix. 18. 1—315.
OU   Eumelius, 'vic. Afr.', *CTh*. ix. 40. 2—316.
SB   Lucrius Verinus, p. 64 f.
SB   L. Aradius Valerius Proculus Populonius, pp. 52 f., 65; ST. I—a. 333.
OU   Menander, *CTh*. iv. 13. 2, viii. 5. 4—322–6.
SB   C. Annius Tiberianus, pp. 71, 112; ST. II—325–7.
SB   Aco Catullinus, Philomathius, pp. 78 f. 338–9.
sb 28   Petronius, *CTh*. ii. 6. 5, x. 15. 3—340.
SB 29   Julius Eubulides, xi. 4181 = D. 1233—344.
OU   Caesonianus, 'vic. Afr.', *CTh*. i. 15. 2—348.
OU   Martinianus, 'v.c. vic. Afr.', *CTh*. xii. 1. 44—358.
OU   Claudius Avitianus, 'vic. Afr.', viii. 7037—362–3.
OU   Antonius Dracontius, 'v.c. a.v.p.p.' D. 758. D. 763, *CTh*. xi. 7. 9,
      xiii. 6. 4—364–7.
OU   Musuphilus, 'vic. Afr.', *CTh*. xiii. 6. 3—368, 370 or 373.
OU   Crescens, 'vic. Afr.', *CTh*. xi. 1. 17, Amm. xxviii. 6. 23—371–3.
OU   Nitentius, 'vic. Afr.', *CTh*. xvi. 6. 2—a. 377.

SB   Virius Nicomachus Flavianus, p. 119; vi. 1782–3 = D. 2947–8; ST. II—
       377.
SB   Faltonius Probus Alypius, Symm. *Ep.* vii. 66; *CTh.* i. 15. 19 ST. II—378.
SB   Celsinus Titianus Symm. *Ep.* iii. 19; *CTh.* xiv. 3. 17, xii. 1. 84 ST. II—
       380.
SB   Alfenius Ceionius Julianus, p. 50; ST. I.—381.
OU   Castorius, D. 1288—a. 385.
OU   Licinius, *CJ.* xi. 60. 1—385.
OU   Fl. Macrobius Maximianus, 'v.c. a.v.p.p.' *AE* 1912, 178—383/408.
OU   Magnillus, Symm. *Epp.* ii. 20, iii. 34; *CTh.* x. 17. 3—391.
OU   Caecilius Severus, 'a.v.p.p.' *IRT* 519—M/L IV.

VICARS OF THE SPAINS FROM THE ACCESSION OF CONSTANTINE TO
       THE DEATH OF THEODOSIUS

NS   Q. Aeclanius Hermias, 'v.p. a.v.p.p.', ii. 2203—306/37.
OU   Octavianus, 'comes Hisp.', *CTh.* ix. 1. 1—316–17.
SB 30 Septimius Acindynus, ii. 4107—c. 325.
SB   C. Annius Tiberianus, pp. 71, 112; ST. II—332, 335.
OU   Severus, 'comes Hisp.', *CTh.* viii. 12. 5—333–5.
OU   Ti. Fl. Laetus, 'v.c. comes', *AE* 1927, 165—337/40.
SB 31 Albinus, *CTh.* xi. 36. 5; *CJ* vii. 62. 20—341.
SB   M. Aurelius Consius Quartus, p. 84 f.—M IV.
OU   Clementinus, *Col. Avell.* ii. 33–8—c. 357.
OU   Fl. Sallustius, 'v.c. vic. Hisp.', D. 1254—a. 361.
SB 32 Volusius Venustus, p. 92; ST. II—362–3.
OU   Valerianus, 'vic. Hisp.'; *CTh.* i. 16. 10—365–6.
OU   Marius Artemius, 'v.c. vic. Hisp.', *CTh.* xi. 26. 1—369–70.
ns   Sextilius Agesilaus Aedesius, 'v.c. vic. Hisp.', D. 4152, Amm. xv. 5. 4,
       14: advocatus, mag. libellor, et cog., sacr. mag. ep., mag.
OU   Marinianus, 'vic. Hisp.', *CTh.* ix. 1. 14—383.

PRAETORIAN PREFECTS

Names in brackets are those of acting praetorian prefects. Though Hermogenes who appears in *Chron. 354* as both urban and praetorian prefect in 349, is not bracketed in the *fasti* of the *PLRE*, his joint tenure of both posts is a pointer to the temporary nature of his appointment. He is recorded in office from 19 May 349 to 26 February 350, a time of civil strife in Italy.

A stroke (–) before a name indicates that the person concerned was of senatorial rank before his prefecture, though not of senatorial birth.

A prefect appointed by one emperor and continuing in office under the next is listed only under the first. But if reappointed after an interval of years, he appears twice, marked (*) the second time.

Constantine's prefect Volusianus is the only one listed here who is not included in the *fasti* of the *PLRE*.

Constantine's Praetorian Prefects

SB   Petronius Annianus, p. 67 ff.; ST. II.
OU   Junius Bassus, vic. It: *CTh.* ii. 10. 4 (326); PPO: *CTh.* xvi. 2. 3 (329).
SB   Petronius Probianus, p. 68 f.; ST. II.
SB   (Acilius) Severus, p. 69; ST. II.
OU   Fl. Constantius, iii. 6751.
OU   Evagrius, *CTh.* xiv. 8. 1, ix. 3, 2, xii. 1. 22.

SB 33   Volusianus, ST. I.
SB   Valerius Maximus, p. 69; ST. I.
NS   Ablabius, *ILT*. 814; Eun. *V.S.* vi. 3. 1–7; Lib. *Or.* xlii. 23. (officialis of
         govr. of Crete); vic. As.: iii. 352 = 7000 = D. 6091; Jer. *Chron.*
         s.a. 338; Christian: Eun. *V.S.* vi. 2–3, Zos. ii. 40. 3.
OU   Felix, *CTh.* iii. 30. 5, xiii. 4. 1, xii. 1. 21.
OU   Gregorius, *CJ.* v. 27. 1, *CTh.* xi. 1. 3.
NS   Papius Pacatianus, *LIT* 814. v.p. praes. Sard: I. 372.
SB   Annius Tiberianus, p. 65; ST. II.
OU   Nestorius Timonianus, *ILT* 814.
NS   Caelius Saturninus, vi. 1704—D. 1214, showing his rise from equestrian
         posts such as 'a consiliis sacris sexagenarius', to his adlection 'inter
         consulares'; PPO: vi. 1705 = D. 1215.
OU   Aemilianus, *CTh.* xi. 16. 4.

PRAETORIAN   PREFECTS   IN   THE   WEST   UNDER   CONSTANTINE'S
                              SUCCESSORS

Constantine II, Constans and Constantius II
OU   Ambrosius, Paul. *V. Amb.* ii. 3–4.
SB   Antonius Marcellinus, p. 77 f.
SB   Aco Catullinus Philomathius, p. 78 f.
SB   Fabius Titianus, pp. 79, 112 ff.; ST. II–III.
SB   M. Maecius Memmius Furius Baburius Caecilianus Placidus, p. 79 f.
         ST. III.
SB   Vulcacius Rufinus, pp. 76, 117 f.; ST. II.
OU   Ulpius Limenius, *CTh.* ix. 21. 6.
(OU   Eustathius, *CTh.* ii. 1. 1, xi. 7. 6).
(OU   Hermogenes, *Chron. 354*).
OU   Anicetus, Aur. Vict. *Caes.* 42. 6; Zos. ii. 43. 3.
OU   Maecilius Hilarianus, *CTh.* vi. 4. 3–4.
SB   C. Ceionius Rufius Volusianus Lampadius, pp. 50, 82; ST. I.
SB   Q. Fl. Maesius Egnatius Lollianus Mavortius, p. 80 f. ST. III.
NS   Fl. Taurus, humble origins: Lib. *Or.* xlii. 24–5. Career: *AE* 1934, 159.
OU   Honoratus, Lib. *Ep.* 386.
OU   Fl. Florentius, Ath. *Hist.* Ar. 22; Amm. xvi. 12. 14.
OU   Anatolius, Amm. xix. 11. 3; *CTh.* xii. 1. 38.
OU   Nebridius, Amm. xx. 9. 5.

Julian
ns   Fl. Sallustius, vi. 1729 = D. 1254, 'vicarius V provinciarum, vicarius
         Hispaniarum, vicarius urbis Romae et comes Consistorii', No sign
         in this detailed *cursus* inscription of a correctorship, consularship or
         proconsulate, so probably non-noble.
OU   Cl. Mamertinus, Amm. xxi. 10. 8; 12. 25; xxvi. 5. 5.

Jovian
OU   Decimius Germianus, Amm. xxvi. 5. 5. First law as PPO: *CTh.* xi. 30.
         30 18 Dec. 362—MSS.; 18 Dec. 363 Seeck, *Regesten*, Still in office
         Apr. 366; *CTh.* viii. 7. 9.

Valentinian I
SB   Sex. Claudius Petronius Probus, pp. 96 f. 111 ff.; 156 f.; ST. II.

*SB   Vulcacius Rufinus, pp. 96 f.; 117 f.; ST. II.
ns   Florentius, CSL: *CTh.* xiii. 1. 6; PPO Gall.: *CTh.* xiii. 10 5.
ns   Viventius, from Siscia, Pannonia: Amm. xxvi. 4. 4; xxvii. 3. 11–12;
     CTh. xiii. 10. 4 and 6.
NS   Maximinus, Amm. xxviii. 1, passim. PPO: Amm. xxviii. 1. 41.

Gratian

ns   Fl. Claudius Antonius, mag. (scrinii): Symm. *Ep.* i. 89; QSP: Ibid.
     PPO Gall.: *CTh.* xiii. 3. 11.
NS   Decimius Magnus Ausonius, Aus. *Grat. Act.* ii. 7, *Ep.* xxii, *Lib. Protrept.*,
     Parent. xi, *ad Lect.*, passim; *Parent*; passim.
–NS   Decimius Hilarianus Hesperius, son of Ausonius, refs. as above.
NS   Julius Ausonius, father of Ausonius, refs. as above.
ns   Siburius, physician from Bordeaux: Marcellinus Empiricus, *de Medica-*
     mentis, praef. 2. Symm. *Ep.* iii. 43. *CTh.* xi. 31. 7. Lib. *Ep.* 963
     (Siburius, govr. of Palestine, son ?).
OU   Fl. Syagrius, brother-in-law of Theodosius: Them. *Or.* xvi. 203. Mag.
     Off.: *CTh.* vii. 12. 2–3.
OU   Fl. Afranius Syagrius, notarius: Amm. xxviii. 2. 5–6. PPO: *CTh.* xi. 30.
     38, viii. 5. 36, i. 10. 1.
–OU   Fl. Hypatius, son of Fl. Eusebius, cos. ord. 347: Julian. Or. iii. 107.
     Brother therefore of Empress Eusebia and Fl. Eusebius junr. Amm.
     xviii. 1. 1, xxi. 6. 4, xxix. 2. 9. Cos. ord. together with his brother, 359.
OU   Fl. Mallius Theodorus, Claud. *de cos. F. Mallii Theodori v.c. panegyris.*
OU   Proculus Gregorius, praef. ann: *CTh.* xiv. 3. 15. QSP: Symm. *Ep.* iii.
     18, i. 95 Aus. *de Fastis* iv dedic., Sulp. Sev. *Chron.* ii. 49, 2–3.

Valentinian II and Theodosius

*SB 34   Sex. Claudius Petronius Probus, pp. 96, 111 ff.; 156 ff. ST. II.
SB 35   Nonius Atticus Maximus, p. 101.
SB   Vettius Agorius Praetextatus, pp. 61, 101.
OU   Fl. Neoterius, notarius: Amm. xxvi. 5. 14. PPO: *CTh.* ii. 1. 16.
OU   Fl. Euodius, Sulp. Sev. *Chron.* ii. 50. 7, Sulp. Sev. *V. Mart.* 20. 4.
OU   Principius, mag off.: *CTh.* i. 9. 2. PPO: *CTh.* xiii. 1. 14.
OU   Fl. Eusignius, procos. Afr. *CTh.* xii. 1. 95 (383). PPO: *CTh.* i. 32. 5.
     Estates in Sic.: Symm. *Ep.* iv. 71.
OU   Trifolius, CSL: *CTh.* vi. 30. 7. PPO: *CTh.* xv. 4. 7.
OU   Constantianus, *CTh.* v. 1. 4.
OU   Felix Juniorinus Polemius, *CTh.* xv. 1. 28.
SB   Virius Nicomachus Flavianus, vi. 1782 = D. 2947, pp. 100, 110 f., 119;
     App. 32; ST. II.
OU   Apodemius, *CTh.* xii. 12. 12–13, xi. 30. 51.
(SB   Fabius Pasiphilus, x. 1692 = D. 792, x. 1694; ST. III).

STATISTICAL TABLES

Office-holders who cannot be placed in a particular reign or group of reigns are not included in these totals but are included in the over-all totals. This means that there are some discrepancies between the reign-totals and the over-all totals. The totals for men of senatorial birth include a few whose nobility is probable though not certain or almost-certain and who are marked 'sb'. These are: the *praesides* Agricola (App. 4), Aemilius Maximus (App. 8), Numerius Albanus (App. 9) and Septimius Januarius (App. 9); and the vicar of Africa, Petronius (App. 28).

Men probably of non-senatorial birth (ns) have regularly been included in the NS totals.

TABLE I

The Social Origins of Western Praesides (284–337)

Diocletian and the tetrarchy

Diocese	SB	NS	OU
Africa	—	17	1
Hispaniae	—	3	1
Britanniae	—	1	—
Galliae et Viennensis	—	2	3
Illyricum	—	1	1
Sardinia	—	3	4
Totals:	—	27	10

Constantine

Diocese	SB	NS	OU
Africa	4	6	—
Hispaniae	3	3	2
Britanniae	—	—	—
Galliae et Viennensis	1	1	1
Illyricum	—	3	—
Sardinia	1	2	1
Totals:	9	15	4

TABLE II

The Social Origins of Western Consulars from Constantine to Theodosius

Diocese	SB	NS	OU
Africa	12	1	17
Hispaniae	2	1	2
Galliae	1	—	1
Illyricum	2	—	4
Italia Suburbicaria et Annonaria	32	2	29
Totals:	49	4	53

TABLE III

The Social Origins of Vicars

Diocletian and the tetrarchy

Diocese	SB	NS	OU
Italia Suburbicaria	—	1	—
Italia Annonaria	—	1	—
Africa	—	1	—
Hispaniae	—	—	1
Galliae	—	—	1
(Aegyptus)	—	1	—
Totals:	—	4	2

Constantine I

Diocese	SB	NS	OU
West:			
Italia Suburbicaria	—	1	3
Italia Annonaria	—	—	2
Africa	3	1	6
Hispaniae	2	1	2
Britanniae	—	1	—
Galliae	—	—	1
East:			
Asiana	—	2	1
Macedonia	—	—	1
Comites Orientis	1	—	4
Totals:	6	6	20

Constantine II, Constans and Constantius II

	SB	NS	OU
West:			
Italia Suburbicaria	—	—	6
Italia Annonaria	1	—	—
Africa	2	—	3
Hispaniae	2	—	3
Britanniae	—	—	2
East:			
Thraciae	—	1	—
Asiana	—	2	3
Pontica	—	1	2
Comites Orientis	2	—	6
Totals:	7	4	25

Julian

	SB	NS	OU
West:			
Italia Suburbicaria	1	—	1
Italia Annonaria	—	—	—
Africa	—	—	1
Hispaniae	1	—	—
East:			
Macedonia	—	—	1
Thraciae	—	—	1
Asiana	—	—	2
Comites Orientis	1	—	1
Totals:	3	—	7

TABLE 111—continued

Diocese	SB	NS	OU
Valentinian I and Valens			
West:			
Italia Suburbicaria	3	3	2
Italia Annonaria	—	—	2
Africa	—	—	4
Hispaniae	—	—	2
Britanniae	—	—	1
Galliae			
East:			
Thraciae	—	1	—
Asiana	—	—	3
Comites Orientis	—	2	2
Totals:	3	6	16
Gratian			
Italia Suburbicaria	—	—	3
Italia Annonaria	1	—	1
Africa	4	—	—
Hispaniae	1	—	—
Totals:	6	—	4
Theodosius and Valentinian II			
West (383–95):			
Italia Suburbicaria	1	—	3
Africa	—	—	4
Galliae	—	—	1
East (378–95):			
Macedonia	—	—	2
Thraciae	—	—	1
Asiana	1	1	1
Pontica	—	—	3
Comites Orientis	—	—	11
Totals:	2	1	26

Totals for period from accession of Constantine to death of
Theodosius:

	SB	NS	OU
West:			
Italia Suburbicaria	8	4	18
Italia Annonaria	2	—	5
Africa	10	1	21
Hispaniae	6	2	7
Britanniae	—	1	4
Galliae	—	—	3
Totals:	26	8	58
East:			
Macedonia	—	2	4
Thraciae	—	3	3
Asiana	2	6	10
Pontica	—	2	9
Totals:	2	13	26
Comites Orientis	6	2	23

TABLE IV

The Social Origins of Praetorian Prefects

	SB	NS	OU
Diocletian	—	3	2
Maxentius	1	—	2
Licinius	—	1	1
Constantine I	6	3	7

West				*East*			
	SB	NS	OU		SB	NS	OU
Constantine II,				Constantius II	1	6	2
Constans and							
Constantius II	7	1	8				
Jovian	—	—	1				
Julian	—	1	1	Julian	—	—	1
Valentinian	2	3	—	Valens	—	—	5
Gratian	—	5	5	Theodosius (378–83)	2	1	2
Valentinian II and							
Theodosius (383–95)	4	—	8	Theodosius (383–95)	—	1	2
Totals:	13	10	23	Totals:	3	8	12

SB total from Constantine to Theodosius:	22
Total of PPOs of known social origin from Constantine to Theodosius:	43
Over-all total of PPOs from Constantine to Theodosius:	85
Constantine's noble PPOs plus noble PPOs in West 337–95:	19
Total of Constantine's PPOs plus all PPOs in West 337–95:	62

LISTS

GP Q. Fl. Maesius Egnatius Lollianus Mavortius—Decatrenses
     (Puteolis), p. 80 f.; ST. III.
     Q. Fl. Maesius Cornelius Egnatius Severus Lollianus—Deca-
     trenses (Puteolis), p. 122; ST. III.
     Sex. Claudius Petronius Probus—Verona (vi. 1751), Capua—
     originalis—pp. 96 f., 111 ff., 156 ff.; ST. II.
     Tyrrania Anicia Iuliana—(priv.) vi. 1714 = D. 1271; ST. II.
GP Q. Clodius Hermogenianus Olybrius—Formiae, Theveste p. 00;
     ST. II.
     Ceionius Apronianus—Cillium, Afr. procos.—viii. 210 = D. 5570
     ST. I.
GP L. Aradius Val. Proculus Populonius—guild in Rome, Puteoli—
     pp. 52–3, 65; ST. I.
GP Anicius Auchenius Bassus—Neapolis, Fabrateria, Vetus, Bene-
     ventum App. 16.
GP Ragonius Vincentius Celsus—Ostia—xiv. 173.
GP Vulcacius Rufinus—Thamugadi—viii. 2403 pp. 96 f., 117 f., ST. II.
     Insteius Lampadius—Thamugadi—viii. 2403.
     Neratius Constans—Saepinum—ix. 2448 p. 117; ST. II.
GP Postumius Lampadius—Capua- cons. Camp., patronus—x. 3860
     = D. 1276 longe a maiorib. originalis, x. 1704 PUR 403–6.
GP Arrius Maecius Gracchus—Salernum p. 90; ST. III.

B: NOBLE COMITES

P indicates a *comes intra palatium* or *intra consistorium*.

P   M. Nummius Albinus Triturrius: comes domesticus ord. pr. vi.
     1748; ST. I.
     L. Turcius Secundus: comes Augustorum—p. 54; ST. I; vi. 1772 =
     D. 1230.
     C. Caelius Censorinus: comes d.n. Constantini Maximi Aug. App. 3.
     Brittius Praetextatus Argentius: comes ord. pr. pp. 140–1; ST. I,
     x. 3846.
P   Memmius Vitrasius Orfitus Honorius: comes ord. pr. iterum intra
     consistorium . . . comes ord. sec. expeditiones bellicas gubernans
     p. 88 f.; ST. III; vi. 1739–42.
P   M. Aurelius Nerius Symmachus v.p.: 'intra palatio comitatus' sub
     Constantino p. 84 f; ST. II; vi. 1747.
P   Neratius Cerealis. p. 115; ST. II; Soz. 4. 6. 15.
P   L. Aradius Valerius Proculus Populonius: comes ord. sec., comes
     ord. pr., comes iterum ord. pr. intra Pal. pp. 52, 65,; ST. I; vi.
     1690 = D. 1240.
     L. Crepereius Madalianus: comes Flavialis, ord. sec. pp. 58 f., 133;
     ST. I. xiv. 4449; comes ord. primi: CTh. xiv. 10. 2.

C. Vettius Cossinius Rufinus: comes Augg. nn. p. 60, x. 5061 = D. 1217.

C. Ceionius Rufius Volusianus: comes d.n. Constantini invicti et perpetui semper Augusti; pp. 44 f., 49, 63; ST. I.; vi. 1707 cf. p. 3173 = D. 1213.

C. Annius Tiberianus: comes Afr., Comes Hisp. p. 71; ST. II; CTh. xii. 5. 1, CTh. xii. 1. 15; Cf vi. 1. 6.

Fabius Titianus: comes ord. pr. pp. 79, 119; ST. II–III; vi. 1717 = D. 1227.

M. Maecius Memmius Furius Baburius Caecilianus Placidus: comes ord. pr. p. 79 f., ST. III; x. 1700 = D. 1243.

P Vulcacius Rufinus: comes ord. pr. intra consist. pp. 76 f., 117 f., ST. II; vi. 32051 = D. 1237.

P Q. Fl. Maesius Egnatius Lollianus Mavortius: comes ord. pr. intra Pal. p. 80 f.; ST. III; vi. 37112 = vi. 1723 + vi. 1757.

C: NOBLE PAGANS

For a full list of pagan priests between 370 and 390 see H. Bloch, *Harvard Theological Review*, 38 (1945), facing p. 244. For the early fourth century see A. Alföldi, *The Conversion of Constantine and Pagan Rome*.

L. Ragonius Venustus—aug. pub. p.R.Q., pont. Vest. mai., taurobol., criobol. 390 consecrated altar 'diis omnipotentibus'. vi. 1760.

L. Aelius Helvius Dionysius—pont. dei Solis. vi. 1675 = D. 1211; p. 40 f.

Vettenia Sabinilla—virgo vestalis. vi. 1675 = D. 1211; p. 41 f.

M. Aurelius Julius—augur. probably pre-Diocletianic, despite *PLRE*; D. 3710.

T. Fl. Postumius Titianus—pont. dei Solis, aug. vi. 1418 = D. 2941.

Brittius Praetextatus Argentius—XVv. s.f. x. 3846; pp. 140–1; ST. I.

Brittius Praesens—pont. mai. vi. 2153; p. 140, ST. I.

Memmius Vitrasius Orfitus—pont. deae Vest., XVv. s.f., pont. dei Solis vi. 1739–42; p. 88 f., ST. III.

L. Turcius Apronianus Asterius—XVv. s.f. D. 1229; ST. I.

Publilius Ceionius Caecina Albinus—(pagan in Macrob.) (? ⸗ Albinus, pagan priest, father of Laeta?) Macrob. *Sat.* 1. 2. 15; Symm. *Ep.* viii. 25; Jer. *Ep.* 107. 1; ST. I.

Q. Aurelius Symmachus Eusebius—pont. mai. vi. 1699 = D. 2946; p. 119; ST. II.

Turcius Secundus Asterius—XVv. s.f. vi. 31118.

Pontius Atticus—(pagan). vi. 31118; App. 23.

Rufius Antonius Agrypnius Volusianus—(pagan). ST. I; Jer. *Chron.* s.a. 377; Pall. *Hist. Laus*, 54, 62; *V. Mel.* (Gr.) 1, 41, 50–6; *V. Mel.* (L) i, ii. 10, 19–35; Aug. *Ep.* 124–6; Jer. *Ep.* 145—Aug. *Ep.* 202; Paul. *Carm.* xxi.

Q. Sattius Fl. Vettius Gratus—aug. p.p.R.Q. *AE* 1923, 61; p. 62.

L. Aradius Valerius Proculus Populonius—aug. pont. mai. XVv. s.f., pont. Flav. vi. 1690 = D. 1240, vi. 1691–4; pp. 52 f., 65; ST. I.

L. Aurelius Avianius Symmachus—pont. mai. XVv.s.f. vi. 1698 = D. 1257; p. 83 f; ST. II.

Clodius Octavianus—pont. mai. ix. 2566; p. 85.

Alfenius Ceionius Julianus Kamenius—VIIv. epulonum, pater sacr. summi invicti Mithrae, Hierof. Hecatae, Arcibuculus die Liberi, XVv.s.f., tauroboliatus deum matris, pont. mai. D. 1264; p. 50; ST. I.

C. Ceionius Rufius Volusianus Lampadius—tauroboliatus—*AE* 1945, 55; pp. 50, 82; ST. I.

Ceionius Rufius Volusianus—tauroboliatus vi. 512 = D. 4154; p. 50; ST. I.

C(eionius) Ruf(ius) Volusianus—'pater ierofanta, profeta Isidis, pontifex dei Sol.' (to be identified with one of the two previous Ceionii)—vi. 846 = D. 4413; p. 50.

Rufius Caeionius Sabinus—'p(ont) m(aior), hierof. d. Hecat., aug. pub. p.R.Q., pater sacror. invict. Methrae, tauroboliatus'—vi. 511 (377); p. 50; ST. I.

Sabina—tauroboliata—vi. 30966 = *IG* xiv. 1019 (377); p 50; ST. I.

Rufia Volusiana—tauroboliata—vi. 509 = *IG* xiv. 1018 (370); p. 50; ST. I.

Petronius Apollodorus—tauroboliatus—vi. 509 = *IG* xiv. 1018 (370); p. 50.

Caecinia Lolliana—Deae Isidis sacerdos. vi. 512 = D. 4154; p. 50; ST. I.

Clodius Hermogenianus Caesarius—tauroboliatus—vi. 499 = D. 4147 (374) p. 50.

Caeionius Alfenius Julianus Kamenius—tauroboliatus—*AE* 1953, 238 (374); (probably to be identified with the previous entry); p. 50.

M. Aurelius Consius Quartus jun.—pont. mai., promagister iterum, XIIv. vi. 1700 = D. 1249; p. 84 f.

Aradius Rufinus—pagan—Lib. *Ep.* 825, 1374; ST. I.

Julius Festus Hymetius—pagan—App. 12; ST. III.

Praetextata—pagan—App. 12.

Marcianus—procos. Afr., Chr. who apostasised in pagan reaction—see App. 22, p. 187, note 1.

C. Vettius Cossinius Rufinus—pont. dei Solis, aug., Sal. Pal. x. 5061 = D. 1217; p. 60.

Publilius Optatianus Porphyrius—pagan—(later convert to Christianity?) *Not. Scav.* 1917, 22; p. 60.

Basilius—pagan—(a relative of Valerius Maximus Basilius, PUR 319–23 in whose family Basilius recurs repeatedly as a signum?) Him. Or. iii. 8.

Postumius Rufius Festus Avienius—pagan. vi. 537 = D. 2944; p. 133 ff; ST. I.

C. Ceionius Rufius Volusianus—XVv.s.f. vi. 2153; p. 50; ST. I.

Fl. Atticus—XVv.s.f.—vi. 2153.

Aco Catullinus Philomathius—pagan. vi. 1780 = D. 1260; p. 78 f.

Fabia Aconia Paulina—sacrata apud Eleusinam Deo Iaccho Cereri et Corae, sacrata apud Laernam deo Libero et Cereri et Corae, sacrata apud Aeginam deabus, tauroboliata Isiacae, Hierophantria deae Hecatae Graecosacraneae deae Cereris—vi. 1780 = D. 1260.

Fabius Titianus—XVv.s.f. D. 8983; pp. 79, 119 ff.; ST. II–III.

M. Maecius Memmius Furius Baburius Caecilianus Placidus—pont. mai., aug. p.p.R.Q., XVv.s.f. x. 1700 = D. 1231; p. 79 f; ST. III.

Vulcacius Rufinus—pont. mai. vi. 32051 = D. 1237; pp. 76 f, 117 f; ST. II.

Q. Fl. Maesius Egnatius Lollianus Mavortius—aug. p.p.R.Q. x. 4752 = D. 1223; Firm. Mat. *Math.* 8. 15; p. 80 f.; ST. III.

(No)nius Tineius Tarrut(enius) Atticus—XVv.s.f. App. 35.

Vettius Agorius Praetextatus—aug., pont. Vest., pont. Solis, XVv.s.f., curialis Herculis, sacratus Libero et Eleusini, Hierophanta, neocorus, tauroboliatus, pater patrum. vi. 1779 = D. 1259; p. 101 f.

Virius Nicomachus Flavianus—pont. mai. vi. 1782 = D. 2947; pp. 100, 110 f., 119; App. 32; ST. II.

Celsinus Titianus—pont. Solis et Vestae. Symm. Ep. I. 68; Seeck: Symm. p. cvi; ST. II.

D: NOBLE HOLDERS OF REPUBLICAN MAGISTRACIES

Anicius Faustus: suff. cos. (cos. ii, 298). Probably *also* pr. urb. vi. 315 = D. 3409 cf. Chastagnol, *Fastes*, 31 f.

Sex. Anicius Paulinus: suff. cos. vi. 1680, ST. II.

M. Nummius Albinus Triturrius: q.k. pr. urb., cos. ord. iterum (i.e. suff. cos, ord. cos.) vi. 1748; ST. I.

L. Turcius Secundus Asterius: q., pr., cos. (suff.) vi. 1772 = D. 1230, ST. I.

Insteius Pompeianus: suff. cos. vi. 32000 = *ILCV.* 60; App. 25.

Ragonius Vincentius Celsus: q., pr. tr., suff. cos. vi. 1760; related to Ragonius Venustus, pagan priest.

(Quintilius) Laetus: suff. cos. Jer. *Ep.* 54. 6. 3 ST. iii.

Pompeius Appius Faustinus: pr. urb. App. 10.

T. Fl. Postumius Titianus: q.k., pr. k. v. cos. vi. 1418 = D. 2941; ST. I.

L. Castrius Constans: suff. cos. D. 8881; *MAMA* vi. p. 35.

C. Caelius Censorinus: pr. k., suff. cos. App. 3.

Cezeus Largus Maternianus: 'praetorio viro', App. 5.

L. Turcius Apronianus Asterius: q., pr. D. 1229; ST. I.

L. Nonius Verus: v. cons., App. 24.

Attius (Insteius T(ertullus Populonius: q.k., pr. k., cos. suff., App. 25.

Attius Insteius Tertullus: q., pr.k., cos. suff., App. 25.

Ceionius Italicus: suff. cos. ('clarissimo atque consulari viro') viii. 7012–3; ST. I.

Memmius Vitrasius Orfitus Honorius: q.k., pr., suff. cos. p. 80 f; ST. III.

Q. Aurelius Symmachus Eusebius: q., pr. VI. 1699 = D. 2946; p. 119; ST. II.

Q. Fabius Memmius Symmachus: q., pr., Symm. *Ep.* v. 22; Seeck, Symm. p. lxxi; ST. II.

Anicius Auchenius Bassus: q.k., pr. tut., App. 16.

Meropius Pontius Paulinus: suff. cos., App. 17.

L. Aradius Val. Proculus Populonius: pr. tut. vi. 1690 = D. 1240; pp. 52 f., 37; ST. I.

Caelius Urbanus: suff. cos. vi: 1705 = D. 1215.

L. Crepereius Madalianus: q.k., pr. suff. cos. xiv. 4449; pp. 58 f, 133; ST. I.

Alfenius Ceionius Julianus Kamenius: q.k., pr.tr. D. 1264; p. 50; ST. I.

Julius Festus Hymetius: pr. urb., App. 12.

Julius Agrius Tarrutenius Marcianus: q.k., pr. k., App. 22.

Q. Fl. Maesius Cornelius Egnatius Severus Lollianus Mavortius jun.: q.k.—x. 1697 = D. 1226; p. 122 f.; ST. III.

Q. Fl. Maesius Egnatius Lollianus Mavortius: q.k., pr. urb. pp. 80 f., 122 f. ST. III.

Sex. Claudius Petronius Probus: q., pr. urb. vi. 1779 = D. 1259; p. 111 ff.

(No)nius Tineius Tarrutenius Atticus q.k., pr. tut., App. 35.

Vettius Agorius Praetextatus: q.k., pr. urb. vi. 1779 = D. 1259; p. 101 f.

Virius Nicomachus Flavianus: q., pr. vi. 1782 = D. 2947; pp. 100, 110 f., 119; App. 32; ST. II.

N.B. The above list takes no account of the ordinary consulship. See p. 12 ff., above.

E. SUFFECT CONSULS

This is a complete list of suffect consuls from Diocletian to Theodosius. For a discussion of them see M. T. W. Arnheim, 'Suffect Consuls in the Later Roman Empire', (forthcoming). For references see List D.

T. Fl. Postumius Titianus
Anicius Faustus
Sex. Anicius Paulinus
M. Nummius Albinus Triturrius
L. Turcius Secundus Asterius
Insteius Pompeianus
Ragonius Vincentius Celsus
(Quintilius) Laetus

L. Castrius Constans
C. Caelius Censorinus
L. Nonius Verus
Attius (Insteius T)ertullus Populonius
Attius Insteius Tertullus
Ceionius Italicus
Memmius Vitrasius Orfitus Honorius
Meropius Pontius Paulinus
Caelius Urbanus
L. Crepereius Madalianus

BIBLIOGRAPHY

Numismatic Sources

BRUUN, P. M., *The Roman Imperial Coinage, vol. VII: Constantine and Licinius*, ed. C. H. V. Sutherland and R. A. G. Carson (London, 1966).

COHEN, H., *Description historique des monnaies frappees sous l'Empire romain*, 8 vols., reprint, Graz, 1955 (Paris 1880–92).

MAURICE, J., *Numismatique Constantinienne* (Paris, 1906–13).

PEARCE, J. W. E., *The Roman Imperial Coinage, vol. IX: Valentinian I to Theodosius I*, ed. H. Mattingly, E. A. Sydenham and C. H. V. Sutherland (London, 1951).

Fasti and Prosopographies

BARBIERI, G., *L'Albo senatorio da Settimio Severo a Carino, 193–285* (Roma, 1952).

CHASTAGNOL, A., *Les Fastes de la Préfecture de Rome au Bas-Empire* (Paris, 1962).

Chronographus a. 354, ed T. Mommsen, *Monumenta Germaniae Historica*, Auctores Antiquissimi, vol. xi (Chronica Minora) (Berlin, 1894).

CLINTON, H. F., *Fasti Romani*, 2 vols. (Oxford, 1845–50).

DEGRASSI, A., *I Fasti consolari dell'Impero Romano dal 30 av. Christo al 613 dopo Cristo* (Roma, 1952).

DESSAU, H., KLEBS, E. AND VON ROHDEN, P., *Prosopographia Imperii Romani, saec. I, II, III*, 3 vols. (Berlin, 1897–8).

GELZER, H., *Patrum Nicaenorum Nomina* (Teubner) (Leipzig, 1898).

GROAG, E. AND STEIN, A., *Prosopographia Imperii Romani saec. I, II, III*, editio altera (Berlin, 1933–).

JONES, A. H. M., MARTINDALE, J. R. AND MORRIS, J., *Prosopography of the Later Roman Empire* (with *Fasti*), forthcoming.

LIEBENAM, W., *Fasti consulares Imperii Romani*, Bonn, 1909.

SCHUURMANS, C., 'De Samenstelling van den Romeinschen Senaat vanaf de troonbestijging van Diocletianus tot aan het einde van de IVe eeuw n.C. (284–400 n.C.), unpublished doctoral dissertation (Ghent, 1943).

SEECK, O., *Regesten der Kaiser und Päpste für die Jahre 311 bis 476 n. Chr.* (Stuttgart, 1919).

Modern Works

ALFÖLDI, A., *A Conflict of Ideas in the Late Roman Empire*, Tr. H. Mattingly (Oxford, 1952).

—— *The Conversion of Constantine and Pagan Rome*, Tr. H. Mattingly (Oxford, 1948).

16

ALFÖLDI, A., *Die Kontorniaten, ein verkanntes Propaganda mittel* (Leipzig, 1943).

—— 'The helmet of Constantine with the Christian monogram', *JRS* 22 (1932), 9–23.

—— 'La grande crise du monde romain au IIIe siècle', *Antiquité Classique* (1938).

ALLARD, P., *Julien l'Apostat*, 3 vols. (Paris, 1906–10).

ANDERSON, J. G. C., 'The genesis of Diocletian's provincial reorganisation', *JRS* 22 (1932), 24–32.

ARNHEIM, M. T. W. 'Vicars in the Later Roman Empire', *Historia* 19 (1970), 593–606.

—— 'Third Century Praetorian Prefects of Senatorial Origin: Fact or Fiction?' *Athenaeum* 49 (1971), 74–88.

ASCHBACH, J., 'Die Anicier', *Sitzungsberichte der kaiserl. Akad. der Wissenschaft in Wien, phil-hist. Kl.*, 64 (1870), 407–10.

BARBIERI, G., *L'Albo senatorio da Settimio Severo a Carino*, 193–285 (Roma, 1952).

BARK, W. C., *Origins of the Medieval World* (New York, 1960).

BAYNES, N. H., *The Byzantine Empire* (London, 1946) (1925).

—— *Byzantine Studies and other Essays* (London, 1955).

—— *Constantine the Great and the Christian Church*, Raleigh lecture, 1929, *Proceedings of the British Academy*, vol. xv.

—— *Historia Augusta, its date and purpose* (Oxford, 1926).

—— 'The Decline of Roman Power in Western Europe', *JRS* 33 (1943) 29 ff.

—— 'Three Notes on the Reforms of Diocletian and Constantine', *JRS* 15 (1925), 195–208.

—— Review of Alföldi, *Conflict of Ideas*, *JRS* 43 (1953), 169 ff.

BERNARDI, A., 'The economic problems of the Roman Empire at the time of its decline', *Studia et Documenta Historiae et Iuris*, 31 (1965), 110–170.

BESNIER, M., *L'Empire Romain de l'Avènement des Sévères au Concile de Nicée* (Paris, 1937).

BIRLEY, E., 'The governors of Numidia, A.D. 193–268', *JRS* 40 (1950), 60–9.

—— 'Senators in the Emperor's Service', *Proceedings of the British Academy*, 39 (1954), 197–214.

BLOCH, H., 'A new document of the last pagan revival in the West', *Harvard Theological Review*, 38 (1945), 199–244.

BOAK, A. E. R., *The Master of the Offices in the Later Roman and Byzantine Empires* (New York, 1919).

—— *Two Studies in later Roman and Byzantine Administration* (London, 1924). (University of Michigan Studies, Humanistic Studies, vol. xiv).

BOAK, A. E. R. *Man-power Shortage and the Fall of the Roman Empire in the West* (London, 1955).

BOISSIER, G., *La Fin du Paganisme: Etude sur les dernières Luttes Religieuses en Occident au IVᵉ siècle* (Paris, 1891).

BORGHESI, *Opera*.

BRATIANU, G. I., *Etudes Byzantines d'Histoire Economique et Sociale* (Paris, 1938).

BRÉHIER, L., 'Constantin et la fondation de Constantinople', *Rev. Hist.* 119 (1915), 241–72.

BRISSAUD, J., *Le Régime de la terre dans la societé étatiste du Bas-Empire* (Paris, 1927).

BROUWERS, A., 'Des préfets du prétoire "clarissimes" antérieurs au règne de Sévère Alexandre', *Latomus* 5 (1946), 41–6.

BROWN, P. R. L., 'Aspects of the Christianization of the Roman Aristocracy', *JRS* 51 (1961), 1–11.

—— *Augustine of Hippo: a biography* (London, 1967).

—— 'Christianity and local culture in late Roman Africa', *JRS* 58 (1968), 85–95.

—— 'The diffusion of Manichaeism in the Roman Empire', *JRS* 59 (1969), 92–103.

BRUUN, P. M., *The Roman Imperial Coinage, vol. vii: Constantine and Licinius*, 313–37 (London, 1966).

—— *Studies in Constantinian Chronology* (New York, 1961).

BURCH, V., *Myth and Constantine the Great* (London, 1927).

BURCKHARDT, J., *Die Zeit Constantins des Grossen*, 3rd edn., Leipzig, 1898 (Basel 1953).

BURY, J. B., *The Constitution of the Later Roman Empire* (Cambridge, 1910).

—— *A History of the Later Roman Empire (395–565)*, 2 vols. (London, 1923).

—— 'The Notitia Dignitatum', *JRS* 10 (1920), 131–54.

—— 'The provincial list of Verona', *JRS* 13 (1923), 127–51.

Cambridge Ancient History (Cambridge University Press, 1923–39), especially vol. xii.

Cambridge Economic History, Ed. J. H. Clapham (Cambridge, 1941). vol. i.

Cambridge Medieval History, Planned by J. B. Bury, ed. H. M. Gwatkin (New York, 1911–36), vol. i.

CAMERON, A. D. E., 'Literary allusions in the *Historia Augusta*', *Hermes* 92 (1964), 363–77.

—— 'The Roman friends of Ammianus', *JRS* 54 (1964), 15–28.

—— 'Gratian's repudiation of the pontifical robe', *JRS* 58 (1968), 96–102.

CANTARELLI, L., *La diocesi italiciana da Diocleziano alla caduta dell'impero occidentale: Studi e documenti di storia e diritto*, xxii (1901), 83–148; xxiii (1902), 50–100; 259–283; xxiv (1903), 143–73, 273–311.

CHASTAGNOL, A., *La Préfecture Urbaine à Rome sous le Bas-Empire* (Paris, 1960).

—— *Les Fastes de la Préfecture de Rome au Bas-Empire* (Paris, 1962).

—— 'La conversion d'une famille de l'aristocratie romaine sous l'empire', *Revue des Études Latines* 33 (1955), 50–3.

—— 'Le sénateur Volusien et la conversion d'une famille de l'aristocratie romaine au Bas-Empire', *Rev. des Etudes Anciennes* 58 (1956), 241–53.

—— 'Les Légats du proconsul d'Afrique au Bas-Empire', *Libyca* 6 (1958), 7–19.

—— 'La carrière du proconsul d'Afrique M. Aur. Consius Quartus', *Libyca* 7 (1959), 191–203.

—— 'Notes chronologiques sur l'Histoire Auguste et le *Laterculus* de Polemius Silvius', *Historia* 4 (1955), 173–88.

—— 'L'administration du diocèse italien au Bas-Empire', *Historia* 12 (1963), 348–79.

—— 'Les inscriptions des gradins sénatoriaux de Colisée', *Akte des IV. Internationalen Kongress für Griech, u. Latein. Epigraphik, Wien*, 1962 (published 1964).

—— 'Les Espagnols dans l'aristocratie gouvernementale a l'époque de Theodose', in Piganiol (ed.), *Les Empereurs romains d'Espagne*, 269–92.

—— 'Les consulaires de Numidie', *Melanges Jerome Carcopino* (Paris, 1966), 215–28.

—— 'La famille de Caecinia Lolliana, grande dame païenne du IVe siècle ap. J-C.', *Latomus* 20 (1961), 744–58.

CLAUSING, R., *The Roman Colonate* (New York, 1925).

COSTER, C. H., *Late Roman Studies* (Cambridge, Mass., 1968).

CUMONT, F., *Les religions orientales dans le paganisme romain* (Paris, 1929).

DAUZAT, A., *Les noms des lieux* (Paris, 1926).

DEMOUGEOT, E., *De l'unité à la division de l'Empire Romain, 395–410* (Paris, 1951).

DIEHL, C., *History of the Byzantine Empire*, tr. G. B. Ives (Princeton, 1925).

DILL, S., *Roman Society in the last century of the Western Empire* (London, 1899).

—— *Roman Society in Gaul in the Marovingian Age* (London, 1926).

DOPSCH, A., *Wirtschaftliche u. soziale Grundlagen der europäischen Kulturentwicklung aus der Zeit von Caesar bis auf Karl den Grossen* (Wien, 1923–4).

DOWNEY, G., *A study of the Comites Orientis and the consulares Syriae* (Princeton, 1939).

ELLISSEN, O. A., *Der Senat im oströmischen Reiche* (Göttingen, 1883).

EMEREAU, C., 'L'archonte-proconsul de Constantinople', *Rev. Arch.* 23 (1926), 103 ff.

ENSSLIN, W., *Zur Geschichtschreibung u. Weltanschauung des Ammianus Marcellinus* (Leipzig, 1923).

—— 'Die Titulatur der magistri militum bis auf Theodosius I', *Klio* 23 (1930), 306–25.

—— 'Die magistri militum des 4. Jahrhunderts', *Klio* 24 (1931), 102–47.

—— 'Der Konstantinische Patriziat und seine Bedeutung im 4. Jahrhundert', *Melanges Bidez*, Univ. Lib. Brux. Institut de Philologie et d'histoire orient., vol. ii (1934), 361–76.

—— 'Der Vicarius praefecturae urbis', *Byz. Zeitschr.* (1936), 320 ff.

FORNI, G., *Il reclutamento delle legioni da Augusto a Diocleziano* (Milano-Roma, 1953).

FORTINA, M., *L'Imperatore Graziano* (Torina, 1953).

FRANK, T. (ed.), *An Economic Survey of Ancient Rome*, 6 vols. (Baltimore, 1933–40).

FREND, W. H. C., *The Donatist Church* (Oxford, 1952).

—— *Martyrdom and Persecution in the early Church* (Oxford), 1965.

—— 'Paulinus of Nola and the last century of the Western Empire', *JRS* 59 (1969), 1–11.

—— 'The failure of the persecutions in the Roman Empire', *Past and Present* (1959), 10–30.

—— 'The Roman Empire in Eastern and Western historiography', *Proc. Cambr. Phil. Soc.* No. 194 (1968), 19–32.

GAGÉ, J., *Les Classes Sociales dans l'Empire Romain* (Paris, 1964).

GANSHOF, F. L., 'Le statut personnel du colon au Bas-Empire', *Antiquité Classique* 14 (1945).

GELZER, M., *The Roman Nobility*, Tr. R. Seager (Oxford, 1969).

GIBBON, E., *The Decline and Fall of the Roman Empire*, 6 vols. ed. J. B. Bury (London, 1930) (1776–88).

GLOVER, T. R., *Life and Letters in the fourth century* (Cambridge, 1901).

GRENIER, A., *Manuel d'archéologie gallo-romaine*, 4 vols. (Paris, 1934–60).

GROAG, E., *Die Reichsbeamten von Achaia in spätrömischer Zeit* (Budapest, 1946).

—— 'Notizen zur Geschichte kleinasiatischer Familien', *Jahreshefte des Oesterreichischen Archäologischen Instituts in Wien* 10 (1907), 282–90.

HARDY, E. R., *The Large Estates of Byzantine Egypt* (New York, 1931).

HARMAND, L., *Le Patronat sur les collectivités publiques des origines au Bas-Empire* (Paris, 1957).

HARMAND, L. (ed.), *Libanius: Discours sur les patronages* (Paris, 1955).

HARNACK, A. VON, *The expansion of Christianity in the first three centuries*, tr. J. Moffat, 2 vols. (London–New York, 1904–5).

HARTKE, W., *Römische Kinderkaiser* (Berlin, 1951).

HATT, J. J., *Histoire de la Gaule Romaine* (Paris, 1959).

HEICHELHEIM, F. M., *Wirtschaftsgeschichte des Altertums*, 2 vols. (Leyden, 1938).

HEITLAND, W. E., *Agricola* (Cambridge, 1921).

HIRSCHFELD, O., *Die kaiserlichen Verwaltungsbeamten bis auf Diocletian*, 3rd ed. (Berlin, 1905).

HODGKIN, T., *Italy and her Invaders*, 8 vols. (Oxford, 1902–9) (1885–99).

—— *The dynasty of Theodosius* (Oxford, 1889).

HOEPFFNER, A., 'Un aspect de la lutte de Valentinien I contre le sénat: la création du *defensor plebis*', *Revue Historique* 182 (1938), 225–37.

HOMO, L., *De la Rome Païenne à la Rome Chrétienne* (Paris, 1950).

—— 'Les privilèges administratifs du sénat romain sous l'empire, et leur disparition graduelle au cours du IIIe siècle', *Revue Historique* 137 (1921), 161–203; 138 (1921), 1–52.

HOWE, L. L., *The Pretorian Prefect from Commodus to Diocletian* (Chicago, 1942).

HYDE, W. W., *Paganism to Christianity in the Roman Empire* (Philadelphia–London, 1946).

JARDÉ, A., *Etudes critiques sur la vie et le règne de Sévère Alexandre* (Paris, 1925).

JONES, A. H. M., *Constantine and the Conversion of Europe* (London, 1948).

—— *The Later Roman Empire, 284–602*, 3 vols. (Oxford, 1964).

—— *The Cities of the Eastern Roman Provinces* (Oxford, 1937).

—— *The Greek City from Alexander to Justinian* (Oxford, 1940).

—— 'The date and value of the Verona list', *JRS* 44 (1954) 21–30.

—— 'The decline and fall of the Roman Empire', *History* (1955), 209–26.

—— '*Capitatio* and *Iugatio*', *JRS* 47 (1957), 88–94.

—— 'Collegiate Prefectures', *JRS* 54 (1964), 78–89.

—— 'The Roman colonate', *Past and Present* 13 (1958), 1–13.

—— 'The career of Fl. Philippus', *Historia* 4 (1955), 229–33.

JULLIAN, C., *Histoire de la Gaule*, 8 vols. (Paris, 1921).

KELLY, J. N. D., *Early Christian Creeds* (London, 1963).

KEYES, C. W., *The rise of the equites in the third century of the Roman Empire* (Princeton, 1915).

KORNEMANN, E., *Reichsteilung und Doppelprinzipat im Imperium Romanum* (Berlin, 1930).

LABRIOLLE, P. DE, *La réaction païenne* (Paris, 1934).

LABRIOLLE, P., BARDY, G. AND PALANQUE, J. R., *De la paix constantinienne à la mort de Théodose*, (*Histoire de l'église depuis les origines jusqu'a nos jours*, ed. A. Fliche and V. Martin) (Paris, 1935).

LAISTNER, M. L. W., *Christianity and Pagan culture in the later Roman Empire* (New York, 1951).

LAMBRECHTS, P., *La composition du sénat romain de l'accession au trône d'Hadrien à la mort de Commode, 117–92* (Antwerp, 1936).

—— *La composition du sénat romain de Septime Sévère à Dioclétien* (193–284) (Budapest, 1937).

—— 'Studien over Romeinsche instellingen. I. De Senaat van het principaat naar het Dominaat', *Philol. Studien* 8 (1936/7), 3–12.

—— 'Les thèses de Henri Pirenne sur la fin du monde antique et les débuts du moyen-âge', *Byzantion* 14 (1939), 513–36.

LAQUEUR, R., *Das Kaisertum und die Gesellschaft des Reiches: Probleme der spätantike* (Stuttgart, 1930).

LECRIVAIN, C., *Le sénat romain depuis Dioclétien à Rome et a Constantinople* (Paris, 1888).

LOT, F., *La fin du monde antique et le début du Moyen Age* (Paris, 1927)

—— *Les destinées de l'Empire en occident de 395 à 888* (Paris, 1928).

—— 'La *Notitia Dignitatum utriusque Imperii*: Ses tares, sa date de composition, sa valeur', *Rev. d. ét. anc.* (1936), 285–338.

McGEACHY, J. A., *Q. Aurelius Symmachus and the senatorial aristocracy of the West* (Chicago, 1942).

McKAIL, J. W., 'Ammianus Marcellinus', *JRS* 10 (1920), 103–18.

MACMULLEN, R., 'Social Mobility and the Theodosian Code', *JRS* 54 (1964), 49–53.

MAGIE, D., *Roman Rule in Asia Minor to the end of the third century A.D.*, 2 vols. (Princeton, 1950).

MANN, J. C., 'The administration of Roman Britain', *Antiquity* 36 (1961), 317–20.

MARQUARDT, J., *Römische Staatsverwaltung*, 3 vols., reprint of 3rd edn. Darmstadt, 1957 (1881–5).

MARTINDALE, J. R., 'Note on the consuls of 381 and 382', *Historia*, 16 (1967), 254–6.

—— Unpublished article on the dating of the praetorian prefects of Constantine.

MATTHEWS, J., 'Continuity in a Roman family: the Rufii Festi of Volsinii', *Historia* 16 (1967), 484–509.

—— 'A pious supporter of Theodosius I: Maternus Cynegius and his family', *Journ. Theol. Stud.* 18 (1967), 438–46.

—— 'The connections of Florus, praetorian prefect (East) 381–3', unpublished MS.

MAZZARINO, S., *La fine del mondo antico* (Milano, 1959).

—— *Aspetti sociali del quarto secolo* (Roma, 1951).

MERLIN, A., 'La mosaïque du seigneur Julius à Carthage', *BCTH* (1921), 95–114.

MICKWITZ, G., *Geld u. Wirtschaft im römischen Reiche des IVen Jahrhunderts* (Helsingfors, 1932).

MOMIGLIANO, A. (ed.), *The conflict between paganism and Christianity in the fourth century* (Oxford, 1963).

MOMMSEN, T., *The Provinces of the Roman Empire from Caesar to Diocletian*, tr. W. P. Dickson (London, 1909).

—— *Römische Staatsrecht*, 3 vols., reprint, Graz, 1952 (Leipzig, 1871).

MORRIS, J., 'Changing fashions in Roman nomenclature in the early Empire', *Listy Filologické* 86 (1963), 34–46.

—— 'Munatius Plancus Paulinus', *Bonner Jahrbücher* (1965), 88–96.

NESSELHAUF, H., 'Die spätrömische Verwaltung der gallisch-germanischen Länder', *Abdhandl. d. Preuss, Akad. d. Wissenschaft, phil.—hist. Kl.* 2 (1938).

NISCHER, E., 'The army reforms of Diocletian and Constantine and their modifications up to the time of the *Notitia Dignitatum*', *JRS* 13 (1923), 1–55.

NISTLER, J., 'Vettius Agorius Praetextatus', *Klio* 10 (1910), 462–75.

NOCK, A. D., 'Deification and Julian', *JRS* 47 (1957), 115–23.

OSTROGORSKY, G., *Geschichte des byzantinischen Staates* (München, 1940).

PALANQUE, J.-R., *Essai sur la préfecture du prétoire du Bas-Empire* (Paris, 1933).

—— *Saint Ambroise et l'Empire Romain* (Paris, 1933).

—— 'L'empereur Gratien et le grand pontificat païen', *Byzantion* 8 (1933), 41–7.

—— 'Sur la liste des préfets du prétoire du IVe siècle', *Byzantion* 9 (1934), 703–13.

—— 'La date de la transfert de la préfecture des Gaules de Trèves à Arles', *Rev. d. ét. anc.* 36 (1934), 358–65.

—— 'Les préfets du prétoire sur les fils de Constantin', *Historia* 4 (1955), 257–63.

PALLU DE LESSERT, A. C., *Fastes des provinces africaines sous la domination romaine* (Paris, 1896–1901).

—— *Vicaires et comtes d'Afrique* (Constantine, 1891).

PARIBENI, R., 'Le dimore die *Potentiores* nel Basso Impero', *Mitt.d. deutsch. arch. Inst. (Rom. Abt.)* 55 (1940), 131–48.

PARKER, H. M. D., *A history of the Roman world from A.D. 138 to 337* (London, 1935).

—— 'The legions of Diocletian and Constantine', *JRS* 22 (1932), 175–89.

PASSERINI, A., *Le coorti pretorie* (Roma, 1939).

PEROWNE, S., *The end of the Roman World* (London, 1966).

PETERSEN, H., 'Senatorial and equestrian governors in the third century A.D.', *JRS* 45 (1955), 47–57.

BIBLIOGRAPHY 235

PETIT, P., *Libanius et la vie municipale a Antioche au IVe siècle après J-C.* (Paris, 1955).

—— *Les étudiants de Libanius* (Paris, 1956).

PFLAUM, H. G., *Le Marbre de Thorigny* (Paris, 1948).

PIGANIOL, A., *L'Empire Chrétien* (325–95) (Paris, 1947).

—— *L'empereur Constantin* (Paris, 1932).

—— 'Dates Constantiniennes', *Rev. d'hist. et de phil. relig.* 12 (1932), 360–72.

—— 'L'inscription de Aïn-Tebernok', *Rev. d. ét anc.* 31 (1929), 142–50.

PIRENNE, H., *Mahomet et Charlemagne*, 2nd edn. (Paris, 1937).

POINSSOT, M. L., 'La carrière de trois proconsuls d'Afrique contemporains de Diocletien', *Mem. soc. nat. ant. France* 76 (1924), 264 ff.

POINSSOT, M. L. AND LANTIER, R., 'Quatre préfets du prétoire contemporains de Constantin', *CRAI* (1924), 363 ff.

RAMSAY, W. M., *Cities and Bishoprics of Phrygia*, 2 vols. (Oxford, 1895–7).

RÉMONDON, R., *La crise de l'Empire romain de Marc-Aurele à Anastase* (Paris, 1964).

RIDLEY, F. A., *Julian the Apostate and the rise of Christianity* (London, 1937).

ROBERT, L., *Hellenica*, vol. iv (Paris, 1948).

ROSTOVTZEFF, M. I., *The Social and Economic History of the Roman Empire*, 2nd ed., 2 vols. (Oxford, 1957) (1926).

—— *Studien zur Geschichte des römischen Kolonates* (Leipzig-Berlin, 1910).

SAUMAGNE, C., 'Du rôle de l'*origo* et du *census* dans la formation du colonat romain', *Byzantion*, 12 (1937).

SAUNDERS, J. J., 'The debate on the fall of Rome', *History* 48 (1963), 1–17.

SCHÖNEBECK, H. VON., 'Beiträge zur Religionspolitik des Maxentius u. Constantin', *Klio* (Beiheft, 1939).

SCHULTEN, A., *Die römische Grundherrschaften* (Weimar, 1896).

SCHULZE, W., *Zur Geschichte lateinischer Eigennamen* (Berlin, 1933) (1904).

SCHUURMANS, C., 'De Samenstelling van den Romeinschen Senaat vanaf de troonbestiging van Diocletianus tot aan het einde van de IVe eeuw n.C.', unpublished dissertation (Ghent, 1943).

—— 'Valentinien I et le sénat romain', *Ant. Class.* 18 (1949), 25–38.

SCHWARTZ, E., *Kaiser Constantin und die Christliche Kirche* (Leipzig, 1913).

SEECK, O., *Geschichte des Untergangs der antiken Welt*, 6 vols. (Berlin, 1895–1920).

—— *Regesten der Kaiser und Päpste für die Jahre 311 bis 476 nach Chr.* (Stuttgart, 1919).

—— *Die Briefe des Libanius, zeitlich geordnet* (Leipzig, 1906).

SEECK, O. (ed.), *Symmachus* (M. G. H., Berlin, 1883).

SESTON, W., *Dioclétien et la tétrarchie* (Paris, 1940).
—— 'Constantine as bishop', *JRS* 37 (1947), 127 ff.
—— 'Recherches sur la chronologie du règne de Constantin le Grand', *Rev. d. et. anc.* 39 (1937), 197 ff.
STEIN, A., *Der römische Ritterstand* (Munchen, 1927).
—— *Die Legaten von Moesien* (Budapest, 1940).
—— *Die Präfekten von Aegypten in der römischen Kaiserzeit.*
—— 'Stellvertreter der *Praefecti Praetorio*', *Hermes* 60 (1925), 97 ff.
STEIN, E., *Geschichte des spätrömischen Reiches*, vol. i (Wien, 1928).
—— '*Agentes in rebus*', *Zeitschr. Sav.-Stift. Rechtsg.* 41 (1920) Röm. Abt. 195–251.
—— *Untersuchungen über das Officium der prätorianerpräfektur seit Diocletian* (Wien, 1922).
—— 'Untersuchungen zur spätrömischen Verwaltungsgeschichte', *Rhein. Mus.* 74 (1925), 347–94.
—— 'A propos d'un livre récent sur la liste des préfets du prétoire', *Byzantion* 9 (1934), 327–53.
STEVENS, C. E., *Sidonius Apollinaris and his age* (Oxford, 1933).
STRAUB, J., *Heidnische Geschichtsapologetik in der christlichen Spätantike. Untersuchungen über Zeit und Tendenz der Historia Augusta. Antiquitas*, Reihe iv, Bd. i. (1963).
—— 'Konstantins Verzicht auf dem Gang zum Kapitol', *Historia* 4 (1955), 296–313.
STROHEKER, K. F., *Der senatorische Adel im spätantiken Gallien* (Tübingen, 1948).
SUERBAUM, W., *Vom antiken zum frühmittelalterlichen Staatsbegriff* (Münster, 1961).
SUNDWALL, J., *Weströmische Studien* (Berlin, 1915).
SUTHERLAND, C. H. V., 'Some political notions in coin types between 294 and 313', *JRS* 53 (1963), 14–20.
SYME, SIR RONALD, *Ammianus and the Historia Augusta* (Oxford, 1968).
THOMPSON, E. A., *The historical work of Ammianus Marcellinus* (Cambridge, 1947).
THOMSEN, R., *The Italic Regions from Augustus to the Lombard Invasions* (Copenhagen, 1947).
VAN BERCHEM, A., 'Note sur les diplômes honorifiques du IVe siècle à propos de la table de patronat de Timgad', *Rev. de Philol.* (1934), 164–8.
VAN SICKLE, C. E., 'Conservative and philosophic influence in the reign of Diocletian', *Class. Phil.* 27 (1932), 51–8.
VASILIEV, A. A., *History of the Byzantine Empire, 324–1453* (Madison and Milwaukee, Wisconsin, 1958).
VINOGRADOFF, P., *The Growth of the Manor*, 3rd ed. (London–New York, 1920) (1905).

Vogt, J., *Constantin der Grosse und sein Jahrhundert*, 2nd edn. (München, 1960).

—— *The Decline of Rome* (London, 1967) (1965).

Walbank, F. W., *The decline of the Roman Empire in the West* (London, 1946).

Walser, G. and Pekary, T., *Die Krise des römischen Reiches: Bericht über die Forschungen des 3. Jahrhunderts (193–284), von 1939 bis 1959* (Berlin, 1962).

Warmington, B. H., *The North African Provinces from Diocletian to the Vandal Conquest* (Cambridge, 1954).

—— 'The career of Romanus, *comes Africae*', *Byz. Zeit.* 49 (1956), 55–6.

Westermann, W. L., 'The economic basis of the decline of ancient culture', *American Hist. Rev.* 20 (1914/15), 723–43.

Wytzes, J., *Der Streit um dem Altar der Viktoria* (Amsterdam, 1936).

Zulueta, F. de, *De Patrociniis Vicorum* (Oxford, 1909).

INDEX

Personal names are listed in order of *nomina*, with the exception of emperors, classical authors and other generally well-known figures, who are registered under their conventional English names.

Flavius (often abbreviated to 'Fl.'), which in the fourth century could evidently be assumed by anyone in the imperial service, is not regarded as a *nomen*. All Ceionii/Caeionii will be found under the shorter spelling.

STEMMATA

1. The Ceionii and Collaterals

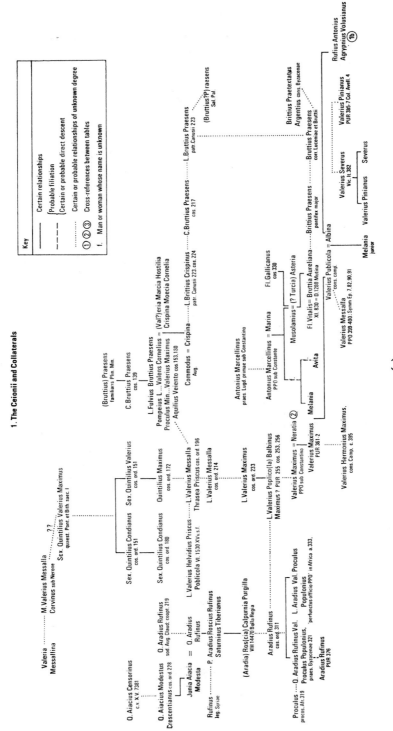

(a)

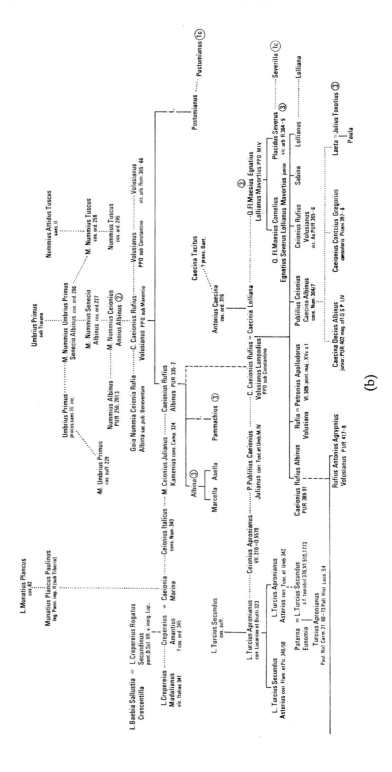

(b)

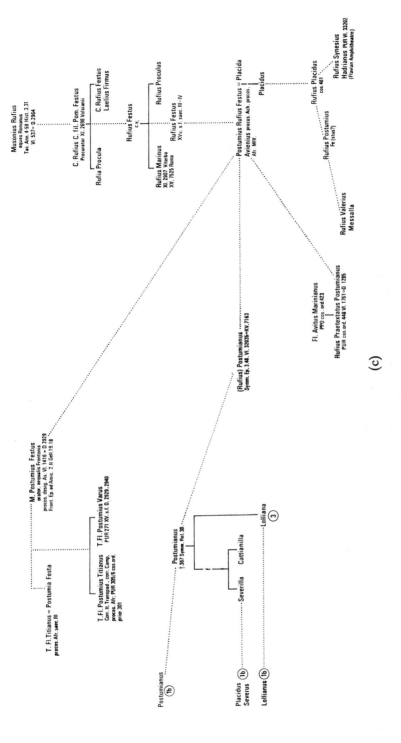

Musonius Rufius
eques Romanus
Tac. Ann. 4.59 Hist. 3.31
VI. 537 = D. 2964

C. Rufius C. fil. Pom. Festus
Procurator XI. 2698 Volsianni

C. Rufius Festus
Laelius Firmus

Rufia Procula

Rufius Festus
c.v.

Rufius Proculus

Rufius Marinus
XI. 2907 Viterbo
XV. 7525 Roma

Rufius Festus
XVv. s.f. saec. III–IV

Postumius Rufius Festus = Placida
Avienius procos. Ach. procos.
Afr. MlV.

Placidus

Rufius Placidus
cos 481

Rufius Synesius
Hadrianus PUR VI. 33202
(Flavian Amphitheatre)

Rufius Postumius
[= stud?]

Rufius Valerius
Messalla

M. Postumius Festus
orator. aequalis Frontonis
procos. desig. As. VI. 1416 = D. 2929
Front. Ep. ad Amic. 2. II Cell.19.18

T. Fl. Titianus = Postumia Festa
procos. Afr. saec. III

T. Fl. Postumius Titianus
Corr. It. Transped. corr. Camp.
procos. Afr. PUR 305/6 cos. ord.
prior 301

T. Fl. Postumius Varus
PUR 271 XV. s.f. D. 2929. 2940

Postumianus
(1b)

(Rufius) Postumianus
Symm. Ep. 3.48. VI. 31205=XV. 7163

Postumianus
†367 Symm. Rel. 30.

Fl. Avitus Marinianus
PPO cos. ord 423

Rufius Praetextatus Postumianus
cos. ord. 448 VI. 1761 = D. 1285

Severilla   Cattianilla

Lolliana
(3)

Placidus
Severus (1b)

Lollianus (1b)

(c)

2. The Anicii and Collaterals

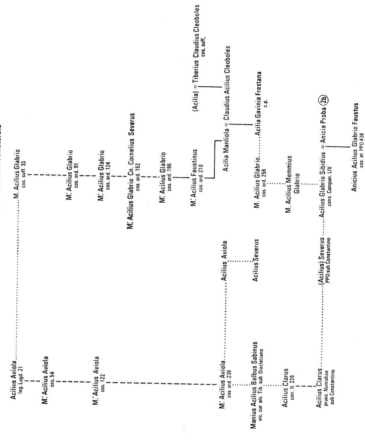

(a)

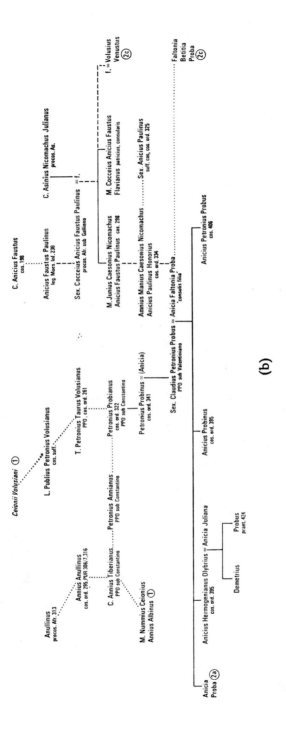

Ceionii Volusiani ①

C. Anicius Faustus
cos. 198

Anicius Faustus Paulinus
leg. Moes. Inf. 230

Sex. Cocceius Anicius Faustus Paulinus
procos. Afr. sub Gallieno

C. Asinius Nicomachus Julianus
procos. As.

f. = Volusius
Venustus
②c

M. Junius Caesonius Nicomachus
Anicius Faustus Paulinus cos. 298

M. Cocceius Anicius Faustus
Flavianus patricius, consularis

= f.

Annius Manius Caesonius Nicomachus
Anicius Paulinus Honorius cos. ord. 334

Sex. Anicius Paulinus
suff. cos, cos. ord. 325

L. Publius Petronius Volusianus
cos. suff.

T. Petronius Taurus Volusianus
PPO. cos. ord. 261

Petronius Probianus
cos. ord. 322
PPO sub Constantino

Petronius Probinus
cos. ord. 341

Sex. Claudius Petronius Probus = Anicia Faltonia Proba
PPO sub Valentiniano   consulis filia

Faltonia
Bettia
Proba
②c

Anicius Petronius Probus
cos. 406

Anullinus
procos. Afr. 313

Annius Anullinus
cos. ord. 295, PUR 306/7.316

C. Annius Tiberianus
PPO sub Constantino

M. Nummius Ceionius
Annius Albinus ①

Petronius Annianus
PPO sub Constantino

Anicius Probinus
cos. ord. 395

Anicius Hermogenianus Olybrius = Anicia Juliana
cos. ord. 395

Demetrius

Probus
praet. 424

Anicia
Proba ②a

(b)

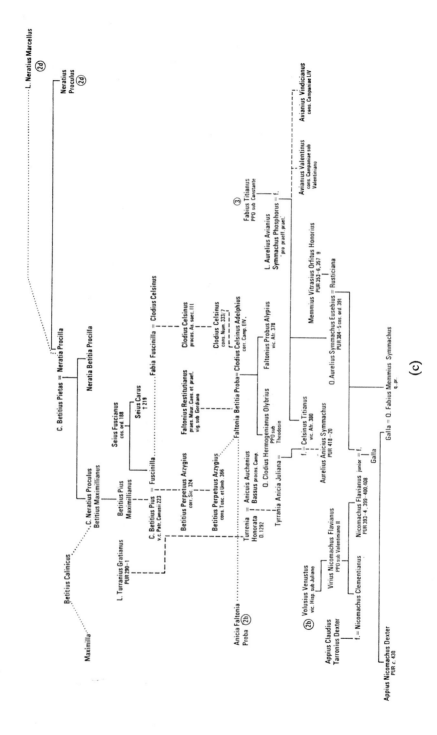

(c)

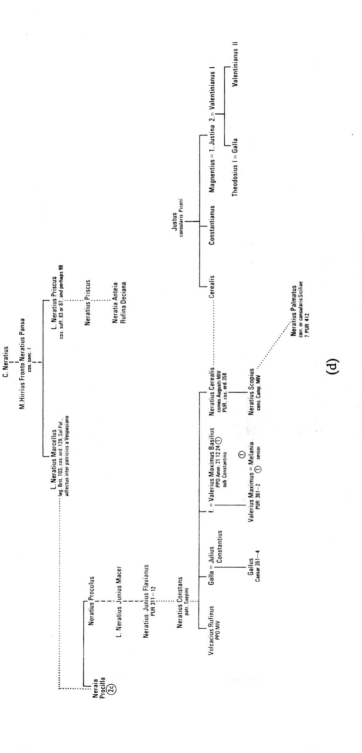

C. Neratius

M. Hirrius Fronto Neratius Pansa
cos. saec. I

L. Neratius Marcellus
leg. Brit. 103. cos. ord. 129. Sal Pal.
adlectus inter patricios a Vespasiano

L. Neratius Priscus
cos. suff. 83 or 87. and perhaps 98

Neratius Priscus

Neratia Anteia
Rufina Deciana

Neraia
Procilla
(2c)

Neratius Proculus

L. Neratius Junius Macer

Neratius Junius Flavianus
PUR 311–12

Neratius Constans
patr. Saepini

Justus
consularis Piceni

Constantianus

Cerealis

Magnentius = 1. Justina 2. = Valentinianus I

Theodosius I = Galla

Valentinianus II

Neratius Cerealis
comes August. MIV
PUR. cos. ord. 358

Neratius Scopius
cons. Camp. MIV

Neratius Palmatus
corr. or consularis Siciliae
? PUR 412

f. = Valerius Maximus Basilius
PPO Amm. 21 12 24 ①
sub Constantino

Valerius Maximus = Melania
PUR 361–2 ① senior

Galla = Julius
Constantius

Gallus
Caesar 351–4

Volcacius Rufinus
PPO MIV

(d)

3. The Maecii, Fabii, Scipiones, Gracchi, and Collaterals

Cornelius Cethegus
cos. 24

Cornelius Cethegus .... Cornelius Cethegus
cos. 170   Sal. Pal. 180

Ser. Cornelius Scipio
Salvidienus Orfitus
(3b)

Cethegus
Furius Maecius Gracchus
Corr. Flam. et Pic. c. 350
? PUR 376–77

Arrius Maecius Gracchus
PUR 415

M. Maecius Memmius
Furius Baburius
Caecilianus Placidus
(3b)

Pammachius = Paulina (3b)
'Furiae germinis decus'

Furia (3b)

Fabiola (3d)

Claudius Marcellus
PUR 292–3

Ceionius Rufius Albinus
PUR 335–7 (1)

C. Ceionius Rufius
Volusianus Lampadius = Caecinia
PPO MIV   Lolliana (1)

f. = Albina

Marcella

Asella

(a)

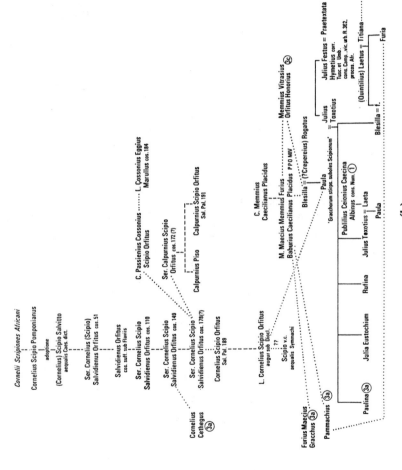

(b)

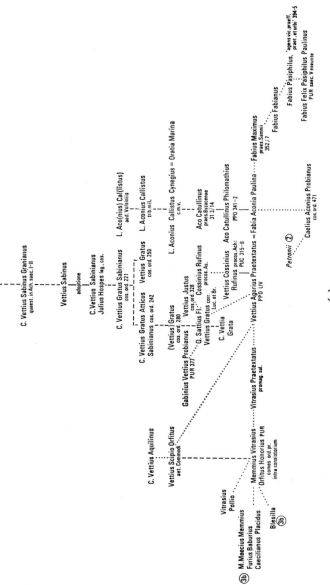

(c)

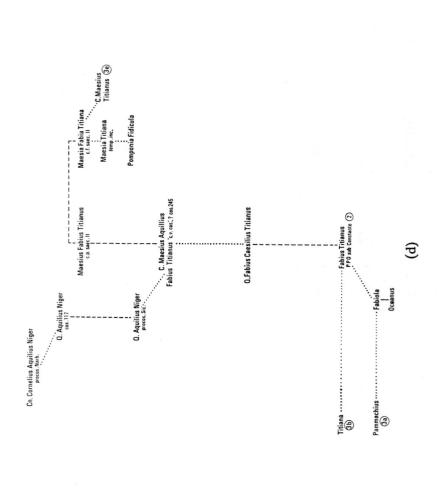

Cn. Cornelius Aquilius Niger
proces. Narb.

Q. Aquilius Niger
cos. 117

Q. Aquilius Niger
proces. Sic.

Maesius Fabius Titianus
c.p. saec. II

C. Maesius Aquillius
Fabius Titianus ᶜc.v. cos.,? cos.245

Maesia Fabia Titiana
c.f. saec. II

Maesia Titiana
temp. inc.

Pomponia Fidicula

C. Maesius
Titianus ③e

Q. Fabius Caesilius Titianus

Fabius Titianus ②
PPO sub Constante

Titiana ①b

Pammachius ③a

Fabiola
Oceanus

(d)

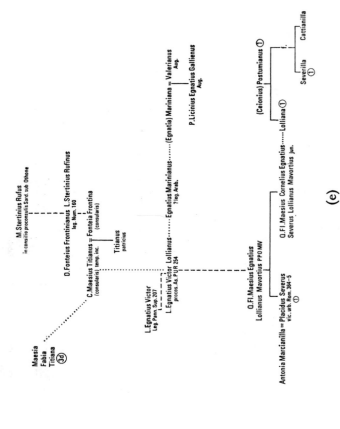

(e)